Capital First Dividend		30000
		109723
	1047506 3	
	7 6 9 7 4 6 2	181725
Discount on Domestic Exc		5221
Bills Payable		5000
City Corporation		3500
F de Lizardi & C.		
Lizardi Hermanos	F 3 6 6 1 6 7 89	455673
	F 440000	
Exchange Suspense		4 4
Bank of Orleans	1 08	
Atchafalaya Bank	6 7 83	
Merchants' Bank		9 7
Branch Bank Decatur		3 7 4 7 0
Branch Bank Huntsville		1 3 3 1 2
Shoe & Leather Dealers' Bk		1 5 3 7 5
Morris Canal & Bank g C.		3 6 1 8
Franklin Bank Cincinnati		3 7 1 8
Leather Manufacturers' Bank		3 4 4 0
Clinton & Port Hudson R R C.		5 3 3
New Haven County Bank		4 5 0 0
Tucker & Carter		2 4 6 0
R W & Thorne & C		1 4 7 5
Washington Keyes Cashier		1 5 9 5
Individual deposites	6 2 1 8 0 6 1 6	
Deposites on Interest	2 8 1 3 6 0 1 0	
Deposites on Certificats	1 3 5 3 2 4 8	916698
Circulation		5 9 0 6 5

FINANCE AND
ECONOMIC DEVELOPMENT
IN THE OLD SOUTH

FINANCE AND ECONOMIC DEVELOPMENT IN THE OLD SOUTH

Louisiana Banking, 1804-1861

GEORGE D. GREEN

STANFORD UNIVERSITY PRESS
STANFORD, CALIFORNIA
1972

Stanford University Press
Stanford, California
© 1972 by the Board of Trustees of the
Leland Stanford Junior University
Printed in the United States of America
ISBN 0-8047-0792-8
LC 73-153817

To Anne

Acknowledgments

ANYONE WHO writes a scholarly monograph realizes the vitality of the mythical "community of scholars" and depends heavily on the labors of those who have preceded him. I have tried to acknowledge my debts to the written work of other scholars in the Notes and Bibliography of this study. Peter Temin's splendid *The Jacksonian Economy* appeared after the completion of my original manuscript, though I did have the benefit of some of his earlier papers, and I have tried to indicate the relevance of this book at several points in the footnotes.

John Gurley and the late David Potter, as my dissertation advisers, guided and criticized the first version of this work and helped to keep my attention on the larger questions. Several others have generously read and criticized earlier drafts of the manuscript: John Clark, Lance Davis, Herbert Dougall, Stanley Engerman, Frank Gatell, Irene Neu, Fritz Redlich, Gerald White, and Harold Woodman. They are certainly not responsible for the errors that may remain.

I am also grateful to many librarians and archivists for their generous help: Mrs. Connie Griffith and the staff of the Tulane Archives; Mr. Virgil Bedsole and the staff of the Department of Archives at Louisiana State University; and others at Stanford University, the National Archives, and the Library of Congress. The endpaper of this book, a Citizens Bank balance sheet for July 1837, was supplied by the National Archives. My sincere thanks also to Mike Edwards and others at the Stanford University Press for their creative and conscientious editorial work.

The Ford Foundation supported my initial research with a dissertation fellowship in economics. The McKnight Foundation honored me with their 1968 Award in American History. And the Charles Warren Center for Studies in American History at Harvard University provided editorial and typing resources. I am grateful for the assistance and encouragement of all three institutions.

Every happily married scholar will understand that my greatest debt of gratitude is to my wife, Anne, to whom this book is affectionately dedicated.

G. D. G.

Contents

Tables

Banking Terms

ACCOMMODATION PAPER. A bill of exchange, promissory note, or draft issued or drawn without commercial collateral; it might be secured by a mortgage or simply by the good credit rating of the borrower. Contrasted with "real bills."

BANKS. *Chartered banks* operated under individual charters granted by the state, which specified allowable interest, reserve ratio, allowable loans or note issues, and so on. *Private banks* had no charters and were not allowed to issue notes. *Free banks* did not have individual charters but were governed by the provisions of a single Free Banking Act passed by the state legislature. *Commercial banks*, perhaps the most typical, were chartered banks whose main business was the granting of short-term loans and the clearing of notes and bills of exchange. *Improvement banks* were required to subsidize and manage the construction of a particular improvement project, such as a railroad or canal. *Property banks* received much of their capital from state bonds, and their charters specified that a certain percentage of their credit had to be issued as long-term mortgages.

BILL OF EXCHANGE. A written order to pay a certain sum of money after a stated interval of time, usually at some distant place. A factor might issue such a bill when selling cotton, ordering payment (in sterling) in New York after 90 days. The cotton buyer would "accept" the bill (and the obligation to pay) by endorsing it.

BONUS (to schools, hospitals, and other state-sponsored institutions). In antebellum Louisiana the term "bonus" was often applied to a regular payment made by a bank in return for the bank's charter privileges.

COMMERCIAL PAPER. The term applied to short-term loans granted for business and trading purposes. Commercial paper matured in 90 days or less and was much more liquid than a mortgage or improvement loan.

COMMISSION HOUSE. A factor's or broker's establishment.

CORRESPONDENT TIE. A formal agreement between banks to exchange information and financial services on a regular basis.

DISCOUNTING. When an interest-bearing note is sold by one creditor to another, the buyer usually deducts ("discounts") the interest in advance and pays the remainder in cash.

DRAFT. Any order to pay, such as a check or a bill of exchange. May be written by an individual or a bank.

FACTOR. An agent who sells merchandise (e.g., cotton) and buys supplies for his clients, charging a commission fee for his services. Factors frequently function as financial intermediaries also.

FINANCE. The method of paying for purchases of goods and services. *Internal* or *self-finance* involves payment out of current income or cash holdings. *External finance* involves borrowing funds by issuing mortgages, bonds, stocks, or other securities. Sometimes external finance is *indirect*, with a bank or other financial intermediary operating between the borrower and the lender.

FORCED SAVING. The economic process by which funds are channeled into savings and investment through monetary inflation, which reduces the purchasing power of consumers while allowing new bank loans to finance investment.

INDEPENDENT TREASURY. The separate institutions established by the federal government (in 1840-41, 1846, and later) to receive revenues and pay government expenditures. Largely replaced the use of "pet" banks as depository and payment agents.

KITING. The practice of paying off a maturing bank loan by drafting a new loan on another bank; essentially a means of extending credit beyond the short term granted by the original loan.

MULTIPLE CONTRACTION. A bank normally maintained only fractional reserves, issuing far more liabilities than it could cover with the reserves on hand. Thus an antebellum bank that lost $1,000 in reserves for one reason or another might have to call in several thousand dollars in notes, loans, etc. to restore its liquidity.

NATIONAL BANK. This was not a central bank in the modern sense, but simply a federally chartered bank that had branches chartered in a number of states.

PAID-IN CAPITAL. The portion of stockholders' subscriptions that have actually been paid for, usually with cash but sometimes with a mortgage or other security.

PET BANKS. The banks selected by the federal government as depositories for the government's funds.

RACEHORSE BILLS. Bills that were "kited" back and forth from one city or state to another, being paid off each time by the drafting of a new bill.

RESERVE. The liquid assets held by a bank to back its outstanding banknote and deposit liabilities. In antebellum Louisiana specie was the accepted reserve, although commercial paper was sometimes allowable.

REAL BILLS. By contrast with accommodation paper, "real" bills were issued to finance an actual commercial transaction, such as a shipment of cotton.

SECURITIES. Evidences of debt (or equity) claims. Would include bonds, mortgages, promissory notes, stocks, and so forth. *Indirect securities* are the debt claims issued by financial intermediaries, such as banknotes, bank deposits, or insurance policies. *See also* Finance.

SPECIE. Gold and silver, in either coins or bullion. The term applies specifically to the monetary function of the metals.

SUSPENSION. A ban on the redemption of banknotes in specie. The most notable occurred during 1837-42.

WILDCAT BANKING. In general, banking that was "irresponsible." A wildcat bank supposedly issued too many loans and banknotes for speculative purposes, and kept inadequate reserves.

FINANCE AND
ECONOMIC DEVELOPMENT
IN THE OLD SOUTH

Introduction

BANKING PLAYS a prominent role in the traditional historiography of antebellum America. Alexander Hamilton has been placed among the financial angels for his leadership in chartering the first Bank of the United States; and Andrew Jackson has descended into financial hell (according to Bray Hammond) but risen into democratic political heaven (according to Arthur Schlesinger, Jr.) because of his leadership in destroying the second Bank of the United States. Even textbooks routinely contrast the sanctity of "hard money" (i.e., specie) and strictly "commercial" banking with the sinfulness of "wildcat" banking, depreciated paper currency, "speculative" booms, and financial "panics."

This traditional moralistic picture of early American banking and finance has several deficiencies. It exaggerates the harmful role of banks in causing financial crises and economic instability, and ignores the effect of banking on economic growth and development. It concentrates on the two federal banks and on national politics, bypassing the subjects of state banks and state politics. Finally, the traditional history of banking often rests implicitly on naïve economic theories of money and banking. This study, by undertaking a theoretically explicit analysis of the political economy of banking in a single important state, attempts to overcome these deficiencies.

The Economic Impact of Louisiana Banking

Most economic historians have sharply criticized the rapid expansion of banking and finance in the United States during the 1830's. They condemn the expansion of state-chartered banks because it ended in, and presumably caused, the financial panic of 1837. Accepting a "boom or bust" theory, they discount a decade of real economic growth as unreal or unsound because it concluded with a depression.[1] The implicit theory underlying this interpretation is often sadly inaccurate. For example, the historian often seems to assume unconsciously that all foreign borrowing is burdensome and unproductive. He may even believe that all paper money, credit, or debt, is fundamentally unsound—that only specie represents "true value." Or he may accept the crudest form of the quantity theory of money and assume that any expansion of the money supply is automatically inflationary. Assumptions like these are usually disguised in historical descriptions of "wildcat" banking (a much misused epithet), or in vague conclusions that banking was "overindulged" or "overexpanded." James Winston's description of New Orleans is typical:

The credit system was practically universal at this time among the cotton planters of the state, and it was through the instrumentality of the banks of New Orleans that landed property and slaves were converted into circulating notes, with which all kinds of speculative enterprises were forwarded. Much of the capital employed in the various enterprises launched during this decade is said to have been raised in Europe by the sale of mortgages, the whole resulting in an immense turnover of business, but unaccompanied by a corresponding accumulation of real values.[2]

The conclusions of this study differ almost completely from the traditional views. Specie, despite its universal acceptance, was a costly and unproductive form of money and wealth. By partially displacing it and substantially supplementing it, the expansive financial system that Louisiana and other states devised in the 1820's and 1830's both permitted and actively encouraged a decade or more of rapid, genuine economic development. The banks in these states accelerated economic growth by concentrating their credit on investment rather than consumption spending. Their financial intermediation increased the supply of saving and allocated it more efficiently among alternative types of investment. Aided by state guarantees of their debts, Louisiana's banks imported $20 million of foreign capital. From this and other sources, they provided credit to New Orleans commerce and plantation agriculture and gave heavy support to transportation and other "social overhead" investment projects. This allocation of bank credit generally followed the optimal development path for Louisiana's economy, given the state's initial economic, social, and political structure.

Between 1835 and 1837, however, the quantity of money and credit expanded more rapidly than did the capacity of the real economy. Here, this study agrees with the traditional view of inflation, though not with the inferences traditionally drawn from the fact of inflation. The monetary expansion and resulting speculative expectations may have contributed to the financial crisis and depression that began in 1837, but they cannot be considered the sole cause. And even during the inflationary years of 1835-37 a case might be made for the favorable effect of expanded banking on economic development, through the mechanism of forced saving.

The years of financial crisis following the panic of 1837 did not produce a modern, Keynesian depression with sharply reduced production and mass unemployment. There may have been some adverse multiplier-accelerator effects on construction, capital goods producers, and retail trade. But most of the hardship seems to have come instead through capital losses, debt burdens, and lower prices for cotton and other staples. Although most contemporaries (and most historians of banking) viewed the banks' suspensions of specie payments in 1837 and 1839 as a great evil that produced serious losses, inequities, and "demoralization," a few recognized it as a form of relief. By partially eliminating fixed exchange rates, suspension modified interregional and international settlements (often disruptively if it was not carried out everywhere). But it also permitted some local credit expansion with less regard to external imbalances, and thus prevented further forced liquidation, deflation, and depression.

In the absence of either a specie standard or a central bank, some interesting problems arose in regulating the money supply during suspension. The New Orleans bankers worked out several gentlemen's agreements to limit their note issues. But when these loose cartels repeatedly broke down in bank rivalries, the authority of government sanctions was sought, and was eventually obtained in the famous Louisiana Bank Act of 1842. In the immediate context of depression and financial crisis the Act was liquidationist in spirit: it led to the resumption of specie payments, but its rigid "fundamental rules" forced the banks into an unnecessarily severe contraction of money and credit.

In pursuing the twin goals of economic stability and economic growth, antebellum Louisiana wrestled with one of the basic dilemmas of the American financial system of that day: the desire for both "sound money" and "easy credit." The root of this dilemma was the existence of a specie standard and fixed international exchange rates together with a fractional reserve banking system. Bankers, merchants, storekeepers, and others had devised a variety of ingenious credit arrangements that minimized the need for specie in most transactions and thus softened the conflict of objectives. But if foreigners, frightened bank customers, or angry legislative advocates of hard money demanded payments in specie, they soon discovered that there was not enough of it to go around in a growing economy; and in the process they usually forced the banks to contract banknotes, deposits, and loans. No set of automatic rules, mandatory reserve ratios, or "commercial" loan policies could erase this basic dilemma.

Beginning in 1842, Louisiana abandoned its practical compromises and departures from the specie standard. The ensuing decade of "sound money" retarded financial expansion and hindered real economic growth, particularly in New Orleans commerce. After 1853 the financial system again became expansive, although it probably had far less impact on real growth than it had had in the 1830's. In short, expansive finance, even when it operated under the shadow of "sound money" and a specie standard, did accelerate growth, whereas restrictive finance retarded growth.

Revisionism from the Perspective of State and Local History

If we wish to study the relationship between banking and the economy, we may naturally ask, why choose Louisiana? Quite simply, a study concentrated on the national level would deal with statistical averages and very broad trends that tend to obscure the structural and institutional changes in particular regional and local economies. Antebellum Louisiana was part of the western frontier, which was then rapidly replacing its primitive economy with commercial agriculture. She also shared many characteristics with other Southern states: an agricultural economy with a mixture of plantations and small farms; an overwhelmingly rural society with tiny interior villages and small river or coastal towns; and a social and political hierarchy with Negro slaves at the bottom and a small slaveholding aristocracy at the top. But the South's one great city, New Orleans, affected the economic, social, and political patterns of all Louisiana, often in most "unsouthern" ways. Antebellum New Orleans was the nation's fifth largest city, and rivaled New York as the nation's greatest emporium. She handled not only basic Southern crops like cotton, sugar, and tobacco, but also a great volume of products from the entire Mississippi Valley. Because of New Orleans' pivotal position in interregional and international trade, the banking system of Louisiana was one of the largest and most important in the country.*

The economy of antebellum America operated within a network of regional and local markets rather than a unified national market; and relatively independent systems of money and credit existed in different states and regions. Thus the financing of American interregional trade in the early nineteenth century was similar to the financing of international trade, involving the purchase and sale of domestic or foreign bills of exchange and the calculation of exchange discounts and risks. To the cotton planter, the rural storekeeper, and the New Orleans retailer, exports to Charleston and New York or imports from Boston and Cincinnati were almost as truly "foreign" trade as dealings with Liverpool, Paris, or Havana. This business was conducted through factors (commission merchants) and other mercantile specialists. Many historians, exaggerating the adverse effect of the planter-factor relationship on economic growth, have failed to notice the factor's economic function in interregional commerce and his usefulness to the banker as an intermediary in the financial structure. And some have confused the welfare of the planters with the welfare of the South as a whole.

The study of a local and regional economy also gives a fresh

---

* Louisiana ranked third (behind New York and Massachusetts) in banking capital, accounting for as much as 12 per cent of the nation's total in 1840; by 1859 she had slipped to fourth (behind Pennsylvania) with 6 per cent. Operated conservatively with unusually high reserve ratios, Louisiana banks held a still larger share of the specie in the nation's banks: 16 per cent in 1830, 10 per cent in 1840, 19 per cent in 1845, and 15 per cent in 1859. For Louisiana data see Table C.1. For United States data, see: USC, [41], pp. 84-85; Fenstermaker, pp. 66-67.

perspective on the economic role of government. In Louisiana, the federal government was a "foreign" agency whose financial transactions shifted funds between the states. Its independent subtreasury plan disrupted economic stability, especially by adhering to a rigid specie standard when the nation's banks were operating with suspended specie payments and flexible exchange rates in 1837-42. The federally chartered second Bank of the United States was intimately involved in the domestic economy of Louisiana until Jackson's famous "war" against the Bank was imported from Washington. Recent studies have shown that antebellum state governments often exerted a much stronger influence on the economy than the federal government did. Louisiana provides us with a dramatic case study of government intervention, since hers was the most heavily subsidized and closely regulated of all the state banking systems.[3]

Theory and Statistics in Historical Analysis

In part, this study is an informal experiment in methodology—an attempt to narrow the gap between the "new" economic history practiced mainly by economists and the traditional economic history practiced mainly by historians. What follows is not quite "econometric" history. Although there is an abundance of statistical evidence, some of it "synthetic" or "figmentary,"* there are no regressions or formal statistical tests.

More important than quantification or statistical procedure, in my opinion, is an extensive and explicit use of relevant economic theory. Many of our traditional histories of American banking and finance have been marred by their reliance on an implicit theory that is often illogical or irrelevant.[4] How often have we read, for example, that paper money is inherently inflationary, or that banks making other than short-term commercial loans are engaging in dangerous "speculation." I do not claim that every theoretical argument in the following pages is beyond challenge or revision; what I do claim is that a more explicit use of theory

---

* The term "figment" is used by Fritz Redlich with reference to data that did not exist in the historical sources but have been derived, or "synthesized," from historical data on the basis of theoretical assumptions or models. A prime example would be the estimates of GNP for the nineteenth century. See Redlich, " 'New' and Traditional Approaches to Economic History and Their Interdependence."

will improve the level of historical discussion and revision in the future. And I have tried to "translate" economic theory into readable English.

As the historical situation becomes more complex, the need for explicit, rigorous use of theory is increased. The approach of traditional historians is likely to result in either of two modes of explanation, both fallacious. The historian's treatment of causal relationships may be oversimplified, based on hidden assumptions, and even flawed by logical contradictions. Or his assertions about causation may be essentially an open-ended "list" of causes, with the ranking or interaction of causes left to his subjective judgment or avoided entirely. The first approach attempts more explanation than the evidence justifies; the second attempts less. A better course is to keep the relevant theory explicit and coherent, extending it as far as possible to allow for institutional changes. The stubbornly unmanageable factors (usually noneconomic) can be discussed in terms of their interactions with the variables within the basic model, as well as in terms of their separate causal roles. Thus most, if not all, of the explanation proceeds within an orderly theoretical framework.

As a model expands to include additional variables and relationships it may well become untestable in the statistical sense. The "new" economic historians would probably respond to this situation either by declaring the problem insoluble or by reducing its dimensions and attempting to estimate ("quantify") or, more often, to dismiss the troublesome new variables by assuming that they are not present. Again, I prefer a more eclectic approach. The simple, precise, and statistically testable models of the economist and the "new" economic historian are useful as a starting point; they can indicate the general magnitude and direction of historical changes and give a rough quantitative idea of the relative importance of the causal variables. From this beginning a theory may be elaborated and extended to other, less aggregative statistics and to traditional qualitative evidence.

The Process of Finance

Let us begin the application of economic theory to history with a simple descriptive model of the process of finance as it operated in antebellum Louisiana. Finance essentially involves paying for goods and services received. Its simplest form is internal finance (self-finance), which meets expenditures out of current income or accumulated savings. In this case, no debt or credit is created, and all transactions are in cash or kind. The alternative is external finance, that is, borrowing to pay for goods and services. In this case, debt and credit are created, sometimes a whole chain of debts and credits. The two crucial participants in external finance are the ultimate borrower (debtor) and the ultimate lender (creditor). The first is some participant in the nonfinancial economy—planter, farmer, merchant, manufacturer, consumer, or government—whose spending exceeds his income. To match this deficit spender there must be an ultimate lender, a similar nonfinancial participant who saves, that is, spends less than his current income. External finance, however complicated it appears in given transactions, always boils down to transferring current purchasing power (i.e., command over goods and services) from the ultimate lender to the ultimate borrower, from creditor to debtor. At some later time, of course, the debt will be repaid, and purchasing power will flow in the other direction, usually augmented by interest. Transactions in external finance can be conducted either directly between borrower and lender or indirectly through a financial intermediary such as a commercial bank.

A very large proportion of the total spending on both consumption and investment in antebellum Louisiana was undoubtedly financed internally. Farmers and planters spent current profits (or utilized their own capital and labor force directly) to acquire more acreage, more slaves, or other improvements. Merchants and storekeepers put their savings into increased inventories. Consumer goods were homemade or were purchased out of current income. Agricultural (and related) income, however, was seasonal, which created a need for much external financing between harvests.

The bulk of external finance flowed directly from lender to borrower. A Louisiana planter often financed his purchase of land or slaves by borrowing from relatives, friends, or wealthy neighbors with surplus funds to invest.[5] A large volume of external finance also arose in connection with the export of Louisiana cotton or sugar and the import of manufactured goods and other supplies. Frequently, this trade credit involved a long, complex chain of direct financial transactions (see Figure 1). The farmer or planter obtained supplies from a local storekeeper, charging his purchase on a running account that he would presumably pay off at harvest time. The storekeeper, in turn, obtained his goods from a wholesale merchant in New Orleans or elsewhere, paying for them on long-term credit (90 days to a year). This chain of credit continued up the line to the manufacturer; and the total credit involved had to cover the value of the merchandise for the full period of time between production by the manufacturer and payment by the farmer, commonly a year or more. The necessary savings (ultimate lending) usually came from a combination of several sources. If the farmer's debt (or the storekeeper's unsold inventory) ran longer than the storekeeper's wholesale credit, the storekeeper had to rely on his own capital or special borrowing

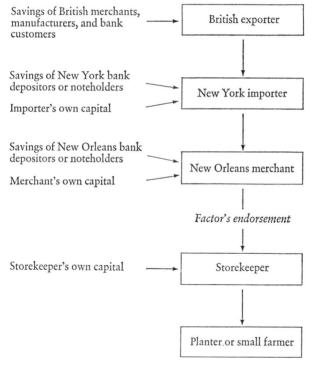

FIGURE I. A TYPICAL CHAIN OF DIRECT FINANCE

to bridge the gap. Similarly, other merchants and middlemen along the chain contributed some of their own capital or borrowed from their local banks and other outside sources.[6]

The pivotal middleman in the chain was usually the factor, who performed a variety of services for planters (and occasionally for storekeepers): marketing crops, purchasing supplies, keeping business records, paying bills, and providing information on general business conditions. In addition, he was the "contact man" or broker between rural borrowers and urban lenders. Generally the factor endorsed or guaranteed the planter's financial contracts, adding his own credit rating as additional security for the lender. Although this endorsement greatly improved a planter's access to urban finance, it did not tie up the factor's own capital unless a planter failed to pay his debts on schedule.[7]

A factor would often involve himself more directly in the chain of credit by acting as a financial intermediary between the borrowing planter and his various creditors (see Figure 2). During the year the factor would directly finance a variety of expenditures for the planter: purchases of basic plantation supplies; marketing expenses for the planter's cotton or sugar (transportation, storage, processing, insurance, commissions, and fees); and purchases of land, slaves, or other improvements. By paying the planter's bills, or providing him with cash to do so, the factor became the planter's major creditor. Ordinarily, the accumulated debt was to be paid when the planter's crop was sold, and any deficiency was carried over against the next year's account.

Usually, very little of the credit that the factor supplied came from his own savings. Instead, he was in turn indebted to others further up the chain of credit. By negotiating delayed payments to merchants who sold goods to the planter the factor shifted some of the credit burden to the importers (see Figure 1). Similarly, by paying for marketing services with time drafts the factor shifted the financing of the staples trade partly onto the buyers of the crop.*

---

* At the factor's request, the planter would write an order (draft) for the factor to pay the marketing firm at some distant date. The factor would then "accept" his obligation to pay by endorsing the draft. The merchant receiving this postdated check could either hold it until maturity (in which case he provided the financing for that interval) or discount it to a banker or other lender, adding another link in the chain of credit. Woodman, *King Cotton*, pp. 39-40.

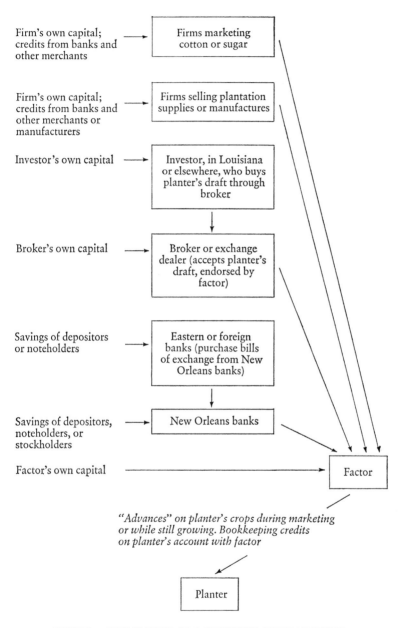

Firm's own capital; credits from banks and other merchants	→	Firms marketing cotton or sugar
Firm's own capital; credits from banks and other merchants or manufacturers	→	Firms selling plantation supplies or manufactures
Investor's own capital	→	Investor, in Louisiana or elsewhere, who buys planter's draft through broker
Broker's own capital	→	Broker or exchange dealer (accepts planter's draft, endorsed by factor)
Savings of depositors or noteholders	→	Eastern or foreign banks (purchase bills of exchange from New Orleans banks)
Savings of depositors, noteholders, or stockholders	→	New Orleans banks
Factor's own capital		→ Factor

"Advances" on planter's crops during marketing or while still growing. Bookkeeping credits on planter's account with factor

Planter

FIGURE 2. THE FACTOR AS A FINANCIAL INTERMEDIARY

The factor also gave the planter access to the New Orleans capital market by endorsing the planter's note and placing it with a broker or exchange dealer for sale.

Another vital link in the chain of finance, to which the New Orleans factors had especially close access, was the banking system. The factors commonly endorsed planters' drafts for discounting at the banks, and also discounted their own local drafts and bills of exchange. Planters had some direct access to bank credit (see Chapter One), but they ordinarily depended on the factors' endorsements or mediation. The banks, of course, were not the ultimate lenders, but simply channels for the savings of others. They mobilized savings within the state by issues of banknotes and deposits, and by local sales of their capital stock. They imported "foreign" savings by selling their stocks and bonds in the East or in Europe, and to a smaller extent by exporting their notes or deposits. Those who held the banks' notes, deposits, or capital, whether Louisianans or "foreigners," were the ultimate lenders who had surrendered their immediate command over goods and services to borrowers at the other end of the credit chain.

So far, we have concentrated on the financing of agriculture and commerce, the two most important sectors of Louisiana's economy. But other sectors were also involved in the financial process. The construction of railroads and other public utilities was almost always externally financed through issues of stocks and bonds; the government and the banking system served as financial intermediaries for these projects. Most routine expenditures of state and local government were financed internally through taxation; but when deficits appeared, the banks played an important role as financial intermediaries. Government bonds were rarely sold to the public except in connection with particular "social overhead" projects—e.g., public utilities or transportation improvements. Little evidence exists on the finance of manufacturing. Presumably, it was accomplished through a combination of internal finance (reinvested earnings), direct finance by owners, and trade credits on raw materials or finished products.

CHAPTER ONE

Banking and the Allocation of Credit

THE ECONOMY of antebellum Louisiana developed along two complementary but distinct lines. Like the other Southern states, she was heavily committed to plantation agriculture, slavery, and the production of cash crops such as cotton and sugar. But unlike the rest of the South (especially her neighbors Alabama, Mississippi, Arkansas, and Texas), Louisiana also developed a prosperous and powerful urban economy in the great commercial center of New Orleans.

Louisiana's agriculture began during the colonial period as rudimentary frontier subsistence farming, producing a few basic commodities that supplied the small forts and trading posts of the area or were exported to the Gulf Coast and the West Indies. Tobacco and indigo were the major cash crops. Slavery had come to Louisiana early in the eighteenth century, and the plantation system was well established by the time of the Louisiana Purchase in 1803. It operated on a small scale, however, serving mainly local markets. At this time most of the state outside New Orleans was unsettled.[1]

Not until the nineteenth century did Louisiana agriculture develop its great export crops, cotton and sugar. In 1803 Louisiana produced less than 5,000 bales of cotton, and at the time of statehood in 1812 only 10,000 bales. But the next decades saw a rapid expansion, and by 1859 output had risen to an antebellum peak of 777,738 bales. From its small beginning along the Mississippi, Louisiana's "cotton belt" spread out to include most of the state by 1860, except for the sugar regions of the delta and the cattle prairies of the southwest.[2] The expansion of sugar and molasses production followed a similar path, though with roughly a decade lag. After nearly a century of unsuccessful experiments, sugar production began in earnest in 1795, when Etienne de Boré produced the first successful and profitable granulated sugar. By 1803 the state produced about 5,000 hogsheads of sugar (roughly 1,000 pounds each); peak production for the antebellum period came in 1853 with an output of about 450,000 hogsheads. The sugar plantations were concentrated in the warm, wet, and fertile lands of the Mississippi delta and the southern bayous.[3]

Although large plantations dominated Louisiana's sugar production and generally occupied the most valuable cotton lands, small farms and plantations remained important. Even in the heart of some of the most fertile river-bottom districts small holdings were scattered among the plantations; and the more sparsely settled areas of northern Louisiana had few plantations throughout the antebellum era. As of 1820, the western half of the state (west of Alexandria and Opelousas) was essentially open prairie devoted mainly to cattle ranching. Even after the expansion of cotton culture into much of this frontier region during the 1830's, the area retained a diversified agriculture, and Louisiana's cattle herds continued to grow until the 1850's.[4]

Except for its large and relatively capital-intensive sugar plantations, Louisiana's agriculture was quite similar to that of other Southern states. But in her development of a great commercial metropolis at New Orleans, Louisiana more nearly resembled New York or Massachusetts. New Orleans had become a major commercial city during the colonial era, while most of the rest of the state lay undeveloped. From at least the time of statehood, over 20 per cent of Louisiana's population lived in the city. In fact, as of the 1840 census Louisiana was the most urbanized state in the nation, with 29 per cent of its inhabitants residing in New Orleans. At that time, the Crescent City was the nation's fifth largest urban area (behind New York, Philadelphia, Boston, and Baltimore.)[5]

New Orleans began her rapid growth under Spanish rule (1762-1800), reaching a population of 5,000 before 1790. And during the early nineteenth century, even before the great expansion of cotton and sugar farming, she gained a place among America's leading commercial cities. By 1815, the city was receiving annually nearly $10 million in goods from Louisiana and the Mississippi Valley. With the westward movement of Southern cotton and Northern agriculture, and with the development of Louisiana's own staples, New Orleans doubled her population and commerce during the 1820's. In 1834-44 her exports matched or exceeded those of New York in value, though she remained far behind the Eastern cities in value of imports. During the 1840's the produce of the upper Mississippi Valley began to flow eastward by river, canal, and railroad; and New York soon regained her leadership of the export trade. New Orleans continued to grow commercially, but she was becoming a more exclusively Southern port.[6]

In some respects New Orleans was an island of urbanization, commerce, and industry in the midst of an otherwise rural and agricultural state. But the temptation to treat New Orleans and rural Louisiana as separate economies or cultures must be resisted, for the two constantly interacted with and influenced each other. New Orleans was the marketing center for the great bulk of the state's agricultural output and the source of most of the state's imported supplies. New Orleans factors and rural storekeepers linked the urban and rural economies. In fact, individual entrepreneurs sometimes pursued simultaneous careers in planting, commerce, and finance. The commerce of New Orleans contributed about as much to Louisiana's total income as did the state's sugar production, and the city accounted for about 70 per cent of Louisiana's manufacturing activity. Urban and rural culture also shared an overlapping social elite; and the two cultures met politically in the state legislature. From the perspective of this study, it is especially noteworthy that New Orleans was the home office for every one of Louisiana's banks.[7]

The Banking System: Basic Structure and Functions

All banks in Louisiana were created by one of three legal routes. A chartered bank was established by a separate, special act of the state legislature; and its charter spelled out the particular rules and restrictions by which the legislature guided its operations. "Free banks" were also creatures of the legislature; but they were regulated by a general free banking law (passed initially in 1853), rather than by separate acts. Besides these two types of incorporated banks, there were unincorporated "private banks," which operated as partnerships or single proprietorships. The private banks had fewer legal obligations to the state than the incorporated banks, but they were subject to general state laws governing financial transactions, maximum interest rates, foreclosure, etc. In particular, they were denied the privilege of issuing banknotes (though they could accept deposits).

The relationship of the two kinds of incorporated banks to the state was not confined to state control of their behavior through the charters. In many ways, they were also economic arms of the government, issuing loans to the state, paying bonuses to state projects, or serving as fiscal agents for state and local government; and the state subsidized or aided some of them. The private banks had no such intimate relationship with the government. The federal government, for its part, exerted no centralized control except for the limited and temporary influence of the Bank of the United States and the irregular leadership of the Treasury. For the most part, then, Louisiana banks were politically regulated only by their state government; and they dealt with the nation and the rest of the world through the financial marketplace, in transactions with other American banks and with the great merchant bankers of Europe.

In addition to the legal structure of the Louisiana banking system, we must consider the structure or pattern of its lending. The greatest variety of chartered banking institutions arose during the expansionary 1830's. Contemporary Louisianans distinguished three kinds of chartered banks. "Property banks," incorrectly called "plantation banks" by some historians, made mortgage loans to planters and urban property owners. "Improvement banks" financed, constructed, and managed internal improvements such as canals, railroads, waterworks, and hotels. "Commercial banks" were more conventional, providing merchants with short-term credit to finance inventories or shipments of cotton, sugar, and other commodities. The channels of bank credit overlapped more than these categories might suggest. But this schematized view accurately reflects the wide range of economic activities that the banks financed. The property and improvement banks were liquidated during the 1840's, but the surviving commercial banks sometimes continued to make the types of loans in which other banks had specialized.

The banking system as a whole was an effective financial intermediary, mobilizing domestic and foreign savings and channeling them to Louisiana's credit-thirsty agriculture, commerce, and social-overhead projects. In addition, it helped provide Louisiana (and adjacent states) with an effective money supply and a mechanism of payments. Throughout the antebellum era Louisiana's banks contributed to the money supply by issuing banknote currency. They also created deposit liabilities; but these did not serve as a general means of payment, since their use as money remained concentrated in the commercial sector of the economy. The banks also aided the payment mechanism by their operations in domestic and foreign exchange; by purchasing and collecting bills of exchange, they especially facilitated payments to and from distant cities.

Louisiana's banks operated within a complex system of international finance whose first axiom was a specie standard requiring that all money of all countries be freely convertible at par into gold or silver. A set of fixed exchange rates between currencies was thus imposed, although the high costs and risks of shipping specie on the open sea permitted a good deal of fluctuation around par values. The specie standard underlay all financial transactions, but the actual system of banking relationships contrived to supplement or displace specie in routine payments. Bankers built up an elaborate network of debts and credits for long-distance payments, using the gold and silver in their vaults to guarantee the convertibility of the various monies in which they dealt. Specie often functioned directly as money in local transactions, especially the petty transactions of retail trade; but even here it was complemented by banknotes and by various bookkeeping credit arrangements.

One of the major themes of this study is the conflict that existed between the credit and the monetary functions of the antebellum banking system. The desire for expanded credit, especially long-term credit, conflicted with the desire for a stable money supply convertible into specie. This conflict was most sharply revealed in the several financial crises that struck the antebellum American banking system. The crisis of 1837-42 was the most severe for Louisiana, and it prompted a basic reorientation of the state's banking policy and practices.

Brief Chronology of Banking and the Louisiana Economy

Although the foundations of Louisiana's plantation agriculture and New Orleans' commercial empire were laid in the colonial era, the French and Spanish left hardly a trace of their presence on the financial system. Their financial policies were implemented almost entirely by the colonial governments. They established no banks, and their various issues of inconvertible paper currencies suffered gradual devaluation. Thus the history of Louisiana banking and finance begins virtually *de novo* in 1804.[8]

With the withdrawal of the Spanish authorities in 1800, the flow of silver from Vera Cruz had ceased, and Louisiana was flooded with depreciated *liberanzas* currency. In 1804, partly in response to this disrupted money supply, a group of New Orleans merchants and businessmen obtained a charter from the territorial governor, W. C. C. Claiborne, and established the Louisiana Bank. Initially capitalized at $300,000, the bank was also given the power to issue banknote currency and to raise its capital to $2 million when expedient; its charter was to expire in 1819. While the Louisiana Bank was still negotiating its charter, Congress approved the establishment of a New Orleans branch of the first Bank of the United States. Thus within two years of the Louisiana Purchase New Orleans had two banks in operation.[9]

When the charter of the first Bank of the United States expired in 1811, the territorial legislature promptly chartered two new banks to replace the New Orleans branch. The Bank of Orleans was apparently a conventional commercial bank, and several of its initial directors were prominent New Orleans merchants who had previously been directors of the Bank of the United States. It was clearly a financial success, for its charter, scheduled to expire in 1826, was renewed in 1823 and extended until 1847. The Planters Bank was apparently set up to provide credit for Louisiana's expanding plantation agriculture, and about half of its directors were planters. Unfortunately, no evidence exists on the actual composition of its loans or on other aspects of its performance. It suspended operations in 1820, and its charter expired in 1826.[10]

The War of 1812 created problems for the Louisiana economy. The British blockade depressed agriculture and commerce, forcing many people to delay or default payments of their debts and taxes. The state government faced a series of deficits, totaling $121,000 by 1815. These deficits were financed by negotiating and renewing one-year loans with the New Orleans banks. Although the amount involved might seem small at first glance, a $75,000 loan granted by the Louisiana Bank in 1815 probably exceeded 10 per cent of its total assets.[11] To meet the crisis a committee of the Louisiana House of Representatives proposed the chartering of a new state bank with a capital of $2 million (of which the state would retain $600,000). The bank would make the usual commercial loans, but in addition it would provide relief for burdened debtors, including the state government. Proponents of the bank argued that the "usurious" interest rates then prevailing proved the need for further banking capacity, and declared: "It is not in times of prosperity that banks are the most useful, but on the contrary in times of distress."[12] The committee's elaborate plan for debt relief through banking was presented in two successive sessions but never brought to a vote. Many of its ideas, however, were later embodied in the charter of the Louisiana State Bank.

After the end of the war in 1815, the state government quickly resumed budget surpluses and within a few years had repaid nearly all of its accumulated debts to the banks. Louisiana's plantation agriculture (particularly cotton) and commerce began a period of rapid growth, greatly aided by the opening of the New Orleans branch of the second Bank of the United States in 1817. By February 1818 the branch had made commercial loans of $1.3 million. At this time, the charter of the Louisiana Bank was about to expire; and in March 1818 the legislature created the Louisiana State Bank, with a $2 million capital stock. The state was to purchase $500,000 of the stock, and would select six of the bank's eighteen directors. Finally, the new charter provided for Louisiana's first banking facilities outside New Orleans; and five branch offices, each with a capital of $100,000, were set up. Louisiana had roughly doubled her state-chartered banking facilities at one stroke.[13]

There is virtually no evidence concerning the "panic of 1819" in Louisiana, and its effect was probably quite limited. The governor, in his annual message to the legislature on January 6, 1819, commented sanguinely: "Agriculture, industry and commerce are in the most flourishing condition. If commerce indeed has for some time experienced and still does experience pecuniary embarrassments, the careful observer will easily discover the cause of it in its very prosperity, or at least in the great extension which the speculating and enterprising spirit which animates and marks the character of our citizens has given to it."[14] By January 1820 he was more concerned about the economic damage resulting from a recent epidemic of yellow fever. His financial worries were negligible; in fact, the state government boasted a healthy surplus and had finally retired its debt.

The major indication of financial pressure was the situation of the new Louisiana State Bank. Because of a "great scarcity of specie," the bank had been forced to limit its discounts severely and to require clearance of all rural discounts through its New Orleans office. In response, the legislature passed an act to remove this limitation on rural loans.[15] The State Bank was allowed to make longer term loans (over 180 days, at 8 per cent per annum interest) and to pay its required "bonus" to the state more slowly; in return, it had to provide its branches with at least $70,000 of initial capital and allow the branches to control (lend on) their own capital and branch deposits. This amendment probably reflected not only a short-run demand for credit in a time of financial pressure, but also the persistent demands of rural Louisianans for greater credit facilities.

The 1820's were a decade of substantial growth for Louisiana's cotton and sugar plantations and for New Orleans commerce; but they were marked by a series of economic misfortunes. Yellow fever struck New Orleans in 1819 and 1822, disrupting all commercial activity and depressing agricultural prices. In 1823 over a third of the state's cotton crop was destroyed by floods, and in 1827 a drought reduced the yield. And the British financial crisis of 1825 cast its shadow over New Orleans markets and finances. These various crises, together with expanded investments in new plantations (especially in capital-intensive sugar plantations), created strong demands for external finance and for expansion of banking facilities.[16] The successive bad years of 1822 and 1823 put especially strong pressures on Louisiana's financial system. The state's planters, in particular, were dissatisfied with high interest rates and the scarcity of credit. In 1834 they were able to force an anti-usury law through the legislature, only to see the governor support the merchants and moneylenders by vetoing the bill. The one expansionary action taken in 1823 was the extension of the charter of the Bank of Orleans.[17]

By early 1824 the pressure for some form of debtor relief was irresistible. The Senate passed a bill to create a state loan office; but the House blocked this proposal by agreeing to charter a Bank of Louisiana, assigning it a capital of $4 million. In return for $2 million of the bank's capital stock, the state issued $2.4 million worth of bonds. The bank sold these to raise specie reserves, and established a sinking fund in order to pay interest and principal on the bonds. Five rural branches were established, each with a capital of $200,000, and two-thirds of the branch capital was required to be lent on mortgage loans. The governor reluctantly approved the new charter, despite provisions for state subsidy, expressing his relief that the law averted the greater evils of "stop laws, paper money, and other similar quackery."[18]

While the Bank of Louisiana was being created in order to expand rural credits, the Louisiana State Bank was coming under attack for reducing them. During much of the 1824 legislative session, the rural-oriented Senate sought to replace all the bank's officers and enforce more liberal lending policies. Apparently the bank's rural debtors were slow to pay in these years of low agricultural incomes, for in 1825 it requested and received legislative permission to close four of its five branches, on condition that its debtors would be given as much as four years to repay their loans.[19] This arrangement relieved the immediate financial problem but reduced the long-term supply of agricultural credit in the state.

By 1827 the rapid development of sugar plantations had created new demands for external finance. The legislature responded by chartering Louisiana's first property bank, the Consolidated Association of the Planters of Louisiana. The planters were to exchange $2.5 million in mortgages on their own property for the bank's $2 million of capital stock. The bank would then use the mortgages as collateral for $2 million of bonds which would be sold abroad to raise a specie reserve. Unable to sell its bonds, the bank sought state support in 1828. And despite some vigorous opposition to "pledging the faith of the State . . . exclusively for the interest of one class of its citizens," the legislature finally agreed to accept the bank's mortgage portfolio (enlarged to $3 million) in return for the issue of $2.5 million in state bonds. The Consolidated Association had further difficulty negotiating the sale of these state bonds, but managed to raise operating capital during the next few years. It soon became clear, however, that one such bank would not satisfy the expanding demand for rural credit.[20]

The 1830's were a decade of great economic expansion in Louisiana, as in most of the nation. The extension of cotton plantations into newly opened territories and a series of exceptionally good harvests at the end of the decade produced a threefold increase in the state's cotton output. Although sugar production remained virtually static, the value of all commerce flowing into New Orleans nearly doubled. All this growth was accompanied by an even more rapid expansion of the state's banking facilities between 1831 and 1836 (see Table 1.1).[21]

Demands for new bank charters deluged the state legislature

TABLE 1.1

The Chartered Banks of Antebellum Louisiana

Bank	Date(s) chartered	Capital (in $ millions)	Remarks
Louisiana Bank	3/12/04	$ 0.3 2.0	Liquidation 1819-23.
First Bank of the U.S. (branch)	1805	—	Charter expired 1811.
Planters Bank	4/15/11	0.6	Suspended operations 1820; charter expired 1826.
Bank of Orleans	4/30/11 3/26/23	0.5 —	Scheduled to expire 1826. Renewed to 1847; into liquidation in 1842.
Second Bank of the U.S. (branch)	1817	—	Charter expired 1836.
Louisiana State Bank	3/18/18	2.0	Became State National Bank in 1870; liquidated 1908.
Bank of Louisiana	4/7/24	4.0	Into liquidation 1865.
Consolidated Assoc. of the Planters of Louisiana	3/16/27 2/19/28	2.0 2.5	Chartered to 1842. New charter, state bonds issued, capital increased; liquidation begun 1843, completed 1883.
City Bank of New Orleans	3/3/31	2.0	Charter expired 1850; assets purchased by Louisiana State Bank.

TABLE I.I (*continued*)

Bank	Date(s) chartered	Capital (in $ millions)	Remarks
Canal Bank	3/5/31	$4.0	Original charter to 1870; reorganized and survived into 20th century.
Union Bank of Louisiana	4/2/32	7.0	Into liquidation Jan. 1844.
Citizens Bank of Louisiana	4/1/33	12.0	Original charter to 1884.
	3/1/36	—	State guarantees bank bonds; into liquidation 1842.
	3/10/52	—	Legislature revives charter; reorganized and survived into 20th century.
Clinton & Port Hudson R.R. Co.	1833	0.5	Charter amended to give mortgage banking powers.
Mechanics & Traders Bank	4/1/33	2.0	Original charter to 1853.
	3/22/50	—	Authorized to begin liquidation; converted to free bank 1853; survived past Civil War.
Commercial Bank of New Orleans	4/1/33	3.0	Into liquidation 1843.
Atchafalaya R.R. & Banking Company	3/10/35	2.0	Banking operations into liquidation in 1842.
New Orleans & Carrollton R.R. & Banking Co.	4/1/35	3.0	Banking powers granted to existing company; these powers surrendered 1844.
New Orleans Gas Light & Banking Co.	4/1/35	6.0	Banking powers granted to existing company and surrendered 1845.
Exchange & Banking Co.	4/1/35	2.0	Into liquidation 1842.
New Orleans Improvement & Banking Co.	2/9/36	2.0	Banking powers granted to existing company; into liquidation 1842.
Merchants Bank of New Orleans	2/25/36	1.0	Into liquidation 1847.
Pontchartrain R.R. & Banking Co.	3/12/36	—	Banking powers granted to existing company but never exercised.
Bank of New Orleans[a]	1853	1.0	First free bank; capital raised to $2 million by 1857.
Southern Bank[a]	1853	1.25	
Bank of James Robb[a]	1857	0.6	Reorganized 1859 as Merchants Bank.
Bank of America[a]	1857	1.0	
Union Bank[a]	1857	1.5	
Crescent City Bank[a]	1857	1.0	

[a] Free bank.

in 1831. Many politicians seemed quite receptive to the idea; and their committee reports emphasized the desirability of mobilizing the "domestic capital in the hands of small traders, mechanics, professional men, and property owners" by allowing interest on bank deposits. The City Bank of New Orleans, a commercial bank, was chartered with a capital of $2 million; it had branch offices in the towns of Baton Rouge and Natchitoches, and each was to lend at least 50 per cent of its $200,000 branch capital on mortgages. The new Canal Bank became the state's first improvement bank; of its $4 million capital, $1 million would finance the construction of a canal from Lake Pontchartrain into the heart of New Orleans; another $1.3 million was designated for four rural branches, at least two-thirds of it for mortgage loans.[22]

The Union Bank bill occupied most of the legislature's energies in 1832. It was a massive undertaking: with $7 million of capital stock, the proposed bank would increase the total capital of Louisiana's state-chartered banks by nearly 50 per cent. Some contemporaries considered this an expansion beyond all reasonable needs. But the bank's supporters replied by pointing to the rapid expansion of the state's agriculture and commerce, and to the anticipated demise of the second Bank of the United States, whose New Orleans branch then held a loan portfolio of over $10 million. The Union Bank, they said, would merely fill the gap left by the departure of the national bank, sustaining the vital flow of credit. The major points of controversy were once again the issue of state bonds on behalf of the bank and the distribution of the bank's lending capacity between New Orleans and other areas of the state (i.e., between commercial and agricultural borrowers). The charter finally provided for eight branch offices with a total capital of nearly $1.8 million (some $1.2 million of it for loans on mortgage); an additional $800,000 was to come out of future profits and was to be lent in parishes not served directly by the branches. Thus the Union Bank would blanket the state with its liberal credit facilities. Whatever its weaknesses as a business proposition, this new charter was a masterpiece of log-rolling politics.[23]

In 1833 the legislature chartered three new banks. The Mechanics and Traders Bank was an ordinary commercial bank with $2 million capital and two branches (combined capital of $500,000). The Commercial Bank of New Orleans was to use about half of its $3 million capital to construct a city waterworks and the rest for commercial loans. But by far the most significant charter of 1833 was that establishing the Citizens Bank, the state's third and last property bank. The bank's authorized capital of $12 million made it the largest state-chartered bank in America at the time (the Union Bank was second). After failing for two years to sell its bonds in Europe, the Citizens Bank finally sold $3 million worth to Hope and Co. of Amsterdam in September 1835. But the sale was conditional on a state guarantee of the bonds; this endorsement was obtained from the legislature in 1836, over strong opposition and only after the bank promised 50 per cent of its stock (and hence of its mortgage loans) to rural areas. Thus Louisiana had now underwritten the bonds of all three of its property banks, incurring a potential obligation of $21.5 million.[24]

In 1835-36 the legislature climaxed its five-year flood of charters by creating six new banks.* One of these, the Merchants Bank, soon became the New Orleans agency for Nicholas Biddle's United States Bank of Pennsylvania (see Chapter Three). The other five were improvement banks. In addition to their banking powers they were given responsibility for the construction or operation of two railroads, two large merchant hotels in New Orleans, and the city's gas streetlights. Because most of their assets were tied up in illiquid improvement projects, and because they had barely begun operations before the Panic of 1837 struck, these institutions suffered extreme financial difficulties in the years ahead. All six had failed or had surrendered their banking privileges by 1847.[25]

At the beginning of 1831 Louisiana had had four banks with a total capital of $9 million. In the next six years the legislature had chartered twelve new banks with an authorized capitalization totaling $46 million. But these figures exaggerate the expansion of banking facilities. Not all of the authorized capital was actually subscribed; some of the paid-in capital went toward improvement projects rather than banking operations; and some of it merely replaced the credit facilities of the New Orleans branch of the second Bank of the United States. When financial crisis de-

---

* A seventh charter, for the Pontchartrain Railroad and Banking Company, was passed in 1836; but the railroad, caught up in the financial crisis in 1837, never exercised its banking powers.

scended on Louisiana and the rest of the nation in March 1837, the era of banking expansion ended. Six years of persistent financial troubles followed, and public policy was restrictive toward banking for some years longer.

The crisis years 1837-42 mark the greatest watershed in the financial history of antebellum Louisiana, and the entire period witnessed a chronic disruption of normal financial and commercial relations. But in Louisiana, at least, this was not a period of sustained economic depression like that of the 1930's. In fact, both earnings from the Louisiana cotton crop and the value of trade through New Orleans reached new peak levels in 1839 and 1840. The greatest economic hardships probably came in 1837, during the sharp financial contraction between March and May; and in 1841-42 there were severe contractions and extensive liquidations, both resulting from efforts to reorganize the banking system and resume specie payments. Between these low points, however, several suspensions and resumptions of specie payments occurred without seriously disrupting the real economy.

During the first years of crisis the banking system was largely under the control of the bankers themselves, acting collectively or individually. The first decisive policy action by the state government was the famous Louisiana Bank Act of February 5, 1842 —essentially a direct attempt to deal with the immediate crisis in the banking system and with the deteriorating financial condition of many Louisiana citizens. The Act was the first attempt by the state to systematically reform and permanently control the banking system. Its several innovations—notably its specie reserve requirements—and its apparent success in subsequent years gave it the status of a "model" law that influenced banking policy in the other states and in Congress.

The Bank Act inaugurated a decade of restrictions and contraction in Louisiana banking. No new banks were chartered, and all but five of the sixteen established banks entered liquidation or closed entirely. From 1843 to about 1846 the state government was controlled by antibank Democrats and supported by a strong popular distrust of banks; and the revised state constitution (1845) prohibited the granting or renewal of bank charters. In addition, because of its own fiscal difficulties, the state temporarily repudiated the bonds that it had issued or guaranteed on behalf of the banks. By 1847 the state had arranged for the payment of its bond obligations, mostly by relying on the resources of the banks or their stockholders. Even as this fiscal recovery was taking place, however, the contraction of Louisiana's banking capacity continued undiminished. Despite the continued contraction of the banking system, the Louisiana economy recovered reasonably well after 1842-43, and agriculture and commerce expanded steadily except around 1848-50. There were, however, a few early signs of shrinkage in New Orleans' commercial empire, and her rising volume of trade focused increasingly on the regional economy of the Gulf states. By the early 1850's an expanding economy had outreached the limited capacity of the state's financial system. Efforts to build several new railroad lines out of New Orleans and across the state in that decade generated particularly strong demands for external finance; and a continued expansion of cotton production and New Orleans trade added to the pressure.

As early as 1849-50 businessmen, journalists, and political leaders began to demand more adequate credit facilities. In 1852 state policy again shifted toward expansion of the banking system. The Citizens Bank was permitted to resume normal operations, although a decade of gradual liquidation had reduced its capital to $1.5 million; it would operate essentially as a commercial bank while continuing to liquidate its mortagage (property bank) assets. A new state constitution (1852) again permitted the legislature to create banks by special or general charter. A year later Louisiana adopted a "free banking" law that made it possible to incorporate a bank by following prescribed rules and procedures rather than by obtaining a special chartering act from the legislature. Louisiana's law was generally quite similar to free banking laws in other states (New York, Massachusetts), except that it incorporated some restrictive provisions like those of the 1840's, notably the reserve requirements of the 1842 Bank Act. Seven free banks were incorporated in New Orleans between 1853 and 1857, more than doubling the state's chartered banking capital and lending capacity.

The expansion of Louisiana's banking system and economy encountered some setbacks in the 1850's because of variations in the cotton and sugar harvests, in foreign financial conditions and markets, and in domestic finances. The most significant interruption followed the panic of 1857, which caused a short liquidity crisis in local banking and depressed some agricultural prices during the early months of the marketing season. But on the whole the crisis was brief and mild, causing none of the massive bankruptcy, debt burden, and disruption that had been common in 1837-42. The state's economy bounced back to normal by mid-1858, and in 1859 reached its peak levels for the entire antebellum era.

The history of banking in antebellum Louisiana, begun so abruptly with the American annexation in 1803, ended equally abruptly under the dictates of war and occupation. The banks of New Orleans suspended specie payments in September 1861 in response to orders from the Confederate government, which was issuing its own inconvertible paper currency. Before New Orleans was occupied by federal troops (April 1862) the banks shipped $6,100,000 of specie out of the state to keep it out of enemy hands. Under federal occupation the banks and merchants were heavily taxed and forced to absorb the losses on outlawed Confederate currency. Finally, the war almost smothered the trade of New Orleans, as well as the Southern economy that generated this trade. By 1865, the few surviving banks were greatly weakened and were poorly equipped to assist the postwar Southern economy.[26]

Commerce vs. Agriculture

The remainder of this chapter will consider the ways in which Louisiana's banking system influenced the distribution of credit among the different sectors of her economy—agriculture, commerce, manufacturing, and transportation or other improvements. The most controversial aspect of this distribution was the division of financial resources between city and country, i.e., between merchant (factor) and planter. There were repeated complaints in newspapers and legislative debates that a few New Orleans factors monopolized the credit of the city's banks, excluding other potential borrowers. This monopoly allegedly produced what planter Henry Huntington called "the system of robbery of our commission houses," by which planters became totally dependent on their factors for credit, the marketing of crops, the purchase of supplies, and a variety of other essential services.[27]

Despite these complaints, we must recognize that indebtedness to a factor was not entirely a misfortune for the planter. It enabled him to sustain his living standard even in years of poor crops, for example. But contrary to the usual interpretation, most planters probably did not incur their debts in order to finance extravagant consumption. In fact, debts grew most during the good years and were merely renewed or extended during the poor years. They were usually contracted for productive purposes, such as the purchase of additional land, slaves, or equipment; and even the wealthiest planters often chose to remain continuously in debt because they expected to profit from the borrowed funds. These expectations were not always fulfilled, and in hard times planters felt free to complain bitterly about debt "burdens" that they had eagerly assumed a few years earlier. Whatever the planters may have said, historians should remember that borrowing from factors often financed permanent additions to the physical capital of the economy.[28]

The factors charged relatively high interest rates and commissions for their services, although competition between factors imposed rough limits on these charges. Seeking lower rates, many planters tried to find other sources of credit, and there were widespread and successful campaigns to establish property banks and branch banking.* But neither of these innovations actually replaced the factors to any notable degree, largely because the bankers preferred to deal with factors rather than with planters. To some extent this preference undoubtedly reflected personal or family ties between New Orleans bankers and factors; and many factors were themselves bank directors. There were other good reasons for the bankers' reluctance to deal directly with planters, however.

As a middleman in the lending process, the factor could provide the banker with detailed information on market conditions and the credit status of individual planters. Moreover, the factor bore the initial impact of delinquent or defaulted debts, thus re-

---

* The free banking campaign of the 1850's was supported by many planters, or at least by their rural political spokesmen, partly in the belief that more "competitive" banking would end the factor's "monopoly" of credit. But strong support also came from the New Orleans business community, and in fact no free banks were chartered outside New Orleans.

ducing the banker's risks. Only if several debtors defaulted simultaneously (as in a general crisis) would the factor be unable to pay the bank. By granting and renewing commercial credit to factors, the bankers indirectly financed more long-term, productive loans to planters than they could have assumed directly; and it was the factors' risk-pooling activities that made this process possible. Given the concentration of banks in New Orleans, it seems probable that the existence of factors allowed a wider dispersion of credit on more liberal terms than the bankers alone could have provided.

As we have seen, planters were not at all content with the concentration of banking in New Orleans. One of the first attempts to provide alternative sources of credit was the establishment of property banks, which would offer planters direct access to long-term mortgage credit. The first such bank, the Consolidated Association of Planters, remained under the control of rural planters despite the admission of city property as collateral for up to one-third of its mortgages in 1836. And a breakdown of the Association's mortgages in 1847 shows 23 per cent granted on city property, as compared to 70 per cent on sugar plantations and 6 per cent on cotton plantations. The other two property banks, the Union Bank and the Citizens Bank, were from the outset largely urban-oriented in their ownership and lending. Even though the property banks did not bypass the New Orleans factors, they did increase by several million dollars the mortgage credit available to planters, particularly during the crucial decade of rapid expansion and capital formation (1827-37); and their failure after 1842 removed a major source of bank credit for both rural and urban landowners.[29]

The second device by which Louisiana's agricultural interests sought to expand their credit facilities was branch banking. The fifteen banks chartered by the state legislature between 1818 and 1836 all had their headquarters in New Orleans. But the same charters authorized the establishment of 46 branch banks in 26 different towns—colonial outposts of the New Orleans banking empire. The chartering of each new bank involved a massive tug-of-war in the legislature, each rural representative seeking a branch for his district while the merchants and bankers of New Orleans lobbied to confine branches to a few of the most profitable towns. Only 36 branches were actually opened, and these were concentrated in the richest cotton and sugar areas along the Mississippi and Red Rivers, and in the sugar and ranching parishes of south-central Louisiana. This network declined sharply after 1837 because of the unprofitability of branches, the liquidation of parent banks, and new legislation that restricted all banking.[30]

As with the property banks, the effort to expand agricultural credit through branch banks was only a partial success. Of the total of $13.4 million authorized as branch capital in the various bank charters, less than $6.8 million was actually allocated by the parent banks. (Usually, this outlay was in proportion to a bank's total paid-in capital, which in several cases did not reach the authorized limit before the crisis of 1837). This branch capital, plus a proportion of the branch deposits (usually a much smaller amount), made up the lending resources of the branches. Not all loans went to planters, however. Roeder estimates that about one-third of branch lending was in mortgages, and some of this went to small-town businessmen. The planters did receive some of the remaining two-thirds, mostly in short-term commercial lending to finance the movement of commodities to market. At its peak, branch banking provided about $7 million of credit to rural borrowers who would otherwise have sought direct finance in New Orleans, borrowed from country stores and other rural sources, or done without. Probably less than half of this $7 million (less in other years) went to finance plantation agriculture. And by 1846, the failure and liquidation of many banks and the closing of the still-surviving Canal Bank's branches had reduced the available branch capital to about $2 million.[31]

The effectiveness of branch banking was limited by conflicting demands for both easy credit and sound money. Independent rural banks, had they existed as an alternative to branch banks, would undoubtedly have encouraged more local entrepreneurship and provided a pattern of lending more responsive to the desires of local merchants, planters, and small farmers. True, each branch bank, once established, had pressed its headquarters for greater lending capacity and had sought greater freedom in extending liberal terms to rural borrowers. But the parent banks, though happy to have their banknotes circulate more widely in rural areas, consistently sought to channel their actual rural lending into the

more liquid commercial loans, avoiding risky, long-term operations (e.g., mortgages). By thus restricting the credit allocation of
their branches, they protected their own liquidity and hence the
"soundness" of their monetary liabilities; they also protected the
commercial supremacy of "imperial" New Orleans from the competition of small-town merchants and factors. Independent commercial banks probably could not have remained liquid enough
to survive in the extremely small towns and one-crop local economies of rural Louisiana (as the lack of small-town free banks in
the 1850's indicates). By pooling illiquid, undiversified rural loans
with the more diverse commercial portfolios of the New Orleans
banks, branch banking gave the entire state a safer money supply.
And the credit it provided, though less than independent rural
banks might have given, was surely much more than New Orleans would have provided to rural Louisiana in the absence of
branches.[32]

In summary, the allocation of finance between New Orleans
and rural Louisiana was as much a question of income distribution between agriculture and the various commercial interests as
a question of economic development. The expansion of financial
activities, mainly through factors, property banks, and branch
banks between 1827 and 1842, did increase the quantity and availability of credit to Louisiana agriculture. Most of this credit apparently went to the larger planters, who could exert political
influence on the location and lending practices of banks, and who
in addition owned most of the valuable fields and slaves that were
preferred as loan collateral. Small farmers and other less-favored
borrowers had to rely on their own savings, personal loans from
relatives or neighbors, and such informal financial intermediaries
as the country storekeeper. The expansion of rural credit facilities
was restrained by the New Orleans bankers and by restrictive legislation after 1842, both aimed at bank liquidity and sound money.
The New Orleans mercantile community encouraged this restraint
in order to protect its own credit supply and inhibit small-town
competitors.[33]

Financing Manufactures and Internal Improvements

Louisiana's banks devoted a negligible proportion of their resources to the support of manufacturing. Unusually detailed rec-

ords for January 1840 reveal that four of the banks held $290,000 in stocks, bonds, and loans on the steam cotton presses owned by two New Orleans firms. There is no evidence of any other such financing, although loans to manufacturers may well be hidden in the totals of loans on mortgage or personal security.[34] By contrast, the banks invested substantial sums to finance the development of canals, railroads, and other "internal improvements." Of course these projects, like the cotton presses, complemented and strengthened Louisiana's commerce and agriculture. They were supported by direct investment and control through improvement banks, and also by more conventional loans and stock purchases.

The improvement banks of the 1830's combined in one corporate charter the right to construct public works projects and the privilege of banking. Usually, construction projects were the primary objective; and several of these banks were originally chartered as simple improvement companies, receiving their banking powers in subsequent amendments. The additional profits to be gained from banking made the stock of the companies more attractive to investors. An improvement bank's issues of notes and deposits could also provide a source of funds to support its construction project, especially at first, when expenses were high and capital subscription was incomplete. Substantial savings were channeled into improvement projects by 1840. The Canal Bank completed a $1.2 million canal from central New Orleans to Lake Pontchartrain. The Gas Light and Banking Company operated a $550,000 lighting network in New Orleans and its suburbs. The Commercial Bank operated a city waterworks worth over $1 million. The Improvement Bank and the Exchange Bank built a pair of large commercial hotels, together spending over $1.5 million. These five banks thus financed and operated about $4.3 million worth of investment property during the decade.[35]

Improvement banks were less successful with railroad projects, mainly because of the 1837 financial crisis. As of 1840, three of the railroad banks could claim about $1 million of railroad capital, but little of this had actually been financed through the improvement banking mechanism. The New Orleans and Carrollton Railroad received its banking powers in 1835 in conjunction with a proposed extension of its original line. Although the bank survived for about eight years, it undertook little railroad construc-

tion after the panic. The Pontchartrain Railroad received a similar charter amendment in 1830, but neither construction nor banking operations got beyond the planning stages before the panic
killed them. The Atchafalaya Railroad and Banking Company,
chartered in 1835, survived as a bank for over a decade but never
constructed its railroad. The Clinton and Port Hudson Railroad
received mortgage banking powers in 1833, which probably
helped it to finance its early construction; but the successful completion of this short rural line was mostly due to a $500,000 direct
loan obtained from the state in 1839.[36]

As agents of economic development, the improvement banks
successfully financed, constructed, and managed, a number of valuable projects. But they were quite insecure as banks—so much
so that one historian has described their operations as "building
America through bankruptcy." Their failure after 1837 imposed
a kind of retroactive "forced saving" on stockholders (many of
them outside the state), noteholders, and depositors. And their
construction projects tied up the bulk of their total assets in an
extremely illiquid form. In this respect the Louisiana improvement
banks were much worse off than similar "investment banks" in
other nations, which usually bought stocks and bonds or made
long-term loans to investment projects. A bank operating in this
way could increase its liquidity simply by selling a portion of its
stocks or other assets. The Louisiana banks, by contrast, owned
their projects directly, and to increase liquidity they had to find
buyers for a canal, a hotel, or a railroad. In addition, Louisiana
investment banking was less diversified than that in other countries, since each bank was deeply committed to only one major
project.[37]

Despite its illiquid assets, the improvement bank was not the
inherently unsound or inflationary institution that many contemporary Louisianans and some historians have believed it to be.
Given enough capital, and enough time to enlarge its deposits and
its notes in circulation, it could acquire sufficient liquid assets
(e.g., commercial loans) to balance its portfolio and survive financial pressures, as the success of the Canal Bank amply demonstrates.

The improvement banks did not carry the entire burden of
financing transportation improvements in the 1830's. Six other

banks invested a total of $400,000 in the stock or debt of the rail-road banks, providing added cash resources and dispersing the risks and illiquidity of the railroad projects throughout the banking community. In addition, the banks directly invested over $300,000 in railroad companies and $192,000 in canal companies that had no banking privileges. The total $1.3 million that all the banks invested in railroads ($1 million in railroad bank property and $300,000 in other railroads) financed 40 per cent of Louisiana's total expenditure on railroad construction and equipment prior to 1840.[38]

By the 1850's most of the earlier bank investments in internal improvements had been liquidated. The Canal Bank still owned its canal ($1 million); the revived Citizens Bank owned the Improvement Hotel (valued at $200,000); and the other three surviving banks owned some $39,000 in canal, railroad, and cotton-press stocks. The constitution of 1852 formally divorced the activities of banking and internal improvement by denying banking privileges to all improvement companies. But the divorce was short lived, and soon the gap left by the withdrawal of the older improvement banks was partly filled by the creation of free banks under the laws of 1853 and 1855.[39]

New Orleans businessmen had already participated in a series of noisy railroaders' conventions, and promotional campaigns for rail links with the Pacific coast and the upper South (Tennessee) were well advanced. James Robb, a prominent banker, merchant, and politician, had led the campaigns for railroads and for free banks, and he clearly recognized how the two objectives might be joined. At first Robb had sought to obtain broad financial support for New Orleans' railroad system from city property taxes. This unpopular and insufficient financing was supplemented in 1854, when the legislature authorized the city of New Orleans to issue $5 million in bonds in order to finance the purchase of an equal amount of stock in the city's three major railroad construction projects: the New Orleans, Jackson, and Great Northern; the New Orleans, Opelousas, and Great Western; and the New Orleans and Mobile. The city would thus act as a financial intermediary, buying the stock of the railroads and selling city bonds to the free banks. New Orleans actually issued $3,671,000 of bonds on behalf of the railroads in addition to its general debt of roughly

$3 million. By 1857, the four free banks held over $2 million in city bonds, and the Louisiana State Bank another $328,750. Even if only 60 per cent of these bonds represented railroad financing (the rough proportion of railroad bonds to total city bonds), this was still a significant share (say 15 per cent) of the $9 million that Louisiana spent on railroads during the 1850's; but it was less than half as large as the 40 per cent share that banks had provided to finance the railroads of the 1830's.[40]

The financing of railroads through free banks in the 1850's was in several ways sounder than similar efforts by improvement banks in the 1830's. The improvement banks owned their railroads directly and often provided the total financing. The free banks were twice removed from the railroads they helped to finance. They did not own railroad property as such, or even railroad stocks; instead, they held city bonds, and the city bore the risk of holding railroad stocks. Moreover, no free bank held a very large proportion of the ultimate financial claims against any one project. The free banks were thus better diversified and more liquid than the earlier improvement banks. Nevertheless, the free banks' suspension of specie payments during the panic of 1857 revealed the risks of mixing a large holding of long-term investment banking assets (bonds) with a large proportion of short-term liabilities (deposits and banknotes). The free banking device diminished the conflict between sound money and easy credit (especially long-term credit for development) but did not eliminate it.[41]

CHAPTER TWO

Finance and Economic Development

THE LITERATURE of American economic history contains remarkably little sustained analysis of the connection between the banking system and the growth of the antebellum economy. In part, this lapse reflects the greater concern of historians for the politics of banking or the role of banks in the recurrent panics of the nineteenth century. It may also reflect the paucity of economic theory on the long-run relationship between money, banks, and economic growth. I will begin this chapter, therefore, by pulling together the relevant economic theory. I will go beyond narrow "monetary" theory to "financial" theory, which encompasses other financial institutions besides banks and other debt and credit issues besides money; and I will go beyond theories of economic "growth" within a given (usually modern) economic structure to theories of economic "development" that consider broad changes in the underlying socioeconomic structure. In applying a theoretical framework to the Louisiana experience one must answer two broad questions: Was the quantity of finance appropriate, and was it allocated properly? Subsequent chapters will build upon and elaborate this discussion in several ways.

Classical economic theory generally denied any close causal relationship between money and economic growth. Money was a "veil." Its expansion could cause inflation in the general price level, and its contraction could cause deflation. But relative prices, interest rates, output, and other "real" variables would be unaffected by changes in the money supply. In this classical model, economic growth could result from growth in the labor supply or from technological advances. But an expansion of physical capital—construction, new tools and factories, and added inventories —was also essential. The rate of investment (capital formation, in this physical sense) was limited by the supply of savings. And interest rates reflected an equilibrium in which the rate of return on investment was balanced against the saver's willingness to forego present consumption. Throughout this real growth process, money was essentially "neutral," and the financial world had no major causative role in the real world.*

It is ironic that John Maynard Keynes, himself a lifelong believer in the economic significance of money, should have initiated a theoretical revolution that for two decades accorded money little or no place in the behavior of the macroeconomy. Keynes argued that under certain circumstances changes in the money supply might have no effect on interest rates, and that changing interest rates might have little or no effect on investment spending. Under such conditions, changes in the money supply would not affect spending, prices, or output, but would simply be offset by changes in money "hoarding." Many early Keynesian economists found confirmation for this theory (now called the "liquidity trap") in the American experience of the 1930's and 1940's. In their view money was not only "neutral" but completely ineffectual. It is hardly surprising that the early Keynesian theories of growth or development (e.g., those of Hansen, Domar, and Kaldor) paid no explicit attention to monetary influences on growth.[1]

With the resurgence of monetary theory in recent years has come an increased interest in the monetary aspects of economic growth. It is not yet entirely clear, however, whether money is still thought to have only a passive, permissive role or whether it

---

* This sketch of classical theory omits the recurring argument (in the "neoclassical" writings of Wicksell, Hayek, and others) that expansion of the money supply could lower the market rate of interest below its "natural" rate, thus stimulating investment and growth. The omission is deliberate, since the argument refers more to economic cycles than to sustained economic growth. That is, an overstimulation of investment could create only a temporary boom, followed by the inevitable decline; and in the long run the growth rate could not exceed the trend dictated by the "natural" (nonmonetary) rate of interest. My sketch also omits the doctrine of forced saving (discussed below), which is recognized in some form by most classical or neoclassical economists and constitutes their main departure from monetary neutrality. See Blaug, Chapters 5, 14 (especially pp. 147-48, 576); Patinkin, Chapter 15 and Supplementary Note J.

is regarded as an independent causal variable in the growth process. Most theorists accept that economic growth occurs most easily when the general price level is relatively stable, and that it is hampered by rapid and persistent inflation or deflation. The simplest model affording price stability is one in which the money supply grows at roughly the same rate as aggregate real output (now commonly measured as GNP). Economists Edward Shaw and Milton Friedman have at least casually suggested that such a model might effectively guide American monetary policy.[2]

The majority of economists, although they do accept the desirability of price stability as a goal (either for its own sake or for the sake of economic growth), have rejected a simple matching of money supply to expanding output. Instead, they have developed several arguments suggesting that money should grow faster than output. In terms of the traditional quantity theory of money, this is equivalent to arguing that the money supply must outgrow output by enough to offset the declining trend of monetary velocity. Gurley and Shaw, for example, have developed a model of this kind to explain the long-term growth of the U.S. money supply. They postulate a very primitive financial system at the beginning, in which both stocks and the rate of issue of primary securities were near zero. In the early stages of development, money (and debt of all types) grew much more rapidly than income; but this monetary growth gradually tapered off as the economy matured. The mature U.S. economy has a relatively stable money/income ratio of about 0.3, that is, a money supply equivalent to about 30 per cent of the nation's annual income.[3]

Following the Gurley-Shaw approach, Rondo Cameron has elaborated some of the institutional changes that account for rapid monetary expansion in the early stages of development. From the start, the population served by the money supply steadily increases as backward sectors of the economy, especially subsistence (frontier) agriculture, are drawn into market-oriented production. As the economy develops, greater specialization and division of labor in production (and consumption) require additional monetary transactions between firms at different stages; thus more and more monetary transactions are needed for a given final output.[4]

Most economists, then, would agree that the money supply must grow faster than real output if economic development is to occur without either inflation or deflation. Some would go beyond this to advocate (or at least urge tolerance of) price inflation as an aid to more rapid development. The most vocal of the contemporary economists holding this view are the "structuralists" associated with the United Nations Economic Commission for Latin America, who argue that in several Latin American economies inflation is caused by structural rigidities such as immobile resources (especially in food supply), a high and inelastic demand for imports, and inflexible prices for labor and industrial goods. The same economies are heavily dependent on a few agricultural or mineral exports, which often have unstable or falling prices in world markets. Under these conditions, it is argued, any attempt to prevent inflation by reducing monetary expansion (or government deficits) will lead to unemployment, depression, and social upheaval. Permitting inflation, on the other hand, will facilitate structural change (industrialization), shifting demands, and a reallocation of resources. This structuralist plan for development through inflation has been sharply criticized by other economists. And despite a partial similarity in the economic structures of modern Latin America and antebellum Louisiana, the model is of little use in our study of a nineteenth-century world living generally by the gold standard and fixed exchange rates.[5]

Another, more traditional, argument for development via inflation is closer to the Louisiana experience. This is the doctrine of forced saving, which asserts that monetary expansion can stimulate investment while suppressing consumption and thus can accelerate economic growth. Banks create new money by making loans to finance investment. The new money results in inflation (full employment is assumed), and higher prices reduce the real buying power of consumers. In this sense consumers are forced to "save" by releasing resources from the production of consumer goods; and these resources are drawn to investment uses by the newly created purchasing power of bank money.

Unfortunately, the process of forced saving is not quite so straightforward and automatic. Consumers can effectively resist the desired shift of resources, both by increasing the proportion consumed out of their original incomes and by using for consumption some of the additional money income that they will gain from the expanded investment sector. Such a battle of money expenditures between consumers and bank-financed investors might well produce a rapid inflationary spiral without any real shifting of resources. The actual effect of forced saving on economic growth depends entirely on the structure of the economy and on the relative responsiveness of consumers and investors to changes in prices and money incomes.[6]

Let us now enlarge the discussion beyond the traditional limits of money and banks to consider all financial assets and institutions, as well as the creation of debt and credit. To do so, we must replace the criterion of an "appropriate" money supply with some index of the quantity of credit or liquidity.

Before proceeding, it is advisable to examine two naïve viewpoints that have often appeared in historical sources and scholarship. The first is the simple equation of credit with capital. This idea had some popularity among antebellum Louisianans. As early as 1804, in a pamphlet published by the Louisiana Bank, James Lyon asserted that the bank would benefit merchants: "They will be enabled to borrow to the full extent of their credit; thus their capital will be at once doubled or trebled." And in 1837 the merchant and banker Samuel Peters wrote, on behalf of the New Orleans Chamber of Commerce: "Whatever possesses exchangeable value, is wealth. But credit possesses exchangeable value. . . . Credit is wealth. . . . Credit acts as capital, and is even more convenient and expeditious, as well as more efficacious in producing accumulation of wealth."[7]

Unfortunately, the social equivalence of credit and capital is based on the fallacy of composition: that what is true for the part (the individual) is therefore true for the whole (the society). An individual may increase his personal command over resources by borrowing, but society as a whole does not grow richer simply because its citizens and institutions redistribute resources and financial claims among themselves. An additional link in the chain of credit may simply add another layer of financial assets (and matching debts), and the creation of new financial assets need not imply the creation of new physical assets.

The second naïve view—nearly the opposite of the first and more popular among moralistic historians and antebellum debtors than among antebellum bankers—is that debt in any form is undesirable and "burdensome." This approach usually assumes that debt is incurred in emergencies (depression, poor harvest, etc.), that it finances unproductive spending on consumer goods, and that the interest charged is to some extent the creditor's exploitation of the debtor's desperate need.[8] Admittedly, some historical cases do fit this characterization; but debt has many other aspects. Aggregate debt has generally declined during depressions and increased during periods of prosperity, although the "burdensome debt" view would imply the opposite. This fact alone suggests that debt is often incurred for productive purposes, to finance capital formation in an expanding economy. Any burden associated with the payment of interest and principal on such debts must be weighed against the earnings received on the capital. Borrowing at 6 per cent in the expectation of earning 10 per cent is a burden that countless businessmen and farmers have happily assumed.

More modern theories of finance and economic growth lead us to expect that an economy will experience a rising debt/income ratio as growth proceeds. (Rising indebtedness, of course, is matched by rising financial assets in other hands; for debt and credit are Siamese twins, born of a single transaction and linked for life.) The rising debt/income ratio is the natural outgrowth of two other financial trends: an increasing use of external rather than internal finance; and a tendency for such finance to be increasingly indirect, moving through financial intermediaries and generating additional layers of financial claims. All three trends vary from country to country (even at a similar stage of development) according to such factors as degree of centralization, reliance on taxes or state enterprises to finance projects, and dependence on foreign borrowing.[9]

Why does the use of external finance generally increase during economic growth? Of the many firms expanding their output and investing in new capacity, larger inventories, and more working capital, some will not have sufficient income or retained earnings to finance internally. The more rapid the growth rate, and the higher its variance between industries or firms, the greater will be the need for external finance. Moreover, as the institutions of production and consumption become more formalized and specialized in their activities, the functions of saving and investment are more often performed by separate institutions. And concurrent improvements in financial markets (brokers, stock exchanges, etc.) by lowering transfer costs, actively facilitate external finance.*

Why is external finance in an expanding economy increasingly conducted through financial intermediaries rather than directly? As the economy grows wealthier, it depends not only on the savings of a few wealthy and knowledgeable "capitalists" but also on a great many small savers who have traditionally preferred self-finance or savings in the form of physical capital (land, gold, jewelry, etc.). If these small savers are to be induced to participate in the financial process, they must be offered financial assets with attractive qualities: short maturity, easy marketability, small denomination, special advantages (such as assured retirement income or insurance protection), fixed return rates, and low risk. But these qualities may not be at all acceptable to the potential debtors (borrowers). Business firms, construction industries, and even the government generally want to borrow on a long-term basis and in large, convenient transactions.

Financial intermediaries are able to reconcile the incompatible desires of lenders and borrowers by issuing their own liquid claims (banknotes, savings accounts, etc.) to the many small savers and purchasing illiquid securities (bonds, mortgages, etc.) from the borrowers. The savers benefit by increased liquidity and reduced risk, since an intermediary can diversify his loans more effectively than an individual saver.† The borrowers benefit by access to a large pool of savings. Operating efficiently and with sufficient funds, the intermediary can often pass along his economies of scale as higher returns to the saver and lower costs to the borrower than either could obtain through direct external finance.

The strength or weakness of an evolving financial system will influence the rate and pattern of economic development in many ways, and it has been generally recognized that inadequate finance will often retard development. For example, when the increase of

---

* Any tendency toward merger or expansion by vertical integration of firms works in the opposite direction, toward greater internal finance. But this trend may itself reflect an inadequate supply of external finance.

† Hugh Patrick has pointed out that both illiquidity and insolvency are risks that confront individuals but not society as a whole. By reducing these risks, financial intermediaries lower the private cost toward the social cost; any resulting increase in saving and investment is therefore a pure social gain at nobody's expense. Patrick, p. 183.

the money supply does not keep pace with the rising demand for money during a growth period, prices should go down. But if prices and wages are "sticky" and resist this deflationary pressure, the economy may suffer depression and stagnation.* Similarly, an insufficient growth of external and indirect finance will very likely retard saving and investment, both by raising the cost of borrowing or lending and by cutting off funds to some potential borrowers.

An inadequate financial system may also retard development by encouraging inefficient structural changes in the economy. The basic inadequacy may take several forms: lack of entrepreneurship among financiers, monopoly or oligopoly in financial institutions, restrictive or inadequate regulation by government, and so on. The rest of the economy will typically respond to these financial constraints with various forms of inefficient centralization—mergers and consolidations of existing business firms, government units, and even family groups—and with greater reliance on internal finance. Business firms tend to retain more earnings for internal reinvestment, even though their own projects may be less profitable and productive to the economy than projects requiring external finance. Consumers will be forced to rely more on their own funds, on borrowing directly from family and friends, or, in emergencies, on the costly funds available from moneylenders and other brokers. Lacking access to remote but profitable investments, consumers with excess savings may either finance less productive investments nearer home or increase their consumption and their holdings of unproductive physical wealth (idle land, gold, inventories, etc.).[10] In all of this, each saver or investor may seem to pursue a rational, growth-oriented strategy; but the economy as a whole is not growing as it could.

Just as the absence of an adequate financial system can retard development, so can its presence encourage development; and in some respects this encouragement will be more than the simple absence of a possible bottleneck. Finance may play an active causal role in accelerating development, as it does when forced saving occurs. The existence of adequate means for external and

---

* Rigidity in the money value of debts and in foreign exchange rates would have a similar depressing influence. See Chapter Six.

indirect finance might also aid development by attracting a larger volume of foreign savings (from other nations or regions), since foreign lenders, with only limited information about investment opportunities in the domestic economy, must rely heavily on the guidance, liquidity, and diversification offered by financial intermediaries, or established securities markets.

Foreign savings are not necessarily an unmixed blessing for the borrowing economy, of course. They are usually invested more cautiously and less innovatively than the savings of well-informed domestic entrepreneurs, so that familiar but stagnant industries are overcapitalized. Or foreign lenders may attempt to impose a "colonial" status on the borrowing economy by backing the production of staple crops or primary resources for export. Finally, there is some risk that foreign capital will be withdrawn in the future. But despite these limitations, foreign savings are likely to stimulate development; and many of their disadvantages can be overcome by a complementary allocation of domestic savings.*

The availability of indirect finance may also accelerate growth by increasing the share of total finance that goes into investment. In a relatively simple economy without extensive corporate saving in the form of retained earnings, most savings will initially accrue to families or to proprietorships (mixed consumer-producer units). Because these are consumption-oriented institutions, their own borrowing for consumption may have a prior claim on savings regardless of interest rates. Moreover, the financial intermediaries typical of a primitive economy—moneylenders, various brokers (in stock, notes, real estate, or commodities), and private bankers—often lend heavily to finance consumption, trade, or speculation. The securities issued to finance development projects in this primitive system are particularly unattractive for direct finance, since they usually involve long maturity, high risk, and uncertain yields. The emergence of more enterprising financial

---

* Many historians, and a few antebellum critics facing large debt repayments, have implied that foreign debts are entirely a deadweight burden on the borrowers. This has often been said, for example, of the debts that Southern merchants or planters owed to Northern or European wholesalers, shippers, factors, and bankers. What is overlooked is that the South generally made productive and profitable use of this borrowed capital, freeing its own savings for even more profitable investment in land, slaves, inventories, etc.

intermediaries may lower the cost of investment finance relative to other uses of funds and thus enlarge the share of investment in total finance.*

Financial development obviously affects economic growth by raising both the total quantity of savings and the proportion of these savings that finances investment. At least as important is the qualitative side of financial development, which improves the allocation of funds (and that of real resources) between alternative uses. Studies by Solow, Denison, and others have indicated that much of the recent economic growth in the United States cannot be attributed to simple increases in the quantity of capital (i.e. overall investment) or labor; rather, it has arisen from improvements in the quality or composition of these factors and in the technology and organizational framework through which they are combined. Simon Kuznets, in criticizing Rostow's *Stages of Economic Growth*, claims that rapidly developing economies have not generally experienced sharp increases in their aggregate levels of saving and investment (as a fraction of GNP). Such evidence justifies a closer look at the microeconomic, allocative, and "qualitative"† effects of finance.[11]

The demand for external finance and the resulting strain placed on the financial system are apt to be greater if development involves major geographical or structural shifts. Financing the migration of labor‡ and physical capital to frontier areas, clearing land, and building towns, industries, and social overheads, would be demanding even for an established financial system; yet a frontier economy must usually import or create its financing (except for such primitive capital accumulation as land clearing, which is usually self-financed). Similarly, the rise of new industries, and to a lesser extent that of new firms in established industries, cre-

---

* This possibility is overlooked in most Keynesian growth models, which make an illogical parallel between lending/borrowing and saving/investing. Such models thus implicitly assume that all borrowing goes to finance investment. More logical parallels would be saving/dissaving, or saving/deficit spending (for whatever purpose).

† The term "qualitative" should not be taken too seriously here. It is merely used as the antithesis of "aggregate quantitative." Some aspects of the microeconomic and allocative effects of finance are at least potentially quantifiable.

‡ The migration of slave labor has unique financial implications. These are developed more fully below, pp. 60-61.

ates a strong demand for external finance and for new institutions to provide expertise and specialized services to borrowers and lenders.[12]

Financial innovations may have an exceptionally great developmental impact on frontier or other nonmarket sectors of the economy. Their effect here is more than the familiar "monetization" of a barter economy, by which more efficient trade and exchange, more price consciousness, and more incentive to save in monetary forms are introduced. Some essentially unmonetized barter economies, in fact, have produced sophisticated credit and financial arrangements that have replaced money quite effectively. For example, country storekeepers, itinerant merchants, and riverboat captains on the American frontier combined the barter of general merchandise for agricultural produce with bookkeeping credits and trade credit. However, further financial expansion in a system of this kind may allow market-oriented production and specialization to replace subsistence production, and the resulting structural change is likely to transform the whole environment in which decisions about saving, investment, and work effort are made. When financial expansion is able to break a closed cycle of self-sufficiency in this way, it can produce striking developmental results.[13]

Finance often interacts closely with technological and organizational changes that are important to economic development. New forms of technology will usually require new investment; and the demand for external finance will be greatest if there are substantial economies of scale in a new process, so that the minimum efficient scale of investment exceeds internal sources of financing. Organizational innovations such as vertical integration or consolidation and the establishment of new production or marketing facilities may similarly require outside financial support. A banker, investment banker, or other financier can mobilize the necessary financing; but if he is a risk-averter or a traditionalist, he may only do so reluctantly, inadequately, or at penalty rates, thus actually retarding development. On the other hand, a financier can as easily go far beyond the mere provision of credit and participate actively in the innovation itself, becoming the promoter or manager of a new enterprise, the negotiator of a consolidation, and so on. Historically, financiers and their institutions have at different times played both the risk-averting and the entrepreneurial role.[14]

The financial system obviously affects economic growth by influencing the allocation and composition of new investment; and it can do the same with existing capital stock. In a financially primitive economy much wealth is tied up in unproductive physical assets—idle land, livestock, housing, inventories, jewelry, and specie. The availability of financial assets, by presenting a profitable alternative for savers, can free this hoarded physical capital for more productive uses. The traditional forms of wealth may be exchanged for other, more productive assets through foreign trade; some forms (e.g., commodity inventories) may be consumed, releasing resources from consumer goods production to build new capital; and some may be allowed to depreciate or wear out, releasing domestic resources from replacement investments. The new financial assets that appear are direct or indirect claims on the new capital resulting from this transformation of resources.[15]

One specific and important example of the improvement of existing physical capital is the declining role of specie in the money supply as more bank notes, deposits, and government token money (coins or paper) become available. The use of specie (or other commodities) as money or a monetary reserve obviously has a high resource cost, since resources must be set aside for this purpose; it also has a high opportunity cost, since the specie might otherwise be used industrially or exported profitably. The gradual displacement of species by "token" money allows a more productive, developmental use of the existing specie supply. Such improvements in the existing capital stock make only a one-time contribution to growth, rather than permanently raising the rate of growth; but their impact may still be substantial.[16]

However finance and economic development are related, one fact must be kept in mind. A financial system is not exclusively, or perhaps even primarily, devoted to the goal of growth and development. Many other objectives shape both conscious financial policy and the less conscious evolution of financial structures: stability in prices, output, and employment; an equitable distribution of income and wealth; separate roles for the private and public sectors of the economy; and a sound mechanism of payments. The pursuit of these goals may often lead to financial changes that inhibit economic development.[17] Probably the best example of conflicting goals has already been mentioned—the simultaneous desire for sound money and easy credit.

The Quantity of Finance and Louisiana Development

Were Louisiana's money supply, banking facilities, and finance adequate, and did they grow at a rate that was optimal for economic development? The first step in answering this question is to measure the Louisiana experience in terms of the theoretically relevant variables. The resulting estimates may be compared with those of the United States as a whole during the same years, and with those of other developing nations, past and present.

In a recent comparative study, Rondo Cameron and his colleagues choose to measure financial development in terms of "banking density"—i.e., the number of bank offices (including branches) per 10,000 population. Considering the experience of several industrializing nations in the past, Cameron defines the following levels of density: over 1.0, "high"; 0.5 to 1.0, "moderate"; below 0.5, "low"; and below 0.1 (one office per 100,000 population), "very low."[18] In Table 2.1, which shows antebellum densities for New Orleans, the state of Louisiana, and the United States, New Orleans rates moderate on Cameron's scale, reaching the high level only in 1820 and 1840. Cameron's index is based on national averages, and one would expect a higher banking density in cities. Compared to similar cities of the day, New Orleans had a moderate density in all years.* The state of Louisiana as a whole ranked generally low in density, at or below the U.S. average; the striking exception was in 1840, at the end of a decade in which banks expanded rapidly and branch banks proliferated across the state.

"Banking density" is admittedly a crude index, mainly because it makes no allowance for variations in bank size or in income levels in the economy. Since Louisiana's banks were much larger than those in other states during the antebellum era, her low bank-

---

* The number of banks chartered for each city can be found in Fenstermaker, Appendix A. Comparing New Orleans with Boston, New York, Philadelphia, Baltimore, and Cincinnati, she ranked fourth, fourth and third among the six cities in 1810, 1820, and 1830 respectively. Interestingly, New York and Philadelphia both ranked lower.

TABLE 2.1

Indicators of Money Supply, Banking, and Economic Growth

Year	Bank money/ La. income ratio[a]	Bank resources/ La. income ratio	Bank density[b] N. Orl.	La.	U.S. data Bank density	Bank money/ GNP ratio	Bank resources/ GNP ratio
1810			.755	.131	.141		
1820			1.100	.195	.192	.146	.405
1824	.14						
1825	.11						
1826	.13						
1827	.16						
1828	.31	.61					
1830	.32	.77	.854	.185	.212	.157	.350
1832	.49	1.86					
1834	.66	.83					
1835	.31	.96					
1836	.72	2.25					
1837	.89	2.65					
1838	.81	2.96					
1839	.69	2.73					
1840	.60	2.40	1.570	1.33	.526	.125	.380
1841	.43	2.30					
1842	.57						
1843	.29	1.24					
1844	.35	1.20					
1845	.44	1.27				.099	.213
1846	.41						
1847	.45	1.00					
1848	.40	.89					
1849	.45	.99					
1850	.44	.91	.601	.560	.353	.104	.197
1851	.30	.58					
1852	.29	.63					
1853	.32	.55					
1854	.47	.91					
1855	.45	.94				.107	.201
1856	.45	.84					
1857	.53	1.04					
1858	.29	.71					
1859	.49	.86					
1860	.41		.712	.184	.496	.110	.211

SOURCES: Louisiana bank money, bank resources, and income from Tables 2.2 and B.4. New Orleans and Louisiana bank density from Tables C.1 and C.4. U.S. bank density: for 1810–30, Fenstermaker, p. 111; for 1840–60, *USC*, [42], p. 70. U.S. money and resource ratios in *USC*, [42], pp. 69–70 (includes second B.U.S. up to 1840). The GNP estimates for 1840–60 (actually 1839–59) are from Robert Gallman's estimates in *Output, Employment, and Productivity*, p. 26; the estimates for 1820 and 1830 were prorated from the 1840 figure by using Paul David's growth index for real per capita output (1840 prices). See David, "Growth of Real Product," p. 184. Population and price index data from *Historical Statistics*, pp. 7, 115.

[a] In contemporary prices.   [b] Bank density equals banks per 10,000 population.

ing density may be misleading. The ratio of bank money to yearly state income does consider bank size and income levels and thus gives a sharper picture (where data are available). According to the theories previously outlined, this money/income ratio should gradually rise during the process of economic development. Gurley and Shaw have concluded, from their study of the experience of the United States since 1800 and that of about 70 countries since 1945, that the ratio is typically 10 per cent or less in the poorest countries and about 30 per cent in the most advanced countries.[19]

The chronology of Louisiana's money/income ratio (Table 2.1) does not fit our theoretical expectations. There is a gradual rise until the early 1830's, but this is followed by a leap to very high levels in 1836-40.* These levels imply an inflationary excess of money during those years, and other price data and qualitative evidence fully confirm this. The sharp drop after 1840 appears to have moved Louisiana's financial system to a new trend line, at a lower level and with slower expansion (if any). The general financial crisis, contraction, and debt default of the period could account for the downward shift, but not for the slower trend.[20] A full explanation of the statistics requires a broader historical approach.

To extend our statistical analysis of finance beyond money and banks, we should first estimate the annual issues of all financial assets, both by ordinary borrowers and by banks or other financial intermediaries. From this, we could construct a ratio of aggregate debt, or financial assets, to income—that is, the kind of ratio that modern theorists have studied. Unfortunately, virtually no data exist on the volume of direct finance in antebellum Louisiana, and we have no way of estimating the issues of bonds, stocks,

---

* To some extent the high levels are a statistical illusion. The income data used in the denominator are the rough and incomplete estimates computed in Appendix B. In the one year for which comparison was possible (1840), my estimate was only 60 per cent of Easterlin's more comprehensive figure. If we boldly assumed the same degree of understatement for all years, we would "deflate" the money/income column to 60 per cent of its original level, lowering the 1845-60 data to a more plausible average of about .27. The adjusted figures are still relatively high, partly because New Orleans was a financial intermediary for the entire Mississippi valley. If the Louisiana banks were actually supplying money and credit directly or indirectly (e.g., through relending by factors) to a larger area, the "true" ratio would reflect the larger regional income and would be correspondingly lower.

mortgages, personal notes, and other securities. This is an important gap: even in modern America, Gurley estimates that only one-third of external finance is handled by intermediaries, and the proportion in Louisiana may have been even lower.[21]

The most comprehensive estimate that can be assembled from available data begins with total bank issues of securities, including deposits, notes, and capital stock (see Table 2.2). But each dollar received for these obligations enabled the bank to purchase a dollar's worth (ignoring reserves) of earning assets—mortgages, promissory notes, bonds, and stocks issued by merchants, planters, and governments. We should therefore double the ratio of bank resources to Louisiana income (Table 2.1, second column) in order to approach the Gurley-Shaw ratio of total financial assets to income.* And even this deliberate double counting of bank assets and liabilities omits the great bulk of financial obligations, which did not pass through the banks.

The adjusted Louisiana data (with financial resources/income ratios doubled) may be compared with the experience of other countries. Gurley suggests that most "poor" countries today have ratios below 0.5. Moderately prosperous countries (e.g., Mexico, Turkey, or Brazil) have ratios of 1.0 to 1.5; and advanced capitalist countries have financial assets two to five times their annual incomes (four times in the U.S.). By this standard, antebellum Louisiana probably falls in the "moderately prosperous" range, with a relatively well-developed financial system (especially in the 1830's).[22]

Even these admittedly crude statistical "tests" tell us certain things about financial development in antebellum Louisiana. All of the state's monetary and financial ratios (even after adjustment) were comparable to those found in financially sophisticated and moderately prosperous economies. The ratios were consistently highest and were growing fastest in the 1830's; after 1845 they were generally somewhat lower and nearly constant. Unfortu-

---

* As before, appropriate reductions in the bank resources figures can partly reflect the proportion of cash reserves (though these would easily be matched as a source of funds by retained profits) and the portion of bank capital that financed canals and similar improvements, especially in the improvement banks of the 1830's. But any upward bias creeping into the data from these sources is certainly overwhelmed by our inability to assess direct finance outside the banks.

TABLE 2.2

Indicators of Monetary and Economic Expansion

Year	Bank money ($ millions, Jan. 1)	La. income (current prices, Sept. 1–Sept. 1 year shown)	Land sales ($ thousands)	Bank money plus capital ($ millions)
1820	$0.79			$1.71
1823			$1.5	
1824		$6.93	4.5	
1825		9.10	0.7	
1826	1.15	9.08	24	
1827	1.28	7.96	143	
1828	2.32	7.46	5.2	4.57
1829	1.52	8.13	39	
1830	3.32	10.38	96	7.99
1831		10.48	86	
1832	3.76	7.71	98	14.38
1833		11.46	112	
1834	9.08	13.77	105	11.45
1835	6.36	20.35	407	19.62
1836	11.51	15.93	1099	35.95
1837	18.50	20.81	289	55.27
1838	14.98	18.55	216	54.92
1839	13.94	20.10	822	54.87
1840	13.85	23.17	229	55.59
1841	9.54	22.32	119	51.25
1842		17.43	57	
1843	6.43	21.95	130	27.36
1844	8.19	23.56	122	28.24
1845	10.52	23.82	117	30.19
1846		30.45	128	
1847	14.32	31.75	139	31.71
1848	12.36	31.23	183	27.94
1849	12.59	28.06	90	27.82
1850	13.28	30.37	125	27.54
1851	13.37	44.56	133	25.74
1852	10.46	35.72	65	22.66
1853	14.96	46.70	173	25.89
1854	18.71	37.55	168	36.07
1855	18.27	40.89	171	38.45
1856	21.97	48.83	91	41.00
1857	22.68	42.64	96	44.41
1858	15.97	54.44	152	38.77
1859	34.15	69.39	245	59.36
1860	31.35	76.02	294	55.85
1861	23.24			

SOURCES: Bank money from Table C.1 and Fenstermaker, p. 2. Louisiana income from Table B.4. Land sales from USC: [3] for 1823–25; [38], p. 9, for 1826–41. Land sales, for 1842–60 from General Land Office, 1843–61. Last column from Table C.1.

nately, these data do not imply a clear historical interpretation of the causal role of finance in economic development. For example, either of two distinct and nearly opposing hypotheses would be consistent with the facts. We might state that the Louisiana financial system was already highly developed by the 1830's, and that its leveling off thereafter was essentially a sign of financial "maturity." Certainly, it had proved itself able to meet the needs of a growing and prosperous economy. Alternatively, we could say that the exceptionally high financial ratios of the 1830's reflected a brief period of inflationary finance and a continuous tendency for Louisiana banks to finance trade and production outside the state. This seemingly healthy financial development ended by 1840, and premature financial stagnation retarded later economic growth. Thus, broadly speaking, the high level of finance suggests financial adequacy, whereas the lack of financial growth suggests financial inadequacy. If we are to choose between these alternative hypotheses, we must have more evidence—further statistics on the behavior of prices and output, information on particular sectors of the economy, and other direct historical evidence.

More detailed data and estimates on Louisiana prices and output (see Table B.4) appear to support the hypothesis that finance permitted or encouraged growth. The period of sharp price deflation (1838-42) was balanced not only by the inflation of 1833-38 but also by inflation in the 1850's. During the entire period, real income was not retarded; and in the 1840's, presumably the period of most restricted finance, it grew more rapidly than it did in either the preceding or the following decade.* The depression of 1839-42 was offset by rapid recovery and expansion after 1842. The 1850's, on the other hand, saw almost no increase in aggregate output until after 1857, despite the expansionist free-banking movement.

At the aggregate level there is little evidence that lack of financial expansion retarded economic growth in Louisiana. But my estimates of aggregate Louisiana income may predetermine this conclusion, since they depend entirely on the available statistics of cotton and sugar production and New Orleans trade. These

---

* This result holds regardless of which variant of "real income" is used and regardless of the dating chosen (1830-1840-1850-1860 or 1825-1835-1845-1855, for example, or similar calculations based on three-year averages centered on the decadal years).

are precisely the economic sectors that were most dependent on external rather than domestic markets, and presumably the sectors that had the easiest access to non-Louisiana finance in times of credit restriction. And even if these favorable aggregate statistics are accepted, they can as easily be used to support our alternative hypothesis of financial retardation. It is possible that Louisiana's growth might have been greater than it actually was if the financial system had been more expansionary. Moreover, the economy may have "escaped" some of the restrictive consequences of financial retardation, either by financial innovations or by substituting alternative techniques for mobilizing resources. Finally, inadequate finance could have retarded particular sectors of the state's economy without noticeably affecting aggregate statistics.

The two most straightforward historical signs of a restrictive financial system in Louisiana are the extensive monetary contraction between 1837 and 1843 and the explicitly restrictive state policies adopted after 1842. By June 1842, financial crisis had reduced the supply of bank money (notes and deposits) to only 16 per cent of its previous peak (that of October 1836); the money/income ratio had fallen by 68 per cent. In response to this disastrous collapse, the state shifted its banking policy from the developmental goal of easy credit to the conservative goal of sound money. The Bank Act of 1842 imposed higher and more comprehensive reserve requirements and began procedures for liquidating several of the banks. Similarly, the new state constitution of 1845, which remained in effect until 1852, prohibited the enactment or renewal of any bank charters. In an environment of post-crisis uncertainty and strict governmental surveillance, the surviving New Orleans banks cautiously maintained their specie reserves well above the 33 per cent required by the Act of 1842; as a result, their lending capacity was greatly reduced.[23]

Even these restrictive measures were largely unsuccessful in achieving the goal of sound money. The constitution of 1845 sought to achieve a sound specie money by gradually abolishing Louisiana bank money—a course that would eventually have led to further deflation or depression. And if the 1845 provisions had remained in effect beyond 1852, they would gradually have been undermined by imports of money from other states, and probably by the introduction of "near money" and other credit devices.

The more sophisticated "reforms" of the Bank Act of 1842 were also less effective than generally supposed, since legally required reserves cannot be used as an emergency source of funds without simultaneously making the bank deficient in legal reserves and forcing it to contract. Nor did the "commercial bills" doctrine espoused by Edmund Forstall automatically guarantee an appropriate and safe money supply (see pp. 120-21).

Before we condemn Louisiana's financial policy out of hand, however, we should ask whether there was a possible alternative policy. In the mid-nineteenth century, the international gold standard and the widespread circulation of specie as part of the money supply severely limited the policy options of any single state. Faith in the specie standard and insistence that all other money must be freely convertible into specie on demand was so nearly universal that alternative ways of coping with the financial crisis of the 1840's were scarcely considered. Yet many alternatives were in daily use, for financial practice was less doctrinaire than financial philosophy. Practical bankers and businessmen had already found ways to minimize the conflict between sound money and easy credit, essentially by compromising or suppressing specie convertibility. Banks arranged for regular settlements of their balances and exchanges of their accumulated banknotes with minimal specie transfers, and circulated small notes that were less likely to be redeemed for specie (until the state restricted this "unsound" practice). Merchants and businessmen relied on bills of exchange and other credit instruments. Government and private banking cartels provided insurance on the monetary liabilities held by the public (as today's FDIC does), served as lenders of last resort to the banks themselves (as today's central bank does), or acquiesced in temporary suspensions of specie payment. Each of these practices permitted a larger and more stable supply of money and credit upon a given specie base; and a wider use of them would probably have been far more effective than the restrictive policies that Louisiana actually adopted.

Despite the favorable statistics for prices and aggregate income, then, it is clear that restricted financial growth retarded Louisiana's economic growth between 1840 and 1853. The state imposed severe limitations on the banks, and could not supply the needed credit on its own. (Indeed, the constitution of 1845 prohibited deficit financing of improvement projects.) There were numerous signs of an unsatisfied demand for finance. Silent evidence came from the exceptionally high profit margins of the surviving banks: even when they were inefficiently run, their monopoly of scarce credit facilities brought returns as high as 30 per cent per year. Quite vocal testimony came from New Orleans businessmen and journalists, who complained bitterly of economic losses and urged the amendment of state policy.[24]

Various financial innovations designed to circumvent government restraints soon appeared. Most notable was the marked expansion of private, unchartered banks; and a few chartered banks from other states also established New Orleans agencies to pick up some of the available business. Although direct evidence is lacking, it is likely that Louisiana businessmen and planters resorted more often to internal or direct finance and sought more direct financing from businessmen in other states. There is less indication of the other adjustments to suboptimal finance predicted by Gurley and Shaw, such as mergers and consolidations.[25]

The greatest impact of the financial restrictions fell on the most vulnerable sector of Louisiana's economy—New Orleans' interregional trade. The city did not suffer a decline in overall trade; on the contrary, her total receipts continued to grow vigorously right up to the Civil War. But she depended increasingly on the export of cotton, sugar, and other Southern products. Grain, pork, lead, and dozens of other products that had once come down the Mississippi were diverted to Eastern cities after 1845, and especially during the 1850's. The New Orleans trading empire shrank even within the South; Kentucky and Tennessee diverted their provisions northward, and Tennessee, Alabama, and northern Mississippi sent more of their cotton eastward to Atlantic ports. The large volume of Western trade that still came to New Orleans was increasingly destined for Southern consumption rather than for export to Northern or foreign markets. This, too, shows the city's increased dependence on King Cotton and other Southern staples, for the specialized Southern planters were among the major customers for Western products.[26]

The major reason for the shrinkage of New Orleans' hinterland was, of course, the transportation revolution that began in the 1830's. By the end of that decade, a network of canals linked the

Ohio River, Lake Erie, and New York City; and in the late 1840's and early 1850's canals were extended westward, capturing an ever larger share of trade in the upper Midwest. In the 1850's the railroads began to divert even more trade away from New Orleans, first through short feeder lines in the Ohio valley and after 1855 through a growing system of trunk lines to the East. Railroads also enabled Charleston, Savannah, and other Southern ports to compete with New Orleans for the trade of the Southeastern states.[27]

No amount of entrepreneurship, railroad building, river and port improvement, or banking expansion in Louisiana could have prevented the ultimate loss of some of the trade of the upper Mississippi and Ohio valleys. New Orleans had received that trade initially because the Mississippi was the only practical route between Western producer and Eastern or European markets, and she was bound to lose a good part of it as new routes were opened. Geography, now wedded to technology, withdrew her bounty from New Orleans and befriended other cities.

But the decline need not have been as great as it was. Much of New Orleans' original empire remained within her grasp, open to competition with other cities. This was particularly true of the lower Mississippi valley (even as far as St. Louis or Cincinnati), and of the areas of Tennessee, Kentucky, and Alabama that had once depended on the tributaries of the Ohio River. Transportation technology alone would not determine the outcome of this competition.

Indeed, technological developments helped New Orleans as well as her rivals. Steamboats made it possible to trade up and down the river with equal ease, and they operated at a much lower capital cost than railroads or canals. Until 1860 the still immature railroad network and the river route through New Orleans were evenly matched competitors, even for the trade of the old Northwest; and in a good year (e.g., 1857) New Orleans was still able to attract Western flour for reexport to the east. As long as the transportation alternatives were nearly even, other factors would determine the commercial fate of New Orleans.[28]

Many factors may have influenced the course of trade—insurance rates (reflecting risks of accident or spoilage), winter freezing and summer heat, mercantile commissions and charges, port facilities, frequency of handling and transshipment en route, and speed of transport. In addition, there were such indirect influences as the changing location of Western agriculture and the relative expansion of consumer markets in different parts of the country.[29] But in the late 1840's and early 1850's, the period of closest competition for trade, many knowledgeable observers placed a large share of the blame for New Orleans' losses on her inadequate credit facilities. Some considered credit as important as transportation:

Grain is now carried from the Wabash to New York, by the canals, at the same cost of freight as is charged by the way of New Orleans. . . . Last autumn the rich regions of Ohio, Indiana, and Illinois were flooded with the local bank notes of the Eastern states, advanced by New York houses, on produce to be shipped to them, by the way of the canals, in the spring. These moneyed facilities enable the packer, miller, and speculator to hold onto their produce till the opening of navigation in the spring, and they are no longer obliged, as formerly, to hurry off their shipments during the winter by the way of New Orleans, in order to realize funds by drafts on their shipments. The banking facilities at the East are doing as much to draw trade from us as the canals and railways which Eastern capital is constructing.[30]

The main burden of the argument was that Louisiana's banking capital, and hence her ability to make loans, was too small for even the existing volume of business. While other cities expanded their banking capacity, the credit facilities of New Orleans steadily declined as bank charters expired. Moreover, the credit terms offered by New Orleans banks were not competitive. Banks in New York, Philadelphia, Charleston, and other rival cities made or renewed loans for six to twelve months, at 6 per cent interest. New Orleans banks confined their few discounts to thirty, sixty, and ninety days, "no matter what amount of country [i.e., small-town merchants'] paper was placed in their hands as collateral security."[31] In part this practice reflected Forstall's restrictive "fundamental rules" of the Bank Act of 1842, which counted only ninety-day, nonrenewable commercial paper as an asset and preferred local merchants to those from out of town.[32]

Having established that restrictive financial conditions retarded economic development in some sectors of the Louisiana economy, we may inquire whether the more expansive financial conditions of the 1830's and the late 1850's actively aided economic development. It is certainly clear that the chartering of new banks and the expansion of credit facilities in 1827-37 was a direct response to unusually strong demands for external finance. The population of the state increased by about 50 per cent during the decade, and that of New Orleans doubled. In the same period, cotton production tripled. When sugar production began its period of rapid expansion in 1827, enormous sums were invested in preparing the land, acquiring slaves, and purchasing sugar-refining equipment (each large plantation required about $20,000 worth). Forstall estimated that the establishment of new sugar plantations between 1827 and 1830 required some $16 million of capital formation. During this agricultural expansion, Louisianans financed the purchase of nearly $2.5 million worth of new land from the federal government, America's original "absentee landlord." There can be no doubt whatever that an expansion of Louisiana's financial system was essential to this rapid growth in population, output, and productive capital.[33]

Louisiana also increased its supply of "human capital" by importing slaves from other Southern states. Historians have often contended that this "drain" of capital inhibited more productive investment in such things as agricultural machinery and improvements or in manufacturing. Since this argument generally confuses physical and financial capital, it is only partly valid. If the new slaves arrived in the company of migrating planters, as sometimes happened, Louisiana obviously received additional human resources at no financial cost.[34] And if the imports were financed by borrowing from residents of the slave-exporting state, Louisiana used none of its own current savings or resources. The profits earned from the new slaves would normally more than cover repayment of the debt, so that foreign borrowing to pay for slaves would actually augment Louisiana's capital rather than draining it.

Only if the interstate slave trade was financed "in cash," out of the savings of Louisiana citizens, did the state immediately surrender any of its own physical capital. A planter might use his own savings, or he might borrow the savings of factors, bank depositors or noteholders, local slave traders, and other Louisiana lenders. In the process, Louisiana was essentially exchanging cotton, sugar, or other goods (and possibly even some specie) indirectly for additional human capital. As long as the Louisiana economy offered no more socially profitable uses for the financial capital of the lenders, slave imports did not harm the state's economic growth.*

The quantitative expansion of banking did more than passively permit the growth of the real economy. Financial growth was an independent cause, an active contributor to real economic growth. As I have suggested previously, this active contribution took three forms: increasing the productivity of existing capital, raising the supply of savings, and improving the allocation of savings between alternative investments.

The most significant improvement in the productivity of existing capital was probably the changing role of specie. As a medium of payment, specie had several disadvantages. Being a commodity money, it was costly to produce, and Louisiana and other states exported some of their output of other goods in order to purchase specie abroad (or from California in the 1850's). It was also costly and risky to transport from place to place, or to store away as a form of wealth. But most of all, specie was idle, unproductive capital that earned no return for its owner or for society. Bank money, by contrast, cost almost nothing to produce and represented savings put to work through loans—that is, active capital. Hence any development in banking or finance that displaced specie enhanced the productivity of Louisiana's existing real capital. As the economy developed, specie was sometimes exported in payment for other goods. But it was more commonly withdrawn from the private hoards of planters, merchants, and frontiersmen, or from monetary circulation, and transferred to bank vaults to serve more productively as a "high-powered" reserve, rather than as low-powered money in circulation. Although this increased the danger of a multiple contraction of the money supply (due to external specie flows), Louisiana was at least making more efficient use of its specie and acquiring a less costly form of money through banknotes and deposits.[35]

Financial expansion also enhanced the productivity of existing

---

* The slave trade within the state obviously involved no loss of physical or financial capital, but simply an exchange of existing assets. However, such transactions may have generated additional demands for external finance. The slaves themselves were acceptable collateral for additional credit.

physical (and human) capital other than specie. By improving access to equipment, slaves, and markets, external finance enabled a frontiersman to give up subsistence farming, or perhaps cattle ranching, in favor of more profitable crops like cotton or sugar. At a slightly more advanced stage of development, external finance sometimes permitted a change from less productive cotton planting to more productive but more capital-intensive sugar planting, or a change to a more efficient technology (steam-powered sugar refining, for example). Each time, the existing land, slaves, and other capital gained in productivity.

The Louisiana financial system, particularly in the 1830's, also accelerated economic growth by increasing the supply of savings. Primarily, these were savings borrowed from other states or from Europe. A large but indeterminate amount of foreign capital entered Louisiana through direct finance, without the help of banks or other financial intermediaries. It sometimes came in the possession of immigrant planters or businessmen but more often in the form of trade credit between merchants. To this direct import of capital the banks of Louisiana added another $20.7 million (up to December 1837) by selling their stocks and bonds abroad.* It is of course conceivable that some of this extra capital would have come to Louisiana without the help of banks. Foreign lenders, however, had little information about the potential profitability of individual plantations, urban lands, or improvement projects. Direct finance from long distance would have been risky under these circumstances, and foreign capital, if available at all, would probably have been prohibitively costly to Louisiana borrowers. We may reasonably credit the banks with attracting a full $20 million of developmental capital.

After 1853, Louisiana's financial capacity was augmented by the revival of the Citizens Bank and the creation of the free banking system. This addition also contributed to economic growth, but its effect was more limited than that produced by the financial innovations of the 1820's and 1830's. The amount of additional

---

* See Table 3.2. The banks also imported an indeterminate smaller amount of capital through their net exports of notes and deposits. The state government facilitated these capital imports by guaranteeing some bank bonds. My estimates (see p. 111) suggest that the state's endorsement lowered the cost of the imports by about 10 per cent.

capital involved was less (about $15 million) and the bulk of it (all but $1.4 million) represented not new savings imported from abroad but merely a new form of holding wealth already within the state. The attractiveness of the stock, notes, or deposits of the free banks as liquid financial assets may have induced savers to transfer specie from private hoards to bank reserves, making the available capital more productive for society. The same inducement may have raised the proportion of saving out of current incomes in the state. But in this period financial innovations probably had less effect on the productivity of existing capital or the supply of savings than on the allocation of investment.[36]

The Allocation of Finance: Consumption vs. Investment

The developmental impact of any given supply of credit obviously depends on the wisdom and efficiency with which it is allocated. In the particular historical context of antebellum Louisiana, the quantity and quality (allocation) of financial assets were closely associated. Many historians have suggested, for example, that in the 1830's an excessive quantity of finance led to unwise resource allocation, chiefly "speculative" investment in real estate and various internal improvement projects. Conversely, they say, the restricted quantity of finance in the 1840's prompted banks to confine their credit to short-term, strictly commercial loans. Obviously, the underlying conditions of the economy as a whole must be kept in mind as we focus more narrowly on the allocation of credit to specific sectors or activities.

From the theoretical viewpoint, we must first ask whether credit allocation in Louisiana accelerated growth by raising the proportion of total output devoted to investment rather than to consumption. Unfortunately, the available evidence permits only the most impressionistic answer to this broad question. There are no statistics on rates of saving or investment for the various sectors of the antebellum economy. And even the reconstruction of such statistics for an economy like that of antebellum Louisiana would be more difficult and less meaningful than a similar reconstruction for twentieth-century America, since the basic economic institutions of that day were less functionally specialized than the modern household or corporation.

In a modern economy one can generally allocate all business (or at least corporate) spending to investment and all household spending to consumption without examining the detailed records of individual firms and families. By contrast, the typical institutions of early Louisiana—plantations, farms, small proprietorships and partnerships—spent their incomes or borrowed funds for both consumption and investment,* and even detailed research will seldom permit a clear division of the two, much less a representative sample sufficient for macroeconomic estimates. Planters and other businessmen did not often separate business and personal expenses in their bookkeeping, and even when they did there is no guarantee that their classification would match that of a modern economist. For example, supplies for a plantation were typically purchased on credit and paid for each year at harvesttime. Was the resulting debt incurred for consumption, or for "working capital" (i.e., investment)? Should we regard supplies for field slaves as investment (since slaves were considered capital) and supplies for the planter's family and household slaves as consumption?

The records of financial institutions contain similar ambiguities, mainly because the banker's description of a loan or the collateral behind it seldom reveals how the borrowed funds were used. Urban mortgages did not necessarily represent real-estate development—on the contrary, the long-term funds they provided were ideal sources of working capital for commerce or business. Similarly, funds obtained from banks or factors on short-term (but renewable) "commercial" loans could be used by planters to finance future production or the purchase of land and slaves.[37]

Despite the lack of quantitative evidence, some educated guesses are possible. The types of collateral most acceptable for external (and especially bank) finance were mortgages on land, buildings, and slaves, or invoices for staple commodities—all sources that encouraged borrowing for investment. The modern practice of lending against consumer durables (furniture, automobiles, etc.) or future income (perhaps without collateral) was almost unknown. Presumably, much of the direct finance supplied by family and

---

* A similar problem exists in modern America, where statisticians have given up trying to separate government "consumption" spending from government "investment" spending. This problem also existed in nineteenth-century government, of course, but it extended to the private sector as well.

friends supported consumption; but most of the indirect finance offered by banks and other intermediaries was at least intended to support investment spending. The clearest exception, a case of frustrated intentions, came during and after the financial crisis of 1837-42, when bankers reluctantly renewed mortgage or commercial loans and thus helped to sustain the consumption of their customers. In this case access to bank finance encouraged an unreduced rate of consumption (i.e., standard of living); but the depression itself was the basic cause of the decline in investment spending.

The banking system probably gave its strongest impetus to investment spending during the decade preceding 1837. Most of the banks chartered at this time were property banks designed to finance the expansion of cotton and sugar production or improvement banks designed to foster particular social-overhead projects. There may have been some forced saving as bank credit financed investment while inflation reduced the consumers' purchasing power. But the argument that forced saving may have aided development is a weak one. In antebellum Louisiana, severe inflation occurred chiefly in the years 1835-37. The pattern of investment became somewhat more speculative, raising the prices of existing capital goods (especially land) rather than encouraging new investment. Moreover, several of the new projects that were begun in those years were interrupted or liquidated during the subsequent crisis. Had the expansionary period lasted a few years longer, it is quite conceivable that forced saving could have made a more lasting contribution.[38]

The Sectoral Allocation of Credit and Economic Growth

As I suggested in the preceding theoretical discussion, finance can affect economic development not only by increasing the proportion of total output devoted to investment but also by allocating that investment more productively. The way in which Louisiana's banking system influenced the allocation of credit among the different sectors of her economy was discussed in Chapter One. Our purpose here is to analyze the impact of that allocation on economic growth.

The cotton and sugar factors of New Orleans exerted a strong influence on the city's banks, and planters frequently complained that the factors charged excessively high interest rates and commission fees. Many historians have argued that these "high" rates, together with the customary price markup for supplies purchased on credit, struck at the heart of Louisiana's economy by raising the planters' costs and reducing their incomes. A planter's indebtedness, they contend, bound him to his factor in near-servitude: he could not seek the best market for his crops or his purchases, and he could not diversify beyond the traditional cash crops of cotton and sugar.[39]

These criticisms of the planter-factor relationship misinterpret its effects on economic growth, mainly by exaggerating the factor's monopoly power and by confusing the welfare of one group, the planters, with that of society as a whole. Factors certainly acquired some market power from their superior knowledge of market conditions, their customary fixed commission rates, and their easier access to both bank and foreign mercantile credit. But their ability to charge monopolistic prices was limited by competitive international markets for cotton and other products, as well as by competition between the factors themselves for the planters' business. The "high" interest charged by factors reflected the scarcity of credit and capital in a growing frontier region, the uncertainty of future crop yields, and the risks borne by the factor as intermediary. These interest rates did mean lower incomes for planters, but the money paid out became income for the factor, banker, or other middleman.* Interest rates and commissions thus determined mainly the distribution of income. The growth rate of total income was affected only to the extent that the middlemen who received income invested a smaller portion of it, or invested it less productively, than the planters would have.

One device by which Louisiana agriculturalists sought to weaken the factors' alleged monopoly powers and augment their own supply of credit was the property bank. Most historians have agreed with Fritz Redlich that the blend of mortgage and commercial banking embodied in these banks was an "unfortunate combination of incompatible functions." And some, accepting the

---

* When these middlemen were "foreigners" the state's total income was indeed reduced. But without factors and their "high" charges, the planters might have imported financial services (and lowered state income) to an even greater extent.

"commercial loan" theory of banking (see pp. 118-21), have flatly asserted that the issue of note or deposit liabilities cannot be "sound" if the issuing bank carries mortgages or other long-maturity assets in its portfolio. However, the success of mixed banking ventures in Germany, Belgium, Japan, and the modern United States (with its "full-service" banks) indicates that this is not always true. The particular circumstances of the antebellum Louisiana economy simply made mixed banking difficult. Mortgage borrowers were concentrated in export-oriented agriculture, giving the banks little opportunity to diversify against the risk of unfavorable market conditions. Moreover, the capital markets for plantation mortgages, or even for the more liquid commercial paper, were poorly developed, giving the banks little opportunity to sell off their assets. The inherent instability of banking under the specie standard also made mortgage banking riskier, since a property bank had few defenses against a liquidity crisis. Despite these handicaps, well-capitalized property banks did provide Louisiana with foreign capital and long-term credit, both essential to more rapid economic growth.[40]

The financial crisis of 1837-1842 buried the property bank idea. And Edmund Forstall's "fundamental rules" in the Bank Act of 1842 made a law of a policy that he and others had earlier sought to impose from within the property banks: the complete separation of mortgage and commercial banking liabilities, with a corresponding division between capital and cash assets. This requirement was intended to create a balanced portfolio of assets that would hopefully be compatible with the mixed investment and commercial banking business involved. But Forstall's bisected version of the property bank received little trial: all three property banks had entered liquidation after 1837, and the Citizens Bank, when it was revived in 1852, essentially became a commercial bank. If the property banks had been guided by Forstall's rules, or by some less rigid assurance of portfolio balance and liquidity, they might have continued to provide vital development credit for many years.

The rural branches of the New Orleans banks were another attempt to increase the credit available to agriculture and small-town business. Branch banks offered less liberal credit and less response to local opportunities than independent local banks might have provided. But they provided a sound money supply and surely did more than the New Orleans bankers alone could have done to develop rural Louisiana. They also accelerated economic growth by "monetizing" the frontier areas of the economy and moving specie hoards into bank reserves, and by mobilizing rural savings for relending locally.[41]

The banks' allocation of credit affected development in less direct ways, most notably by helping to finance the various large-scale improvement projects of the 1830's—the canals, great commercial hotels, and public utilities promoted by the government as necessary for the continued growth of private enterprise in New Orleans. Later, the free banks financed the large railroad projects of the 1850's. In addition, the Louisiana banks contributed to less tangible forms of social overhead. Several bank charters required an annual payment to support education. And in a few cases bank financing may have facilitated the adoption of improved technology (for example, the application of steam power to sugar refining and cotton processing).

More significantly, individual bankers were the promoters or entrepreneurs of many developmental projects. When the Pontchartrain Railroad ran short of construction funds in 1831-32, banker Samuel Peters, himself one of the directors of the railroad, lent his personal credit and also arranged loans from his bank. Edmund Forstall founded New Orleans' first great sugar refinery (in 1831) and was active in several other projects. In the 1850's banker James Robb led the campaign for railroad development and became the first president of the New Orleans, Jackson, and Great Northern line. Robb put his personal fortune and the resources of his bank completely behind the project, almost single-handedly carrying the railroad through the financial crisis of its early years. In the relatively small, personalized business community of antebellum New Orleans a banker's decisions were not limited to strictly financial matters. In his active promotion of community service and development projects, the Louisiana banker resembled the influential small-town banker or the powerful investment banker of Morgan's day more than the specialized, relatively passive urban banker of today. His general entrepreneurial activities may well have been as important to the state's development as his strictly financial activities.[42]

It is clear that Louisiana's banks participated actively in the expansion of New Orleans commerce, and that particular banking innovations were intended to encourage economic growth in agriculture, and certain social overheads. On the other hand, the banks apparently contributed relatively little to the finance of manufacturing in Louisiana. This contrast suggests the need to go beyond examining the impact of banking and finance on the growth of particular sectors of the economy. Did the banks influence Louisiana's economy as a whole toward or away from its "optimal" pattern of development? This larger question will be considered at length in a later chapter.

CHAPTER THREE

Financial Ties to the Outside World

LOUISIANA'S economy was very much an "open" one in the ante-bellum era, having extensive contacts with foreign countries and other states. This chapter views the operations of the Louisiana banking system in the context of international and interregional trade and finance, with particular attention to the external ties arising from the financial operations of the federal government and the Bank of the United States.

Balance of Trade and Payments

The ideal method of describing and analyzing the flow of international and interregional trade and finance would be to construct balance-of-payments accounts for antebellum Louisiana. These would show the receipts and payments arising from trade through New Orleans, from services such as shipping and insurance, and from the income (interest, dividends, or profits) on previous "foreign" borrowing and lending. They would also show the movement of capital in and out of Louisiana and the flow of specie that balanced the overall account. Unfortunately, the data available will not permit even rough estimates of most categories in Louisiana's balance of payments. We have some evidence on the balance of trade as such—the flow of merchandise in and out of the state. There is also partial evidence on certain capital and specie flows. But for most of the nonmerchandise categories, one can only guess whether they involved net receipts or net payments.

New Orleans had a strongly favorable balance in international trade, and she was a major channel for the receipt of foreign exchange and payments. From the 1830's until the Civil War, she rivaled New York as the leading outlet for America's exports. This leadership depended primarily on the shipment of Southern staple crops—especially cotton, a product that accounted for over half of the total money value of United States exports from 1830 to 1860. But New Orleans was not merely a Southern port. As we have seen, she was also the major outlet for produce from the entire Mississippi basin until canals and railroads diverted this traffic (mainly after the late 1840's). Although a major export center, New Orleans never developed a corresponding import trade, and her imports were usually one-fourth to one-half the value of her exports.[1]

Louisiana's large net exports in foreign trade were partly offset by net imports in her trade with other American states. The traditional interpretation (by Louis Schmidt, Douglass North, and others) has been that specialized Southern plantations required large imports of Western foodstuffs; but recent research by Robert Gallman and others indicates that the cotton plantations essentially fed themselves. The city of New Orleans certainly consumed some of the Western products arriving on its wharves, but most of them were reexported to Northern or foreign ports. The conclusion that Louisiana's trade deficits with the West remained small is supported by the estimates of interregional trade (1839-69) made by Albert Fishlow. Instead, the large and steadily growing net imports into New Orleans came from the North. Further net imports also entered Louisiana through Natchez and other river towns, and a lesser amount probably came overland, particularly in the livestock trade.[2]

The "visible" merchandise trade, of course, is only one component of the overall balance of payments for Louisiana. Data on "invisible" and capital-account items are scattered, unreliable, and unsystematic. We may presume, however, that Louisiana generally had net payments for travel and net receipts for mercantile services (though the South as a whole had net payments here). Capital flows varied widely; apparently there were large net imports of capital during periods of rapid economic expansion and net exports in times of depression. The specie flow also fluctuated. Data on gross specie imports into New Orleans from 1842-43 to 1860-61 show an average of $7 million annually over the period, somewhat higher in the 1850's than in the 1840's and reaching

TABLE 3.1

Specie Imports into New Orleans

Year[a]	Value of specie imports	Year	Value of specie imports
1843	$10,415,531	1853	$7,865,226
1844	7,748,723	1854	6,967,056
1845	2,249,138	1855	3,746,037
1846	1,872,071	1856	4,913,540
1847	6,680,050	1857	6,500,015
1848	1,845,808	1858	13,268,013
1849	2,501,250	1859	15,627,016
1850	3,792,662	1860	8,444,857
1851	7,937,119	1861	14,627,375
1852	6,278,523		

SOURCE: New Orleans *Price Current*, annual issue in September or October of each year.
 [a] In 1843–47 the accounting year ended on September 30; in the remaining years it ended on August 31.

peaks after financial crises (see Table 3.1). We may hazard the tentative conclusion, then, that in years of normal prosperity Louisiana's surplus on merchandise trade and her imports of capital were balanced by slight net payments for services and by net imports of specie. During depression years, the trade surpluses were smaller, the capital inflows much smaller, and the net specie imports correspondingly less (sometimes becoming net exports).[3]

What role did Louisiana's banks play in this international and interregional system? For the most part, they shared even the financial responsibilities of trade with other institutions. Much of the credit in Anglo-American trade came from English merchants, who generally dealt through agents in New York or other Eastern cities. The foreign-exchange business at various times was in the hands of private brokers (bankers) or the Bank of the United States. But from about 1825 on, the financing and servicing of the major trade and capital flows was handled chiefly by a few English merchant bankers and by American chartered banks, including those in Louisiana.[4]

Correspondent Ties, Discounts, and Exchanges

Because of New Orleans' involvement in national and world trade, nearly every Louisiana bank maintained a correspondent relationship with some bank in New York, Philadelphia, or Boston, and with some European city (usually London, but often Liverpool, Paris, or Amsterdam). For example, the Commercial Bank, which concentrated on the Western trade and earned its profits largely from its wide correspondent ties, maintained accounts with 71 banks and had "active correspondence" with 40 of these.[5] One of the first concerns of a newly opened bank was to establish correspondent ties. Customarily, it contacted a bank that had no connection with any other New Orleans bank; this allowed for a free flow of services and confidential information on market conditions. Initially, a correspondence agreement usually provided for the collection of bills of exchange payable in the other bank's city, for the purchase or sale (on commission) of foreign bills, and for the interest to be paid on balances between the two banks.[6]

As the correspondent relationship became established, and as the Louisiana bank established its credit rating, an agreement was often expanded to permit open credits or advances; that is, the correspondent bank would pay drafts without funds on hand, up to some specified limit (usually from $10,000 to $100,000). Louisiana's banks commonly enjoyed this overdraft privilege with Eastern or European correspondents, and smaller Western and Southern banks sought similar privileges in New Orleans. In periods of tight money, correspondents tried to limit or halt overdrafts, sometimes reprimanding the debtor bank and as a last resort actually refusing ("protesting") the drafts. In 1837, New Orleans banks were involved on both sides of this process, receiving complaints and protests from Eastern correspondent banks and complaining to the smaller Mississippi banks indebted to them.[7]

Much of the banks' out-of-state business was devoted to domestic and foreign exchange transactions. An important characteristic of the exchange business was its extreme seasonal variation. Virtually at a standstill from July to October, it revived as the early cotton, sugar, and Western produce shipments arrived in late fall and reached full volume from about January to May. During the peak season, the banks discounted so much trade paper that they sometimes had to "ration" other forms of credit. Because the seasonal peak in cotton exports did not coincide with the peaks in imports or other exports, foreign exchange rates were lowest in January-April when the exports of cotton were heaviest. This seasonal imbalance was also reflected in domestic exchange. Bills of exchange and similar paper claims generated by Southern (or Western) exports flowed from New Orleans to the West and North, where they helped to finance the surplus of imports (and the regional imbalances) in those areas. The banks, through their correspondent ties, played a leading role in these financial settlements.[8]

As suggested by the presence of seasonal trade imbalances and strictly financial settlements, not all the bills of exchange discounted by the banks arose directly from shipments of goods. Antebellum bankers distinguished in principle between two types of bills: commercial paper "founded on real business transactions" (i.e., on shipments of goods), and "accommodation" paper (all other bills). The influential "banking school" of monetary theorists argued that by limiting all credit to real commercial paper one would automatically provide a quantity of credit appropriate to the economy, since purchases of "real business" paper merely enlarged the supply of bank money and credit to meet the legitimate needs of trade. Accommodation paper, by contrast, was generally considered speculative, and by purchasing it the banks were supposedly contributing to unsound credit expansion and unhealthy increases of currency in circulation. Unfortunately, these "commercial loan" or "real bill" theories were incorrect, and restricting the type of credit offered did not automatically maintain the right quantity of money and bank credit. Whenever the banks purchased either type of paper and paid for it with their own banknotes (or perhaps with deposits), they automatically increased the money supply by a corresponding amount. Thus either type of transaction could have inflationary consequences.[9]

One especially notorious use of accommodation paper was the system of "kiting" or "racehorse bills." Catterall has described this practice with reference to the branch offices of the Bank of the United States. "A racehorse bill is the payment of one bill of exchange by the purchase of a new one. Thus a bill sent from New Orleans to Nashville for collection would not be collected; but instead the Nashville office would allow the debtor to draw a new bill on another office. The bills kept running to and fro without being paid, and hence were called racers or race-horse bills."[10] If one mentally substitutes "bank" for "office," the same description would apply to the Louisiana banks.

New Orleans banks apparently participated in kiting operations with banks in several other western and southern cities. But Robert Roeder has determined that the practice was concentrated in operations between New Orleans and Natchez during the years before the panic of 1837. Factors with partnership houses in each city would advance credit to planters on four-month bills, which were then discounted with a bank in one of the cities. If these real business bills matured before the factor had received funds from the sale of the planter's cotton, the factor could extend the credit for an additional four months by issuing a draft on his partnership firm in the other city. He (or his partner) would discount this accommodation bill with a bank and use the proceeds to pay off the maturing bill. Through this spiral of bills, factors were able to provide extended credit for planters, to hold cotton inventories for sale at maximum prices, and eventually to obtain Eastern or foreign exchange funds and retire the debts.*

Roeder emphasizes the detrimental effects of these kited bills, blaming them for the catastrophic collapse of credit and the flood of bankruptcies after 1837. Most antebellum Louisianans apparently held the same low opinion of racehorse bills, and of accommodation paper in general. But what seemed clear-cut in principle was often obscure in practice. Since bills of lading and other trading documents did not customarily accompany bills of exchange during the antebellum era, it was often difficult to distinguish accommodation bills from "real" bills.[11]

Despite these adverse opinions (and the preventive measures actually adopted in Louisiana), one can defend accommodation paper, and even racehorse bills, under certain conditions. Edmund Forstall's rival, banker Samuel Jarvis Peters, defended the system of accommodation credits even in December 1837, in the wake of the first panic failures, arguing that it had increased the productivity and output of the state's economy. Historian Walter B. Smith has arrived at a similar favorable opinion of the operations

---

* Roeder, "New Orleans Merchants," pp. 262-70. Drawing and redrawing between merchants, which amounted to a circular flow of private credits, had been common practice before 1800. Once banks began to create credit and purchasing power, this form of mercantile credit gradually died out. The really innovative feature of the New Orleans and Natchez transactions was the acceptance of merchant drafts by the banks, which converted mercantile credit into bank credit. I am indebted to Fritz Redlich for clarification of these points.

of Biddle's bank in domestic exchange—the same operations that Catterall attacked. Monetary theorists today would presumably offer a qualified but favorable judgment. Racehorse bills may be viewed as very similar to short-term renewable loans; as such, they could partially reconcile the planters' and factors' desire for long-term credit to span the seasonal flow of trade and finance with the bankers' desire for liquidity. We should also distinguish between racehorse bills issued in an attempt to avoid repaying debt altogether (probably an uncommon practice) and the same bills issued to finance genuine trade flows through limited extensions of the credit period.

The complaint by Roeder and by many antebellum Louisianans that "kiting" brought on or augmented the financial crisis of 1837 involves a misunderstanding. It was not the form of the transactions but their total volume that mattered. If the economy's resources were fully employed, any further expansion of money and credit, whether for "commercial" or "speculative" purposes, could not increase the output of goods and services. Instead, the extra bidding for existing resources and commodities would merely raise prices, and with higher prices the "needs of trade" would justify still further credit expansion to finance the larger value of trade (the same volume, but at higher prices). The restriction of banking to strictly commercial loans could not have prevented this inflationary spiral or the subsequent crisis.[12]

Notes, Deposits, and Specie Movements

Operations in domestic exchange were only part of the ties between Louisiana banks and those in other states. Other funds were transferred by the movement of banknotes, the accumulation of deposit balances, and the flow of specie. Several of these flows were directly linked to exchange operations, of course, but they also occurred independently.

Banknotes moved in both directions across Louisiana's borders, with the notes of Louisiana banks circulating in other states and those of "foreign" banks circulating in Louisiana. It would be very useful to have estimates of these opposing flows in order to estimate the actual money supply existing in the state, but the data simply do not exist. One may only guess, on the basis of scattered qualitative evidence, that on balance Louisiana banknotes circulating outside the state usually exceeded "foreign" banknotes circulating within. If so, the published estimates of circulating medium in Louisiana, which are based on the volume of notes issued by Louisiana banks, somewhat overstate the actual money in circulation within the state.*

It is clear that Louisiana banknotes circulated throughout the Mississippi valley. One slightly romantic reminiscence of the early days of the Citizens Bank even credits the bank's upriver circulation as the source of the term "Dixie Land," since its familiar $10 notes were called "dixies" (Fr. *dix,* or ten). The same source explains how the wide circulation occurred:

The steamboatmen became of great service to the bank, as the major part of the sum of their collections was carried out of the city to be disbursed throughout the Mississippi Valley, in payment for fuel, wharfboat dues, stores, wages, port charges, etc. Thousands upon thousands of dollars were taken out of the city every week by packets bound for points on the Mississippi, Missouri and Ohio rivers and their tributaries, the Wabash, Tennessee, Arkansas and Red. In this manner, throughout the wide territory from Pittsburgh, Pa., St. Paul, Minn., and St. Louis, Mo., to the Gulf these notes were kept in constant circulation until they became better known than those of any bank in the South, or in the Union, and the circulation of the bank mounted up to four or five millions of dollars, then an unprecedented sum.[13]

Most Louisiana banknotes, however, circulated within the immediate New Orleans trading hinterland—Arkansas, Kentucky, Tennessee, Alabama, and above all Mississippi. A good many notes reached these areas through normal trade and finance, but there were some interesting special arrangements. Several towns in Mississippi (and probably in other states as well), through local merchants, insurance companies, or branches of their banks, obtained the notes of New Orleans banks to replace less acceptable local currencies. This currency reached them in $10,000 bundles (usually of small notes) and was paid out over the counter in routine business. The New Orleans bankers were naturally delighted with this opportunity to circulate money in areas from which it was less likely to return for redemption.[14]

The banknotes of neighboring states also entered Louisiana, and the Louisiana banks did not appreciate this "foreign" com-

---

* An exception must be made for the years 1837-43 when the Louisiana banks contracted their note circulation much more sharply than banks in neighboring states (especially Mississippi). Cashier of Holmesville branch of Commercial Bank of Natchez to Thomas Henderson, May 12, 1837, in Holmesville Branch Letterbook, Commercial Bank of Natchez collection.

petition. They were frequently able to appeal to the public's fear and uncertainty about the soundness of these outside notes, but it was not always easy to agree on a remedy. In 1836 the City Bank proposed that the New Orleans banks jointly hire an agent to gather and redeem the local circulation of Mississippi bank-notes, but the Citizens Bank (led by Edmund Forstall) vigorously rejected the idea. Some years later, many of the representatives to the Louisiana constitutional convention of 1845 proposed to abolish all banking and "return to the good old system of hard money," but they could not decide how to prevent an influx of banknotes from nearby states.[15]

Just as banknotes could move across state lines in both directions, so too could bank deposits in the form of personal or cashiers' checks. Many deposits in New Orleans banks were held by residents of other states, and individual Louisiana citizens likewise accumulated deposits in other states—particularly in the East, where wealthy Southerners generally spent their summers. Unfortunately, the banks did not record these deposits by state of residence, so the amounts are unknown. The flow of personal deposits in and out of Louisiana was probably highly seasonal, reflecting the timing of trade and travel.

In addition to the deposits of individual citizens, there were funds held by one bank for another, which probably accounted for much of the interstate movement of deposits. Louisiana bank customers could conveniently obtain funds in a distant city without maintaining their own deposits there, simply by purchasing drafts on the deposits maintained by their bankers.[16]

Detailed data on the interbank deposits of individual New Orleans banks are available for December 1837 and February 1857. An apparent rise in deposits owed to other banks prior to 1837 seems to have resulted from the special relation of the Merchants' and Gas Light Banks to the Bank of the United States and its Pennsylvania successor. Margaret Myers has contended that "large amounts" of interbank deposits were concentrated in New York between 1840 and 1860. And she says of New Orleans: "The growing trade of New Orleans after 1850 made it worthwhile for many of the southern and southwestern banks to keep balances there, but the effect upon New York deposits was to increase rather than to diminish them, for it enabled the banks of New Orleans to maintain larger balances in New York than formerly."

Close examination of the detailed 1857 data available forces a rejection of this conclusion. There was no marked rise in deposits by other Southern banks in New Orleans, and only a few New Orleans banks showed any tendency to concentrate their deposits in New York. As far as the New Orleans banks were concerned, then, there is very little evidence before 1860 of the pyramiding of reserves in large city banks, a practice that became common late in the nineteenth century.[17]

Besides handling external flows of banknotes and deposits, the Louisiana banks apparently arranged most of the large specie movements in the state, often with transactions running to several hundred thousand dollars. During most of the antebellum period New Orleans imported more specie than any other city in the nation. Between 1843 and 1852, for example, she brought in over 60 per cent of the total U.S. specie imports. Louisiana's commercial proximity to the specie supplies of Mexico and Havana was one reason for this. The banks (or merchants) usually purchased Cuban or Mexican silver with sterling bills of exchange drawn against their British balances, so that the imports of specie were closely attuned to changes in the rates on foreign exchange; when exchange premiums rose too high in New Orleans, specie could be sold more cheaply from Mexico directly to London. The flow of specie through New Orleans to other states was similarly sensitive to domestic exchange rates.[18]

Exchange rates were not the only factor to influence specie movements through Louisiana's banks. Western tradesmen withdrew significant amounts of specie for dispersal in their states, and these withdrawals were unaffected by exchange rates. The New Orleans banks also served as agents for banks in other states on occasion, importing specie reserves on a commission basis. In times of financial crisis they desperately tried to import specie for their own use, even at substantial expense. Periodic suspensions of the convertibility of banknotes to specie facilitated specie hoarding by both the banks and the public; this, too, disrupted the usual interstate flow. Finally, Louisiana's supply of specie was cut off at its source in Mexico on several occasions.[19]

Movements in Bank Stocks and Bonds

Of all the external transactions conducted by Louisiana's chartered banks, dealings in bank stocks and state bonds played the greatest role in importing funds from other states and nations. The process of borrowing from abroad by exporting bank securities occurred almost entirely in the 1830's and was partially reversed in subsequent years. But its significance may be gauged by the fact that the $22 million imported by Louisiana's banks during the 1830's accounted for about 12 per cent of the total capital imported by the entire country during that decade.[20]

The most detailed information available on the location of the owners of Louisiana bank stocks was collected at the end of 1837 and is summarized in Table 3.2, which shows the net result of all external flows of bank stocks (and the bonds of the property banks) prior to December 23, 1837. The banks did not participate equally in the importation of funds. Over 70 per cent of the European funds, for example, were acquired through the sale of state bonds for the three property banks, which raised all their

TABLE 3.2

Holders of Louisiana Bank Stocks, December 23, 1837

Bank	Total stocks	Stockholders' location		
		Louisiana	Other U.S.	Foreign
Atchafalaya	$767,885	$767,885		
Canal	3,999,750	381,350	$1,601,700	$2,016,700
Carrollton	1,948,850	1,258,300	176,550	514,000
Citizens	5,300,000			5,300,000
City	2,000,000	928,300	918,600	153,100
Commercial	3,000,000	1,959,300	742,900	297,800
Consolidated Assoc.	2,523,000			2,523,000
Exchange	793,700	559,510	233,560	
Gas Light	1,854,455	872,045	939,210	43,200
Improvement	1,397,732	1,397,732		
Bank of Louisiana	3,997,480	2,375,580	56,300	1,565,600
Louisiana State	1,929,520	602,300	325,040	1,002,180
Mechanics & Traders	1,998,390	921,440	883,950	193,000
Merchants	1,000,000	35,000	965,000	
Bank of New Orleans	424,700	214,300	102,900	107,500
Union	7,000,000			7,000,000
TOTAL	$39,943,832	$12,273,043	$6,945,710	$20,725,080
Per cent of total		31%	17%	52%

SOURCE: *USC*, [36], No. 471, p. 56.

capital abroad. December 1837 was not quite the high-water mark for the external holdings of Louisiana bank notes, however; the peak was probably reached in early 1842. The Citizens Bank undoubtedly accounted for most of the increase by selling an additional $1.8 million of state bonds in Europe during this four-year interval.[21]

In the 1840's and 1850's, Louisiana banks reversed the pattern of the 1830's by importing securities and exporting capital. Detailed data are available on the ownership of bank stocks in February 1857 and they may be compared to the data for December 1837 (see Tables 3.3 and 3.4). Even though 1837 was not the peak year for external holdings of bank stock and 1857 was not the low point (which probably came in 1853), a dramatic decline in exter-

TABLE 3.3

Holders of Louisiana Bank Stocks, February 1857

Bank	Total stocks	Stockholders' location		
		Louisiana	Other U.S.	Foreign
Canal	$3,164,000	$1,600,000	$964,000	$600,000
Citizens[a]	1,000,000	876,000	53,000 (Md.)	20,500 (Fr.)
			21,000 (N.Y.)	5,300 (Eng.)
			2,500 (Mo.)	20,000 (Neth.)
			1,500 (Va.)	45,800
			78,000	
Bank of La.[b]	3,993,400	2,216,900	862,000	914,500
Louisiana State	2,000,000	1,267,800	185,100	547,100
Mechanics & Traders[c]	1,000,000	459,400	519,600	21,000
Bank of New Orleans[c]	2,000,000	1,904,500	77,500	18,000
Southern[c]	1,250,000	543,500	701,500	5,000 (Eng.)
Union[c]	1,500,000	1,420,300	60,000 (Va.)	8,500 (Eng.)
			5,000 (N.Y.)	6,200 (Fr./Ger.)
			65,000	14,700
TOTAL	$15,907,400	$10,288,600	$3,452,700	$2,166,100
Per cent of total		65%	22%	13%

SOURCE: LS, [21], 1857, Appendix.
  [a] Plus $500,000 of stock for the mortgage department, virtually all owned in Louisiana.
  [b] Estimated by dividing capital between locations according to division of share holdings.
  [c] Free banks, chartered during the 1850's.

TABLE 3.4

Changes in Bank Capital, 1837-1857

Bank	Reductions in total capital	Reductions in foreign capital
Atchafalaya	$767,885	0
Canal	835,750	$1,416,700
Carrollton	1,948,850	514,000
Citizens	4,300,000	5,254,200[a]
City	2,000,000	153,100
Commercial	3,000,000	297,800
Consolidated Assoc.	2,532,000	2,532,000[b]
Exchange	793,070	0
Gas Light	1,854,455	43,200
Improvement	1,397,732	0
Bank of Louisiana	4,080	651,100
Louisiana State	(70,480)[c]	455,080
Mechanics & Traders	1,998,390	193,000
Merchants	1,000,000	0
Bank of New Orleans	424,700	107,500
Union	7,000,000	7,000,000[d]
TOTAL	$29,786,432	$18,617,680
Added by free banks	(5,750,000)	(58,700)
NET REDUCTIONS IN CAPITAL	$24,036,432	$18,558,980

SOURCE: Tables 3.2 and 3.3 and their sources.
[a] Bonds outstanding in 1857, $5.6 million.
[b] Bonds outstanding in 1857, $1.1 million.
[c] Parentheses indicate a negative figure in the column considered.
[d] Not known how many (if any) bonds outstanding in 1857. The great majority of these bonds of the property banks were probably held in Europe; the figures in the table would thus overstate the drop in foreign capital (though only the Citizens Bank, of the three, remained in active operations with its capital).

nal holdings is evident. As the tables show, stock held in other states fell by $3.5 million, and foreign holdings by $18.6 million.

Several adjustments must be made in these figures in order to obtain a more reasonable estimate of capital exports resulting from the repurchase of bank securities previously held in Europe. We may start from an approximate peak of $22.5 million in 1841-42 (adding $1.8 million in Citizens Bank bonds to the 1837 total of foreign holdings). To our 1857 "trough" figure of $2.2 million must be added $6.7 million of property bank bonds still outstanding in 1857. The resulting differential of $13.5 million must then be lowered to reflect the fact that Europeans received less than par value on their shares of liquidated banks.* A final differential of $10 million, though only a rough estimate, is probably reasonable. This would indicate that about half the funds imported through the export of bank securities in the 1830's were returned to Europe in the succeeding two decades.

Federal Finance in Louisiana

Besides participating in the usual variety of international and interregional financial relations, Louisiana was part of America's unique "federal" monetary structure. Side by side with the state's own financial institutions were the New Orleans branches of the federally chartered first and second Banks of the United States (hereafter B.U.S.), the first operating from 1805 to 1811, and the second from 1817 to 1836. Other federal agencies were also present—customs collectors, a branch mint at New Orleans, land offices, the "independent treasury" system, and so on. In addition, several state-chartered banks served as depositories for federal funds. Through all these institutions the federal government not only conducted its own business but also attempted to enforce a monetary system based on a rigid specie standard. Even when the government withdrew funds to its own independent subtreasuries after 1836, it continued to influence the supply of specie and bank money. And its adherence to the specie standard became highly disruptive whenever the rest of the economy compromised or suspended that standard.

It is beyond the scope of this study to explore the full impact of federal fiscal policy—revenues, expenditures, and debt (or surplus) management—on the Louisiana economy. Doing so would involve a massive research effort to assemble statistics of federal receipts and expenditures on a state-by-state basis. These data could then be used to describe the regional impact of customs and land-sales revenues, expenditures on the military, and so on.†

---

* Most of the reduction in foreign holdings arose not from the sale of stock in surviving banks but from a mixture of default and partial repayment on the stocks and bonds of failing banks. Thus the par value of the stock of failing banks is a biased, upper-limit estimate of the funds actually returning to European investors.

† An exploratory study by Lance Davis and John Legler suggests that despite customs revenues collected at New Orleans and a considerable income from the sale of federal lands, the federal budget more often showed deficits than

Ideally, this study should at least examine the specifically monetary implications of the federal budget. Federal transactions continually moved funds in and out of Louisiana, and depending on the institutional context of the moment, these movements had differing effects on the money supply and credit conditions in the state. Unfortunately, even this more limited approach requires the same geographically disaggregated budget data as the broader analysis. It will be possible, then, to deal with federal fiscal policies and transactions only when we can focus on certain "critical" policies or periods, such as the Specie Circular and Surplus Distribution of 1836-37 or the periods of suspended specie payments.

Three institutions served as the depositories and fiscal agents of the federal government in Louisiana: the first and second B.U.S., certain state-chartered banks, and the various federal offices composing the independent treasury system. Over the years, these three institutions alternated in their service to the federal government, and sometimes their operations blended or coexisted. The state-chartered Louisiana Bank bridged the gap between the first and the second B.U.S.; and in 1833 other state-chartered banks took over federal deposits from the second B.U.S. long before it was actually dissolved. When deposit banks were operating, such federal officials as land-office receivers and customs collectors often kept their funds independently or in "special" deposits. Conversely, under the independent treasury system some officials used the banks for deposits or for transfers of funds when the Treasury did not.[22]

The monetary impact of a given movement of federal funds depended on which fiscal agency was employed, and on whether the funds involved were deposits, banknotes, or specie. The receipt, payment, or transfer of funds in banknotes or checks on bank deposits had a direct, proportionate effect on the bank's balance sheet. But if the government operated through a deposit bank and dealt in specie, its transactions had a multiple effect on monetary and credit conditions, since specie was the reserve of

---

surpluses in Louisiana and Arkansas. (Data are given only for the two states combined, at five-year intervals and with no breakdown of receipts or expenditures by type.) This deficit spending, ordinarily amounting to only a few hundred thousand dollars per year, probably did not have much effect on the total Louisiana economy. Lance Davis and Legler, pp. 529, 531.

the banking system. Each dollar of specie retained in government deposits might enable a bank to lend several dollars to its customers, using the specie as a fractional reserve; and each dollar removed might force a multiple contraction of loans. The monetary effect of a government transfer was probably even stronger when it was conducted through the B.U.S. Since this institution was an unofficial regulator and a source of emergency reserves to the state banks, any monetary expansion or contraction that it experienced was often transmitted and magnified through the state banks.

Under the independent treasury system, set up in 1840, the government conducted all transactions in specie through its own officials. Contemporary proponents of the system thought of it as divorcing the government from the banks, and believed that this separation would eliminate the multiple expansions or contractions that had occurred when government specie transactions were conducted through deposit banks. But this was a misconception. Ordinarily, any specie flow in or out of the community indirectly affected the specie reserves of its banks. Specie paid to the government was often obtained from banks in exchange for notes or deposits, and specie received from the government was often deposited in banks. The banks responded to changes in their specie reserves by the multiple contraction or expansion of credit and money, just as they had done under the deposit banking system. Thus the independent treasury system, too, had a "high-powered" monetary effect.[23]

Little is known about the operations of the New Orleans branch of the first B.U.S., which opened in 1805. The initial board of directors was dominated by prominent members of the American commercial group in New Orleans, so it is unlikely that the branch did much to fill the banking needs of the rival French merchants. Whatever the operations of the branch, they were undoubtedly facilitated by its receipts of federal deposits (over $200,000 by 1806,) since a portion of these funds could be lent out. When the first B.U.S. expired in March 1811, federal deposits were shifted to the Louisiana Bank.[24]

The second B.U.S., chartered by Congress in 1816, operated 26 branches in 22 states by 1830. Through these, it anchored the domestic and foreign exchange transactions of the nation and sought to provide a uniform money supply. Because of its size and its national leadership, the B.U.S. strongly influenced the activities of the state-chartered banks. It had a branch in New Orleans from 1817 to 1836, and under its subsequent Pennsylvania charter it maintained an agency there until 1841. Particularly under the leadership of Nicholas Biddle (from 1823 to 1839), the B.U.S. was the most influential of all the federal financial institutions in Louisiana. In turn, the New Orleans branch office was one of the most important to Biddle's overall financial strategy for the B.U.S.[25]

The New Orleans Branch Within the B.U.S. System. The real importance of the B.U.S. in New Orleans began with the selection of Nicholas Biddle as the Bank's president in 1823. Previously, during the presidency of William Jones, the New Orleans branch had participated in the Bank's general expansion of Southern and Western offices. But New Orleans had not expanded beyond the legitimate credit needs of her area nearly as much as other branches, which consequently suffered much heavier losses in the financial crisis of 1819. When the time came, under the contractionary presidency of Langdon Cheves, for assigning fixed capital to the various B.U.S. branches, the overexpanded offices received little or none and were forced to contract their operations. New Orleans, however, was assigned a branch capital of $1 million, a relatively modest reduction from the $1.7 million she had had in mid-1819.[26]

Soon after his appointment, Biddle began to expand the Bank's dealings in domestic bills of exchange.[27] New Orleans occupied the pivotal position in these transactions, linking the Western and Eastern branches. Biddle himself described a typical sequence:

This plan of circulation is governed entirely by the course of trade, and regulates itself. The crop of Tennessee is purchased by merchants who ship it to New Orleans, giving their bills founded on it to the branch at Nashville, which furnishes them with notes. These notes are in time brought to New York for purchasing supplies for Tennessee. They are paid in New York, and the Nashville bank becomes the debtor of the branch at New York. The Nashville branch repays them by drafts given to the branch at New York on the branch at New Orleans, where its bills have been sent, and the branch in New York brings home the amount by selling its drafts on the branch at New Orleans; or the New Orleans branch remits.[28]

The New Orleans branch carried out several distinct types of transactions within this network of domestic exchanges. First, it was the major recipient of Western bills, which were bought by the Western branches and sent to New Orleans for collection at maturity. Another type of domestic exchange generally involved the New Orleans branch in sending funds northward. There were two common variations on this theme. The branch might purchase domestic bills arising from the sale of goods to Northern manufacturers or merchants and send these northward for collection. Many of these "domestic" bills, particularly on cotton, financed foreign trade, with the Northern merchant (or banker) acting as both financial and shipping intermediary between the South and Europe. A second approach was for the New Orleans branch to buy foreign exchange (usually sterling bills based on cotton sold to English agents). The Northern B.U.S. branches, particularly the New York office, were happy to receive sterling bills as a remittance for adverse Southern (or, indirectly, Western) balances, since these could easily be resold to Northern merchants making payments in England.[29]

Most of the domestic exchange transactions of the New Orleans branch followed this pattern. In his public statements, Biddle emphasized the intimate connection of these exchange flows with the nation's internal trade. The traffic in "real" bills was desirable because it was thought to be self-regulating—in Biddle's words, "governed entirely by the course of trade." Samuel Jaudon, the B.U.S. cashier in New Orleans, revealed the political significance of this emphasis on "real" bills in a letter to Biddle, and also indicated the nature of the exceptions to the rule.

A statement of the exchange business, to show the rise and fall of our line of bills according to the periods of the gathering, shipment and sale of the crops, will be necessary to prove that this is real business. Great pains are taken [by political enemies of the Bank] to show that it is all an accommodation business, and that the Bank encourages it to make an usurious interest. The extracts from our letters which instruct the offices very particularly to confine their purchases to real business bills, and a copy of the New Orleans resolution levelled at redrafts, may do good.[30]

The bills of exchange that flowed against the main current were usually purchased at New Orleans and payable at Western branches up the Mississippi valley. Some of these were undoubt-edly real bills that financed the upriver shipment of goods (such as Louisiana sugar). But the marked increase of these reverse financial flows after crop failures, depressed markets, or similar difficulties indicates the use of "redrafts"—that is, kiting. When a merchant could not pay his bill at maturity, it might be met at New Orleans by drawing a new bill on the Western branch. If de-pressed prices or overoptimistic debt-financed farming continued for several seasons, this makeshift extension of credit became bur-densome indeed. A typical situation of this kind occurred in Octo-ber 1832: bills held by the New Orleans branch and payable at Nashville then totaled $828,000, as compared to $63,000 in March 1830.[31]

Whether real bills or otherwise, the domestic exchange trans-actions of the New Orleans branch were of great value to the B.U.S. The exchange business itself was profitable, and the New Orleans branch accounted for about 20 per cent of the total B.U.S. profits from 1829 to 1835. But beyond the direct profits earned, the exchange system pivoting on New Orleans facilitated several other aspects of the Bank's operations. An efficient domestic ex-change system was the key to Biddle's successful increase in the issue of notes and branch drafts, since the exchange of bills pro-vided funds to redeem in the East notes and drafts issued at South-ern and Western branches. And because many of the notes and branch drafts remained in circulation, the linking of exchange and notes permitted the expansion of the B.U.S. and improved its com-petitive position with the state banks. The exchange system also helped the Bank transfer funds to meet the needs of the federal government; for example, the purchase of cotton bills in New Or-leans and their sale in New York could aid in the transfer of trea-sury deposits between the same two cities.[32]

Other aspects of New Orleans branch operations, though less important than the business associated with domestic exchange, were nonetheless important to the Bank's overall strength. For the B.U.S., as for the state banks and the nation, New Orleans was a major source of specie. In the first months of his presidency Biddle developed a successful program for expanding the flow of im-ported Mexican silver through New Orleans to Philadelphia and New York. Even some Jacksonians reluctantly recognized that this "drain" of specie from the New Orleans branch was largely a natural process of distributing imported specie around the country.[33]

The role of foreign exchange receipts at New Orleans (sterling bills based on cotton sales) in the domestic settlements between B.U.S. branches has already been discussed. But the sterling bills purchased at New Orleans were also useful in handling the Bank's own foreign accounts. In 1832-33, purchases in New Orleans were the key to an unusual arrangement between the B.U.S. and Baring Brothers of London. In a swap of credits fully as clever as any between modern central bankers, Barings provided the B.U.S. with sterling funds to pay off $4.2 million of U.S. federal bonds then maturing in Europe; in return, the New Orleans branch provided sterling funds to meet payments on $5 million of Union Bank of Louisiana bonds, for which Barings was the English sales agent. Such offsetting credits saved both institutions the expense and inconvenience of large dealings in foreign exchange markets.[34]

By rejuvenating the B.U.S. and expanding the role of the New Orleans branch, Biddle had realized his basic policy goals. Unfortunately, these goals have been somewhat obscured by studies that attempt to impose modern central banking theory on the policies of an earlier day. Biddle himself explicitly renounced the central banker's primary function of using monetary policy to stabilize the economy: "It is the imperious duty of the bank to remain perfectly passive . . . leaving individual enterprise to seek its own employment. It is the duty of the bank to take the state of the country as the country has chosen to make it; to deal with the existing condition of things, but not to assume upon itself the charge of regulating the domestic industry, and the foreign trade of the Union." Biddle's own objectives were more specific: (1) to provide the nation with a uniform, undepreciated currency; (2) "to facilitate the internal exchanges of the produce and labor of the citizens of every part of the Union . . . [and] to bring down these exchanges to the lowest cost to them all"; (3) to be an efficient fiscal agent of the federal government. For each of these purposes the New Orleans branch was essential, especially in its operations connected with domestic and foreign exchange, banknote issues, and specie transfer.[35]

The B.U.S. and the New Orleans Community. The New Orleans branch was valuable not only to the B.U.S. but also to the New Orleans business community. In many ways it functioned essentially as a local bank—providing credit through local discounts and bills of exchange, issuing deposits, notes, and drafts to augment the area's money supply, and handling specie. The branch was most vital to the community in the 1820's, when the state banks were smallest. In 1820 the B.U.S. in Louisiana exceeded all of the state banks together in total lending, specie holdings, and notes issued. In 1830 its local discounts were still over 60 per cent as large as all loans and discounts of the expanding state banks. But the rapid growth of the state banks in the next few years reduced this to just 14 per cent by January 1834. The branch's absolute volume of local lending reached a peak in 1832, before Jackson's attacks on the B.U.S.; thereafter, the branch's lending declined absolutely, and virtually disappeared relatively, as a source of credit to New Orleans merchants. In terms of relative size, the B.U.S. in New Orleans was more of a "monster" in the 1820's than in its more controversial last years.[36]

As far as can be determined, the New Orleans branch remained on remarkably friendly terms with the state banks. Thomas Govan has asserted that the state banks were generally antagonistic to the B.U.S. during the regime of Langdon Cheves (1819-22) but "ceased complaining" and became friendly collaborators when Nicholas Biddle took control. He attributes the change to Biddle's expansion of B.U.S. note issues and loans, which reduced its accumulation of state banknotes and consequently its claims on the specie held by other banks. Banks that expanded together lived happily together.*

There is little indication that the New Orleans branch was as unpopular as those in other Southern and Western states, even before Biddle took office. Not having expanded as much before

---

* Govan, pp. 85-86. Notes (or deposits) issued by a bank in making loans circulated freely, some of them passing through other banks. A bank lending (creating new notes or deposits) faster than other banks in its area (or while other banks were asking their customers to pay off existing loans), had to incur an increasing debt to the less expansionary banks, since they acquired its notes or deposits faster than it acquired theirs. Jean Alexander Wilburn has recently presented a more comprehensive analysis of state bank and other economically motivated support for the B.U.S. See her *Biddle's Bank*, Chapters 4 and 5. My own explanation, arrived at independently, is similar to hers.

1819, it did not have as far to contract when Cheves imposed restrictions; thus it did not press the state banks for the redemption of their notes to the extent that other branches did. Relations between the state banks and the New Orleans branch continued to be good during the Biddle years. In fact, three state banks—the Canal Bank, the Bank of Orleans, and the Louisiana State Bank—petitioned Congress for the renewal of the B.U.S. charter in 1832, explicitly mentioning the Bank's "liberal policy towards State banks."[37]

Remarkably, these cordial relations existed despite Biddle's deliberate program to strengthen the B.U.S. branches and increase their competition with the state banks. Soon after taking office in 1823, Biddle sent new general instructions to the New Orleans branch, concentrating on its traffic in bills of exchange. He concluded frankly: "[The] object is to place you on the eminence which you have a right to command, to give you an influence and control over the monied operations of N. Orleans & an ascendency over all the state institutions. ... As this course tho' evidently proper and reasonable may excite sensation among those to whom every novelty is a source of wonder, it should be conducted with great prudence." As already noted, this was the beginning of Biddle's expansion of the Bank, which led it to dominance in the domestic exchange business from which state banks had previously profited, and to an enlarged circulation of notes and branch drafts that competed with the notes of state banks.[38]

Louisiana's state banks, instead of resenting the increased competition, seem to have been grateful for the benefits of a generally expansionary policy—the growth of Western trade with New Orleans, the greater opportunities for state banks in local discounting after the B.U.S. emphasized bills of exchange, and the lesser risk resulting from more predictable exchange rates and more uniform (undepreciated) currencies. Having larger commercial interests than most Southern states, Louisiana had more experience of the usefulness of banks in general and of a national bank in particular.* The operations of Biddle's B.U.S. seemed to leave ample

---

* Antebellum Americans used the term "national bank" to refer to the first and second B.U.S. or to any similar federally chartered institution. Such an institution was "national" not only in its charter and in the geographical extent of its branches, but also in its presumed responsibility to assure a sound na-

profit opportunities for state banks in the 1820's and early 1830's. This background of amicable relations partly explains the failure of Jackson's "bank war" in Louisiana.[39]

Politically, as well as economically, the B.U.S. found Louisiana more favorable than most Southern and Western states. Although Jackson won large majorities there in the presidential elections of 1828 and 1832, Louisianans did not favor Jacksonian candidates in state elections during the same period. The state was quite evenly divided politically, but the National Republicans (largely followers of Henry Clay) and the Whigs controlled the governorship (1828-42) and most of the Congressional seats (1828-36); and they held slim majorities in most of the state legislatures. Moreover, the leading Jacksonian politicians in Louisiana in the 1830's were not of the hard-money, antibanking school. Many of them were active in Louisiana's state banks, and at least four were also directors of the New Orleans branch of the B.U.S. itself—John Hagan (1823-32), William G. Hewes (1826), Martin Gordon (1829), and Maunsel White (1826-32).[40]

It is not surprising that Jackson's political war against the B.U.S., as fought in Louisiana, has been called an "imported" disagreement, a clash that would probably never have developed in the state without outside stimulus. In Congress, the Louisiana representatives voted unanimously in favor of the recharter bill of 1832, which the rest of the South and Southwest solidly opposed and which Jackson vetoed. Again, in 1834, Louisiana's representatives unanimously favored recharter and the return of government deposits to the B.U.S. With all these votes on record, anti-Jacksonians continued to win in state elections. But despite the seeming artificiality of the conflict and the consistent defeats of the Jacksonians, there were times when the B.U.S. aroused genuine political and economic controversy in Louisiana. One such period came during the spring and summer of 1832, climaxing in Jackson's veto of the recharter bill in July. In the spring, Biddle ordered the New Orleans branch to reduce its local loans and shift funds to the East to assist in the Bank's large European payments

---

tional currency and financial system. This concept of a single national bank should not be confused with the multitude of "national banks" chartered by the federal government after 1863. The former had some of the characteristics of a modern "central bank"; the latter were just ordinary commercial banks.

on maturing federal bonds. The financial pressure in New Orleans was severe enough to bring protests even from the Bank's supporters. By October, however, the crisis had passed.[41]

The events of 1832 were only a prelude. Soon after Jackson ordered the withdrawal of the government's B.U.S. deposits, beginning in October 1833, Biddle instructed the New Orleans office to cease its purchases of bills on the Western offices. By early 1834, as New Orleans entered its busiest trading season, the financial pressure had become severe. Interest rates as high as 18-24 per cent were reported, and some capitalists refused to lend at any rate. The state banks did not dare expand their credit facilities because they were being pressed for specie to settle the balances that the B.U.S. had accumulated against them. Local businessmen increasingly pressed the New Orleans branch to expand credit and relieve the pressure. The branch directors apparently tried to comply in March 1834, but Biddle overruled them and continued to tighten credit. Not until July did the Bank adopt a more expansive policy, and by then the New Orleans commercial season was virtually over.[42]

Some of the financial pressure struck New Orleans businessmen directly, through the reduction of local discounts by the B.U.S. and the state banks. But greater damage came indirectly. Tight credit in the North inhibited the usual purchases of Southern crops. Biddle's restrictions against bills on the Western branches disrupted the Mississippi Valley trade that normally flowed through New Orleans, and also caused hardship for Louisiana sugar producers dependent on Western markets. Senator Waggaman of Louisiana estimated the season's losses at $4 million on cotton shipped through New Orleans, $1.5 million on sugar, $4 million on Louisiana bank stocks, and perhaps another $4 million on the Western produce trade.[43]

Such severe economic distress was bound to have some political impact, but reactions varied widely. Following their fixed political line, many Jacksonians blamed the B.U.S. for the crisis and accused Biddle of engineering a depression to coerce the nation into rechartering his bank. Likewise, many anti-Jacksonians blamed the President for autocratically withdrawing federal deposits and madly attacking a national bank that they considered essential to the nation's financial health. Perhaps more interesting are the political responses that did not follow partisan lines. Many of the Bank's political defenders publicly objected to its restrictive policies and urged it "to extend succor to your suffering fellow-citizens and under no circumstances to be the instrument of oppressing them." On the other hand, many Jacksonians questioned the wisdom of Jackson's policy and urged the return of government deposits to the B.U.S.[44]

An Ex-National Bank in New Orleans. When the federal charter of the B.U.S. expired in 1836, the branch in New Orleans would have to be closed. In November 1835, the New Orleans loan portfolio was sold to the recently chartered Gas Light Bank for $3.5 million, payable over a four-year period. Meanwhile, in anticipation, the Louisiana Legislature had already chartered several new banks to carry on the branch's deposit and lending functions.[45]

But the B.U.S. did not disappear when its federal charter expired (March 1836); almost immediately, it was reborn as the United States Bank of Pennsylvania. Under its new state charter the Bank had no power to establish branches in other states, and Biddle sought another way to maintain its nationwide influence and business. The solution was to establish financial agents in distant cities—either individuals or state banks that might be purchased. In June 1836 Biddle began negotiations with representatives of the Merchants Bank of New Orleans. This bank had received its Louisiana charter in February, and its stock (nominal capital $1 million) was controlled by a group of about twenty men. Biddle paid the original stockholders a tidy 10 per cent premium on their nominal capital and thus obtained his New Orleans agency by September. While the Gas Light Bank was collecting the loans of the old B.U.S., the Merchants Bank would conduct the operations of the new one.[46]

Biddle sought to strengthen his Philadelphia bank by using the New Orleans outpost to collect debts due from other Southern banks and to purchase bills of domestic and foreign exchange for sale in the North. But the New Orleans officers and directors were more eager to satisfy local credit demands, and Biddle repeatedly urged them to restrain this tendency. He was apparently unsuccessful: by December 1837, the Merchants Bank was devoting over 80 per cent of its total resources to local lending and less than 20 per cent to the type of assets that Biddle preferred.[47]

Although the United States Bank of Pennsylvania conducted most of its Louisiana business through the Merchants Bank, it also pursued an independent set of transactions that had a much more direct and widespread effect on the Louisiana economy: Biddle's famous dealings in cotton (1837-39). Biddle had several reasons for involving his bank, family, and business associates in these massive transactions. For his bank, cotton sales provided foreign exchange to replace that formerly received from federal fiscal operations (Southern taxes were often paid in foreign exchange) and Southern branch operations; foreign bills were especially needed after 1837 to meet the Bank's own debts in Europe. For Biddle's son and business associates, the sales provided opportunities for personal profits. And for the nation, support of the cotton market meant a greater income to Southern planters and merchants (who shared the business with Biddle's "bank ring"), as well as a source of foreign funds to pay for its imports and service its foreign debts. While it succeeded, Biddle's cotton "speculation" brought profits to Louisiana and the rest of the South. It finally failed in 1839, when adverse market forces overwhelmed the Bank's power to influence the price of cotton.[48]

Many contemporaries criticized Biddle's cotton dealings, and some historians have condemned them as mere speculation, even though Biddle's primary purpose was not personal gain or profits for his bank. Leland Jenks, accepting this critique, links Biddle's "speculation" with the fate of the state banks: "The apparent success of Biddle's undertakings was corrupting the financial mores of every American state. Following the example of the Bank of the United States, each commonwealth in turn sought to support the cotton market by chartering new banks and selling fresh issues of stock. Wild-cat banks sprang up throughout the South and West."[49]

Jenks obviously errs on one point with regard to Louisiana, where the wave of new charters came before 1837 and not during the subsequent years of financial turmoil. Still, his remarks raise a related issue that also concerned contemporary Louisianans: did Biddle "corrupt" the existing state banks by initiating the cotton speculations in which they all became involved? In 1840 a committee of the state legislature, investigating recent transactions in cotton by the Louisiana banks, learned that six banks out of seventeen reporting had purchased over $1.3 million of cotton on their own account for sale in Liverpool or Le Havre. But further testimony from the banks involved does not support Jenks's argument. The cotton operations were obviously limited in scale and were undertaken only "as a last resort" when domestic and foreign exchange, the usual financial devices, had broken down. The objectives were to recover debts owed by banks in other states (who could not pay except in local banknotes, which could purchase cotton) and to meet the pressing financial obligations of the Louisiana banks in New York or Europe. These were hardly cases of "wildcat" banking.[50]

Besides the cotton "speculations," the United States Bank of Pennsylvania undertook several other transactions that affected the Louisiana economy. First, Biddle promoted the sale of state bonds in England as a means of meeting American debts there, and these sales included some Louisiana and Mississippi bonds used to raise banking capital. Second, he fought New York and London to postpone the resumption of specie payments from the spring of 1838 until later in the year or even until early 1839. Third, he provided extensive loans to aid Southern banks in their own resumption of payments. His loans of $1.5 million to three Mississippi banks required the withdrawal of $600,000 of badly needed specie from New Orleans. To reassure the New Orleans bankers, Biddle offered them more direct support:

We are preparing a large amount of the issues of the Bank, which will be sent to New Orleans, with the instructions to use them freely, not only in the immediate business of the bank, but whenever they can be made to contribute to the defense of the banks of New Orleans. . . .The Bank of the United States has, in some forms of its existence, been connected with New Orleans from almost its first introduction into the American family, and feels a deep interest in its prosperity, which we shall always be ready and willing to promote.

This last rhetorical flourish merely repeated what circumstances had already made clear: that the fate of Louisiana's banks was still tied to that of the B.U.S.; or rather, that both the B.U.S. and the Southern banks had joined their fates to Southern cotton. It was King Cotton who ended this long-standing partnership in 1840-41, burying the B.U.S. and leaving the state banks to fend for themselves.[51]

The "Pet" Deposit Banks. The Bank of the United States was certainly the most influential of the federal financial institutions operating in antebellum Louisiana, at least in its impact on the rest of the state's financial system. But it was not the only institution to serve as a federal fiscal agency. Unfortunately, there are no available sources that would permit any systematic study of the "independent treasury" system as it affected Louisiana. The rest of this chapter, therefore, will concentrate on the fiscal activities of the state-chartered banks; but there will be some reference to the independent system as well, since the two coexisted historically.

Previous studies of the "pet" deposit banks have focused primarily on the possible influence of partisan politics in their selection, and very little attention has been given to the concurrent influence of Jacksonian monetary "reforms" and economic crisis on both the selection and the actual operating experience of these banks. As the federal government increasingly restricted the holding and use of its deposits, the banks found depository status less profitable and were less enthusiastic to become pet banks. The only major instance of partisan politics in the selection of Louisiana's deposit banks occurred in the initial choices of November 1833 (see Table 3.5). The Jackson administration had established only vague guidelines, seeking two deposit banks in each state wherever possible, to avoid local "monopoly," and favoring well-established and financially "sound" institutions. Six New Orleans banks applied, attracted by the increased profits and stature that would accompany the unrestricted use of government deposits. The two banks selected were those recommended to Secretary of the Treasury Roger Taney by John Slidell and John Nicholson, the leaders of one of the Jacksonian political factions in New Orleans. The choice of one, the Union Bank, could easily be defended on strictly economic grounds; but the Commercial Bank, chartered in March, had only raised one-fourth of its capital and was not even prepared to begin operations.[52]

The receipt of federal funds permitted some expanded lending by the New Orleans deposit banks, but their expansion was restrained and its economic impact offset by the simultaneous contraction of the B.U.S. branch. The Louisiana business community did not feel the expansionary influence of enlarged federal deposits in the state banks until mid-1835, when the retirement of

TABLE 3.5

The Selection of Federal Deposit Banks

Date	Event	Sources[a]
1833		
9/26	City Bank recommended; refused.	See Note 52
10/1	Bank of La. recommended; refused.	same
10/15	Mechanics & Traders Bank and La. State Bank recommended; refused.	same
10/27	Commercial Bank applies; accepted 11/19.	[2], p. 330
11/19	Union Bank applies; accepted 11/20.	[2], pp. 330, 334
1835		
11/18	Gas Light Bank applies; refused 12/3.	[4], p. 332; [11]
1836		
2/11	Citizens Bank applies; refused 2/27.	[12]
1837		
5/13	Suspension of specie payments: de facto independent treasury except for special deposits.	[5], p. 272
6/13	Offer to Citizens Bank.	[13]
7/3	Offer conditionally accepted.	[21]
7/11	Citizens Bank declared ineligible.	[13]
8/3	Offer to Consolidated Association; declined 8/21.	[6], p. 181
1838		
7/10	Citizens Bank applies; accepted 1/9/39.	[14] and [15]
1839		
12/12	Citizens Bank on special deposits basis only.	[16]
1840		
6/30	Independent treasury system passed.	
1841		
8/13	Independent treasury system repealed.	
8/27	Citizens Bank applies; accepted.	[6], pp. 165, 168
8/30	Merchants Bank applies; no action taken, and bank soon into liquidation.	[6], pp. 156ff
12/13	Offer to Union Bank; conditionally accepted.	[16]; [6], p. 175
1843		
5/8	Offer to Bank of La.; reluctantly accepted.	[6], p. 178; [16]; [17]
1845		
10/11	Offer to La. State Bank; declined.	[6], p. 115
10/14	Offer to City Bank; declined.	[6], p. 116
10/17	Offer to Mechanics & Traders Bank; declined.	[6], p. 117
10/28	Offer to Canal Bank; accepted 11/29.	[17]; [6], p. 138
1846		
8/1	Independent treasury system reestablished.	
1847		
11/13	Canal Bank closes account with Treasury.	[17]

[a] Bracketed numbers refer to items listed under Treasury Department in the Bibliography.

the federal debt and the boom in federal land sales led to a great increase in federal deposits all across the nation (see Table C.3). And in 1835-36 the banks used these new deposits to finance expanded loan programs, which proved so profitable that several other New Orleans banks applied for a share of the federal depository business.[53]

The chance for profit in deposit banking was reduced somewhat by the Deposit Act of June 24, 1836, which required each deposit bank to pay 2 per cent interest whenever government deposits exceeded one-fourth of the bank's paid-in capital, to post collateral security as a guarantee of faithful performance, to halt the circulation of small-denomination banknotes (initially, those under $5), to keep specie reserves as specified by the Secretary of the Treasury, and to redeem all notes in specie. Many of these restrictions, Jacksonian "reforms" designed to preserve a money supply convertible into specie, became especially burdensome after the suspension of specie payments in 1837.[54]

The pressures for contraction and adjustment began well before the Panic of 1837; in fact, the suspension of specie payments in May 1837 was essentially a consequence of these earlier pressures. As early as May 1836, Secretary of the Treasury Woodbury began urging the New Orleans banks to increase their specie reserves, and the banks (not only the deposit banks) began making strenuous efforts to comply. Jackson's Specie Circular of July 1836 may have slightly increased the scarcity of specie in the banks after it became effective in August, but evidence of its quantitative impact in Louisiana is lacking.[55]

In early 1837 another problem confronted the two New Orleans deposit banks: large government transfer drafts began moving federal funds to Northern cities. Between January 1 and June 1 the New Orleans depositories were scheduled to lose (net) nearly $2.25 million. The government's $37 million surplus had been allowed to accumulate in the few banks initially receiving the revenues. But with that surplus due to be distributed during 1837, and with heavy government expenditures in the East, it became necessary to shift funds.* Richard Timberlake has argued that the dis-

---

* It should be realized, however, that federal deposits in the New Orleans banks had increased by $1.8 million between June and December, 1836; most of the funds scheduled for departure had only recently been received by the banks. *USC*, [34].

tribution of the surplus did not involve large transfer drafts or specie flows between states. In a very narrow sense he is correct, since the actual payments of the surplus to the states came mainly from deposit banks within each state. The transfers by Louisiana deposit banks on the first two installments totaled just over $500,-000; all but $34,000 went to the state of Louisiana (remaining in one of the state's banks, at least initially), and the excess presumably went to neighboring Arkansas. But in a more significant sense Timberlake is incorrect. The small, innocuous intrastate payments from banks to state governments were preceded by huge and disruptive interstate transfers between banks, which moved funds to the states where installments on the surplus (and other expenditures) would be paid.[56]

For most banks, the suspension of specie payments brought relief from pressure, an end to forced liquidation, and the chance to worry less about liquidity and more about solvency. But for the deposit banks, suspension brought no relief. They still had to do business with the federal government—the one institution in the economy that clung stubbornly to the specie standard. As soon as payments were suspended the deposit banks became ineligible to receive further federal deposits. The government canceled all unpaid transfer drafts and ordered the banks to remit their funds directly to Washington. They were urged to contract their operations, call in their loans, repay their debts (especially those to the government), and resume specie payments as soon as possible. Meanwhile, the government surplus was rapidly disappearing through distribution and through declining revenues. This loss reduced the government's flexibility in maneuvering its various deposit balances and forced the Treasury to put even greater pressure on the deposit banks for remittances to Washington. In response, the New Orleans banks reduced their federal deposits from $4 million in March 1837 to $330,000 in December. The Commercial Bank never fully recovered from this forced liquidation of its portfolio, and ceased its banking operations in 1843. The Union Bank, larger and stronger to begin with, survived but was hurt. The banks' debtors, too, were under severe pressure, being called on to repay their loans in such difficult times.[57]

During the suspension periods between 1837 and 1839, the Treasury could find no banks willing or eligible to serve as deposit banks, since the Deposit Act of 1836 would have required them to redeem their notes and deposits in specie. The worst effects of the independent treasury system came from its unofficial implementation during suspension. The government remained on a specie basis while the rest of the country did not; as a result, the deposit banking system collapsed, and the banks and their customers suffered. But the dual monetary system, specie and nonspecie, disrupted the financial system in countless other ways. For example, customs duties had to be paid in specie. This requirement caused great alarm in New Orleans, and a public meeting of the Chamber of Commerce expressed to Congress its fears of impending "disorder, violence, and resistance to the laws" if the ruling were not modified. On the smaller end of the scale, a New Orleans woman wrote to a friend: "A piece of silver of any size is quite a curiosity now. I have kept a little to pay my post office bill." At some points the government relaxed its interpretation of the law, or sought to adjust its arrangements for transferring and receiving money in order to minimize its demands for specie. But its basic viewpoint remained liquidationist: the country must suffer whatever was necessary to return it promptly to the sacred specie standard.[58]

Deposit banks were reappointed in 1839 and operated until the permanent creation of the independent treasury system in 1846 (except for the interval from June 1840 to August 1841; see Table 3.5). During the 1840's, however, the Treasury further tightened the rules, "to prevent the employment of the cash standing to the credit of the Treasurer for discounts or any of the operations of the Bank whatever." Several New Orleans banks found these regulations unattractive and declined the Treasury's offers of depository status.[59] Being a deposit bank had been a lucrative business in 1833, enough so that bankers sometimes needed political influence to acquire a franchise. But the financial pressures, suspensions, and government restrictions that came after 1836 completely disrupted the deposit banking system. When the independent treasury was formally established in 1846, few bankers mourned the passing of the old deposit system.

CHAPTER FOUR

Public Policy Toward Banking

IN HIS SURVEY of the history of American commercial banking, Paul Trescott has stated the basic dilemma of public policy toward banking: How to reconcile the banks' responsibility toward credit with their responsibility toward money. "The former dictated liberality; the latter, conservatism." Banks that responded generously to the demands of farmers and businessmen for long-term credit ran great risks of failing in their monetary obligations. Illiquid loan portfolios and inadequate specie reserves often forced them to suspend the conversion of their banknotes or deposits into cash on demand. A more conservative lending policy, on the other hand, assured a stable, convertible money supply but necessarily restricted the supply of bank credit and left many unsatisfied borrowers.[1]

Louisiana's policies toward her banks vacillated between "sound money" and "easy credit" during the antebellum years. Sometimes she emphasized regulation of the banks to maintain a stable money supply. To most men of the day, this meant maintaining the convertibility of bank notes (and sometimes deposits) into specie. Emphasis on meeting demands for credit, by contrast, led to a more promotional, expansionary banking policy in which the state often tried to force the banks to allocate credit toward certain sectors of the economy, particularly toward agriculture. These two basic policies—regulation of banking for the sake of sound money and promotion of banking for the sake of easy credit—often appeared together in a single piece of legislation. But the relative emphasis on each varied greatly over time, influenced by internal or external economic conditions, prevailing theories of money and banking, and partisan politics. The major turning point in state policy came in the crisis years 1837-43, during which strongly promotional banking laws gave way to strict regulation. Beginning with the Bank Act of 1842, the state also adopted new techniques for controlling the banks, supplementing old-style control through bank charters with more general laws and stronger administrative agencies to enforce the laws.

Early Regulation by Charter

At first, Louisiana regulated her banks almost entirely by writing specific rules into their charters.* By 1830, certain specifications, repeated almost verbatim in each charter, had become more or less standardized—mostly basic rules dealing with routine matters such as the procedure for electing directors, the types of property a bank might own, and so on. But alongside these were other regulations designed to achieve the government's broad objectives of economic policy.

Most bank charters contained regulations to guide the lending practices of the banks. For example, the state attempted to control the geographical distribution of loans by prescribing the minimum sizes and locations of branch offices or the specific distribution of loans among parishes and congressional districts. Similarly, the banks were often required to allocate a certain proportion of their funds to loans on mortgage security or other long-term credit. Such regulations were obviously intended to expand bank lending to borrowers outside New Orleans, and particularly to planters. And in almost every legislative debate on a new or amended bank charter, the advocates of larger rural lending proposed amendments, though only a few of these proposals were actually adopted. Other rules sought to limit preferential lending and to protect the banks against bad loans. The most direct approach simply limited the total amount that could be lent to any single borrower; this restriction was more often imposed on rural branches than on the New Orleans offices, which dealt with large merchant firms. Most charters also limited loans to the bank's

* Throughout this chapter references to the provisions of bank charters will be identified in text or note only by naming the bank. Specific charter citations are given in Table 1.1. References to subsequent charter amendments, all located in *Acts of Louisiana*, will be identified by date.

directors, and loans for which the bank's own stock served as collateral.[2]

The charter regulations also showed concern for a sound money supply. The most obvious device was a clause (universally written into charters after 1824) that provided for the payment of a severe 10-12 per cent penalty interest rate on all banknotes if the bank should suspend specie payments. And beginning in 1831 (City Bank charter), the legislature required automatic forfeiture of a charter if a suspension should last over 90 days. These provisions may have helped protect noteholders against the circulation of depreciated notes by an individual bank, but they were completely ineffective during a general suspension by all the banks.

Other customary charter provisions attempted to guarantee that the bank would be able to redeem its notes at par with specie, usually by limiting the expansion of certain of the bank's assets or liabilities in relation to the capital paid in. The specific limitation varied in early charters. But the standard form, first seen in the City Bank charter, limited both debts due by the bank (but excluding deposits) and debts due to the bank to twice the capital paid in. Deposits were excluded from the limitation because of the belief that a "deposit" of specie (or "specie funds") added a safe asset to match the liability and hence carried no risk of over-expansion.[3]

Bray Hammond, analyzing the charter limitations on bank expansion, characterizes them as crude attempts to define the fractional cash reserve behind liabilities—crude because they wrongly assumed that bank capital was actually paid in specie and retained as specie in the bank's possession. In Hammond's framework, then, and probably in the minds of some antebellum Louisianans, the limitation of liability/capital ratios was supposed to maintain liquid reserves. The regulations failed in this purpose, since they did not provide adequate specie reserves behind banknotes; but they did set an effective absolute limit on each bank's contribution to the supply of banknotes. And the practice of limiting both assets and liabilities (debts to and from the bank) in terms of capital makes it obvious that the legislature's intention was in fact to limit monetary expansion rather than to provide specie reserves.*

---

* The charter of the Merchants Bank of New Orleans confirms this interpretation. It had the usual limitation of earning assets and liabilities (except de-

The Regulation of Bank Deposits

Historians of banking have sharply criticized the early charter regulation of deposit liabilities. In modern banking practice, it is clear: (1) that deposits are an important part of the money supply, since they are a direct means of payment when transferred by check from one person to another; (2) that additions to the total volume of deposits (as distinct from transfers of existing deposits) are mainly "loan-created deposits" issued in conjunction with bank loans (or bank purchases of bonds and other securities) rather than "lodged deposits" issued in return for currency or coin deposited with the bank. Projecting this modern understanding of deposits into the past, historians have found that most early regulations or opinions on deposits were irrational and ill-informed. For example, there was never a reserve requirement or expansion limitation for deposit liabilities, and there was always an implicit assumption that deposits represented specie funds received and held by the bank.[4]

Were antebellum thinking and policies on bank deposits really so irrational? Not in Louisiana, at least; and, I suspect, not in other states. The projection of twentieth-century banking theories into the early nineteenth century is certainly inappropriate, and it depends on flimsy evidence at best. For example, Bray Hammond, the most ardent critic of early deposit regulations, gives virtually no evidence to show that deposits were in fact loan-created, or that they were generally used directly as a means of payment.[*]

Fritz Redlich and his colleagues have exhibited a better historical sense in their efforts to trace the evolution of bank deposits and checks. Redlich concludes that the earliest individual

---

posits) to twice the paid-in capital; another separate section also required that the entire capital be paid in specie, and that the bank should "at all times retain within her vaults, in specie, one-third of the amount of her capital stock paid in." In this one exceptional case, the combination of the two charter rules —expansion limit and retention of specie capital—did effectively guarantee a specie reserve behind note liabilities of at least one-sixth. Bray Hammond, *Banks and Politics*, pp. 132-37, 142-43, 191. See also Miller, p. 149.

[*] Evidence from balance sheets on the volume of deposits, as compared to the volume of banknotes or loans, is no proof of either assumption, since it shows neither what transactions created deposits nor what transactions transferred or eliminated them. Bray Hammond, *Banks and Politics*, pp. 137, 189.

deposits were mainly savings deposits received by the banks for "safekeeping." Early checks were used primarily to withdraw cash (specie or banknotes) from one's own deposit account, to settle other accounts with the bank (e.g., loan payments), and to make payments to local creditors who could cash (or "deposit") a check at the bank in person. Not until the late 1830's were checking deposits commonly used as a means of payment for other than local transactions. And loan-created deposits were not common until well after the Civil War.* If the uses of bank deposits actually did develop gradually, then antebellum theory and regulation appear much less irrational than Hammond describes them. The lag between changing practice and changing regulatory policy was often a short one.[5]

The very limited evidence available on early Louisiana bank deposits seems to fit Redlich's description. The deposit liabilities of Louisiana banks exceeded their banknote liabilities by 1830, but many of these early deposits were undoubtedly not loan-created and not used as means of payment. Some of the demand deposits were probably retained as savings rather than being used for payments. But the only objective indication that deposits were not used as money would be the proportion of time or savings deposits to total deposits. An isolated scrap of evidence shows that the City Bank, in January 1834, held 67 per cent of its deposits as time deposits. Without accepting this figure as representative of other banks or other dates, we may at least presume that a great many bank deposits were savings deposits not used as a means of payment. Given this limited monetary role of deposits, it is perhaps more understandable that Louisiana did not attempt to regulate bank deposits directly until after the panic of 1837.[6]

Regulation and Promotion by General Law Before 1837

Although nearly all regulation of money and credit in Louisiana before 1837 was accomplished through individual bank charters, there were a few general laws for this purpose; and these laws

---

* As Appendix A demonstrates, the modern distinction between lodged and loan-created deposits was not as meaningful or relevant for the antebellum monetary system. Lodged deposits were truly "created," and could lead to (or result from) an expansion of bank credit. The distinction also sheds no light on the important question of whether bank deposits were used as money.

regulated direct lending between individuals as well as the indirect finance conducted by the banks.

One legal condition that had important practical implications for the pattern of lending was the legal residence (*domicil*) of the borrower. In case of default on a loan, a bank ordinarily had to sue its debtor in the parish of his domicil; and a New Orleans bank obviously took extra risks if it had to bring suit in a rural parish sympathetic to its debtor. One common way around this problem was to require that rural loans be endorsed by reputable residents of New Orleans, usually merchants or factors already doing business with the borrower. But because this arrangement would not satisfy all potential rural customers, a law of 1818 provided an alternative procedure: a rural borrower could "elect" a domicil in a town with a bank, perhaps giving the address of the bank office itself. He thus granted the bank the right to bring suit in more favorable courts. The promotional intent of this legislation was clearly stated, "the intention of the legislature being merely to establish a particular privilege in favour of the banks [but not other creditors], which may actuate them in lending their funds for the encouragement of agriculture."[7]

Of far greater concern to Louisiana than "election of domicil" was the regulation of interest rates—that is, anti-usury laws. Bank charters had always imposed strict ceilings on interest rates, but these restrictions did not prevent private usury. In fact, many observers suspected that just the reverse was true—that the bank limitations contributed to the existence of higher nonbank interest rates. Favored customers of the bank could easily borrow at the regulated bank rates in order to relend at higher rates. Two groups particularly accused of "monopolizing" bank credit for this purpose were the "brokers and shavers" and the large factors who provided credit to the planters.[8]

Government policy took two quite different approaches in dealing with the banks' influence on nonbank lending. The more direct method was to tighten lending regulations. Clauses inserted into several bank charters prohibited loans to any person intending "to discount paper or notes in the market at a higher rate than the conventional [6 per cent] interest allowed by law," and legislative investigations sought to enforce the restriction. The second approach was to abolish usury by expanding competitive bank lending. Rather than tightening regulations to suppress the usual market response to unsatisfied demands (higher interest), this approach sought to balance the market by expanding credit to meet the demand at conventional interest rates. A legislative report of 1831 commented:

The establishment of new banks . . . must favor the industry and encourage the zeal of enterprising citizens by enabling these persons to obtain capital at a reasonable rate of interest; and by creating a competition between monied institutions which will tend to destroy that system of usury, so long and so injuriously practiced in the city of New Orleans. Our predecessors often thought of abolishing usury, and your committee are of the opinion, that one of the surest means of arriving at that salutary object is the incorporation of new banks.[9]

The major attempt to regulate nonbank interest rates directly was the Usury Bill of 1823, passed in a period of financial distress after a series of bad crop years and partly intended to ease the debt burdens of planters and farmers. The Bill provided that third parties might sue to recover the interest and principle on any usurious loans; thus the law did not rely on the often desperate borrowers to expose the illegal interest rates. Exchange brokers were to be licensed and bonded by the state, and their charges and commissions regulated. Finally, the Bill attempted to plug any loopholes through which disguised usury rates might be paid, such as hidden payments in kind, overvaluation of assets, or fictitious bills of exchange.[10]

Reaction to the Usury Bill was violent. Planters generally favored its restrictions, but New Orleans merchants vigorously opposed it, in public discussions and in petitions to the legislature. Governor Robertson finally vetoed it and sent a strongly worded message to the legislature giving his reasons. He argued against government interference with the "freedom of action" and "freedom of contract" of individuals, or with the "market price" mechanism. Legislation alone could not make money cheap and abundant because "the movements of specie and its price were as independent of human ordinances as the currents of the ocean, which ebbing and flowing seek their level." The opposition of knowledgeable merchants and businessmen should be respected: "The money of the country will vanish from circulation when banks and capitalists find themselves shackled with vexations and in-

convenient regulations and surrounded by terrors of fines, forfei-
tures, penalties, unusual punishments, and destructive litigation."[11]

The state Senate voted unanimously to override Robertson's
veto, but the House could not muster the two-thirds majority required to do so. The next session of the legislature sought other
ways to bring financial relief to debt-burdened planters. This time,
the regulatory approach (that of the Usury Bill) gave way to the
promotional approach. Eventually, a House bill to charter the
Bank of Louisiana won out over the Senate's proposal to create a
state loan office. The creation of new banks would abolish usury.[12]

Promotion of Banking: Means

We have seen that state regulation of banking was used to promote easy credit as well as to protect sound money. Thus the
chartering of rural branch banks and the "election of domicil"
law favored more liberal credit to agriculture, and anti-usury laws
sought to make credit cheaper. But Louisiana also used much
stronger methods to promote expanded banking—more so, before
1837, than any other state.

The major forms of state promotion were the issue of state
bonds and the guaranteeing of bank bonds by the state. While
most other states were subsidizing the construction of canals,
railroads, and turnpikes, Louisiana was subsidizing five of its
chartered banks (see Table 4.1). The $24,050,000 in bonds autho-
rized by the Louisiana legislature between 1824 and 1838 (over
40 per cent of the nation's total state loans for banking purposes)
placed the state second only to Pennsylvania in total accumulated
debt. The bonds actually sold by Louisiana amounted to only
$18.7 million, but even this figure was surpassed only by the state
debts of Pennsylvania and New York. Altogether, these loans had
raised almost half of the state's banking capital as of 1838. By any
measure, Louisiana's state subsidy of banking was extraordinarily
large.[13]

The state's loan to the Bank of Louisiana in 1824 and its small
loan to the Mechanics and Traders Bank in 1833 both involved
a simple exchange of state bonds for bank stock. But 86 per cent
of the total subsidy went to the three property banks, for which
the basic transaction was slightly different. The planters or other
propertyholders who subscribed for the stock of these banks paid

TABLE 4.1

Bonds Issued or Guaranteed by the State of Louisiana in Favor of Banks

Bank and issue	Authorized bonds	When payable
Bank of Louisiana		
($2.4 mill., issued 7/1/24)	$600,000	7/1/34[a]
	600,000	7/1/39
	600,000	7/1/44
	600,000	7/1/49
Consolidated Association		
($2.5 mill., issued 12/31/28)[b]		
Union Bank of Louisiana		
($7 mill., issued 10/1/32)	1,750,000	11/1/44[c]
	1,750,000	11/1/47
	1,750,000	11/1/50
	1,750,000	11/1/52
Mechanics & Traders Bank		
($150,000, issued 5/9/33)	150,000	5/9/53[d]
Citizens Bank of Louisiana		
($12 mill., issued 2/1/36)	2,400,000	2/1/50[e]
	2,400,000	2/1/59
	2,400,000	2/1/68
	2,400,000	2/1/77
	2,400,000	2/1/86
TOTAL AUTHORIZED ISSUES	$24,050,000	
TOTAL ACTUAL ISSUES	$18,742,888	

SOURCES: USC, [7] p. 670. AL, bank charters and other acts dated 3/25/44, 4/6/47, 12/19/48, 2/8/50, 3/10/52, and 3/17/58.

[a] First two installments paid on schedule. Last two installments paid by selling state stock in bank, 1844; payment completed 1850.

[b] First group of bonds postponed to 1848 by act of 3/7/36. By 1843 debt listed at $2,380,000 plus $360,775 accumulated interest. Apparently the full authorized amount never issued. Debt reduced to $1,376,000 by 1850. Extensions and refinancing continued until well after Civil War.

[c] First installment paid $850,000 in cash and the rest by new bonds of bank without state endorsement (four groups of $225,000 each, maturing in 1845, 1846, 1847, 1848). Hidy, *House of Baring*, p. 333.

[d] Debt assumed by bank 1844. Paid.

[e] Only $7,188,888 sold of $12,000,000 authorized. A series of extensions granted by acts of 1847, 1852, and 1858. Debt reduced by 1850 to $6,468,000 plus $577,888 in accumulated interest.

their initial subscriptions with mortgages on their real estate. The mortgage portfolio of each bank was then transferred to the state as collateral for state bonds. By selling the bonds in Europe, the bank then raised cash to begin its operations.[14]

The nature of Louisiana's subsidy to her banks should not be misunderstood. In issuing its bonds for the banks the state considered itself to be assuming only a contingent liability. If all went according to plan, no taxes would ever be raised and no state funds directly expended on behalf of the banks. Just as the rail-road or canal bonds of other states were to be repaid out of tolls and other earnings from the improvement projects, Louisiana's bank bonds were to be repaid out of banking profits and the mort-gage payments of the bank subscribers.* The state was merely "lending" its superior credit rating to the banks to assist them in borrowing abroad. Since the bank itself would be repaying the loan, the net benefit of the state's aid would be measured not by the full amount of its bond issues, but by the differences in sales price and other contract terms that could be attributed to the state's guarantee.

From data available for the Citizens Bank, one can roughly esti-mate the reduction in borrowing cost produced by the state's guarantee of bank bonds. The Bank first negotiated a preliminary contract for the sale of its own bonds abroad, and then replaced it with a contract under which the bonds bore the state's endorse-ment. It was estimated at the time that the resulting higher bond prices and lower commission charges saved about $1.06 million on a total loan of $9 million. If we boldly extrapolate this 12 per cent differential to cover the entire $18.7 million issued for all the banks, it would appear that the state's superior credit rating saved the banks about $2.2 million.†

Although the issue of state bonds was the most visible and sig-nificant form of direct aid to banks, it was certainly not the only one. Nearly every bank was exempted from taxation by its char-ter, although a few had to pay annual bonuses to the state in ex-change for their exemptions. Also, bank stocks were purchased directly as well as being received in exchange for state bond issues. The state paid cash for $100,000 of Louisiana State Bank stock, and authorized the city of New Orleans to buy stock in the Gas Light Bank ($100,000) and the Commercial Bank ($500,000).[15]

In addition to direct state financial support from bond issues,

---

* Unlike many other states, Louisiana did have to assume its indirect liability, since several banks were unable to meet their bond payments in the 1840's. But the state managed to evade nearly all these demands on the public treasury.

† The savings estimate is based on McGrane, *Foreign Bondholders*, pp. 174-75. It is composed of $720,000 in higher bond prices, $270,000 in lower loan com-missions, and roughly $71,000 in lower commissions on annual interest pay-ments (my computation). McGrane's original source may have introduced some upward bias into the estimate, since it was attempting to justify the newer contract. But this is offset by the fact that the older contract was also too high—enough so that the bonds were unsalable under its terms.

tax exemptions, and stock purchases, Louisiana's banks received indirect encouragement and promotion. A bank charter, for example, was a promotional as well as a regulatory device, and the common charter privileges of corporate identity and limited liability were as useful to banks as to other businesses. The privilege of issuing notes was an obvious source of profits, and one available only to the chartered banks. Somewhat later came the provision for paying interest on deposits, which first appeared in the charter of the City Bank and was promptly extended to all other chartered banks. The promotional intent of this measure was clearly revealed in a legislative report on the City Bank charter. "A banking institution with a small capital which borrows at 4 percent and lends at 6 percent, would do good business provided the amount of deposit obtained was large. . . . The amount of deposit in the banks without interest is considerable, and the committee have reason to believe, it would be very much increased by offering an interest on deposits."[16]

Promotion of Banking: Objectives

In chartering, encouraging, and subsidizing the banks, Louisiana's political leaders had a variety of objectives in mind. In the broadest sense their purpose was always to promote the economic development, but there were always many differences in the economic circumstances of a particular decision, in the sector receiving benefits, and in the means chosen to provide them.

A new bank charter did not always reflect a policy of expanding banking facilities to encourage economic development. In fact, one of the most common circumstances that justified chartering a new bank was the expiration of an old one. The demise of the first Bank of the United States in 1811 was the occasion for founding the Planters Bank and the Orleans Bank. And the Louisiana State Bank (1818) anticipated the expiration of the old Louisiana Bank in 1819. Even in 1834, after a three-year flurry of new charters, it was argued that little increase of banking capital had actually resulted, primarily because the New Orleans branch of the B.U.S. had shrunk during the same period.[17]

Even when new banks did not merely replace old ones, they were not necessarily founded to promote economic expansion. In periods of economic distress, new banking capacity was viewed as a means of extending relief to embarrassed debtors. In 1813 this argument was unsuccessful, and the state bank proposed at that time was not chartered until 1818. In 1824 the policy had at least partial success: rejecting a simple loan office as the means of providing relief, the legislature chartered the Bank of Louisiana and required it to lend $2 million to distressed planters. Finally, both the Union and Citizens Banks were set up in part to rescue Louisiana's sugar planters from the effects of a series of poor crops and a lower tariff on imported sugar.[18]

Even allowing for the banks chartered to replace old ones or to relieve financial distress, much banking legislation did indeed have the promotion of Louisiana's economic development as its primary objective. For example, the Consolidated Association of Planters was chartered (1827) and subsidized with state bonds (1828) during a period of rapid expansion in Louisiana's sugar planting. But the real wave of promotional bank charters began in 1831 with the Canal Bank and reached its peak in 1835-36, when six new banks appeared. During this six-year period two commercial banks, three large property banks, and seven improvement banks were chartered; and at least six other banks were proposed in the legislature but not chartered. No new charters were issued after 1836. Until 1839 the legislature remained eager to charter new development banks, but its enthusiasm was frustrated by vetoes from Governor André Roman.[19]

The most direct link between banking and development was the frequent use of banking profits to promote specific improvement projects, as was the case in the improvement banks. Banking privileges were generally conceived as subordinate to the improvement project in these banks, and were often provided as an amendment to the original charter of the project itself. The expectation of banking profits, it was felt, would help sell the company's capital stock, making it easier to finance the improvement project. Corporations did not always implement this legislative policy, however, and they sometimes chose to develop their banking powers fully while delaying or ignoring the improvement project. This tendency was most pronounced in the railroad banks chartered just before 1837; they had time to begin their banking operations, but the panic interrupted most of their construction projects.[20]

The second policy device for aiding specific projects of internal improvement was the requirement of bonuses from the banks. A bank's charter might require it to purchase stock in an improve-

ment company, invest directly in a project, or contribute a specified amount of support annually. For example, the Gas Light Bank
was to provide $600,000 of subsidies to a canal, a brick company,
and two railroad projects; and the New Orleans Carrollton Bank
was to lend $80,000 to the city of Lafayette to finance street pav-
ing. The state used the banks to support its social welfare objectives as well as its economic objectives, and several banks were
required to provide modest annual subsidies to such institutions
as schools, orphanages, and charity hospitals.[21]

The guidance of economic development through banking policy
was not limited to the promotion of specific improvement projects. Banking legislation was also used to influence Louisiana's
economic structure, particularly by promoting agriculture and
commerce. Eugene Genovese finds it quite natural that the banks
should have promoted agriculture, since he assumes that Louisiana's planters dominated all other economic groups and controlled state politics as well:

> The merchants either became planters themselves or assumed a servile
> attitude toward the planters. The commercial bourgeoisie, such as it
> was, remained tied to the slaveholding interest, had little desire or op-
> portunity to invest capital in industrial expansion, and adopted the
> prevailing aristocratic attitudes. . . . Southern banks were primarily de-
> signed to lend the planters money for outlays that were economically
> feasible and socially acceptable in a slave society: the movement of
> crops, the purchase of land and slaves, and little else. . . . [The system]
> tied the bankers to the plantations. The banks often found it necessary
> to add prominent planters to their boards of directors and were closely
> supervised by the planter-dominated state legislatures. In this relation-
> ship the bankers could not emerge as a middle-class counterweight to
> the planters but could merely serve as their auxiliaries.[22]

This monolithic planter-dominated economic aristocracy may
have existed in other parts of the Old South, especially those lacking a large, powerful commercial center like New Orleans. But
Genovese's description is certainly quite wrong in the case of
Louisiana. Although the New Orleans business and commercial
"aristocracy" did have many economic and family ties with the
planters, it was hardly subservient to them. The planters themselves often complained of their servile dependence on merchants
and factors, who responded with the sort of rhetoric one expects
of a dominant group: a soothing affirmation of the "harmony of
interests" between merchant, banker, and planter.[23]

Genovese's remarks on Southern banking are also inaccurate when applied to Louisiana. Once we recognize a division of interests between merchants and planters, we should distinguish between bank credit going to factors and merchants for "the movement of crops" and bank credit going directly to planters for the "purchase of land and slaves." Bank credit for the commercial movement of crops was relatively abundant, since short-term commercial paper was easily negotiable and more compatible with a banker's portfolio than the long-term mortgage paper of the planter. And contrary to Genovese's assertion, New Orleans merchants and factors, not rural planters, generally had the greatest influence on the management and lending policies of the banks. With these advantages, the commercial sector of the economy needed little special promotion or subsidy from the state government beyond the issuing of new bank charters to provide greater banking capacity. The state's deliberate attempts to promote lending to agriculture might thus be seen not as proof of the planters' absolute hegemony but as an attempt to compensate for the competitive weakness of rural borrowers in the private credit market. And the frequent defeat of these planters' campaigns in the legislature suggests that the planters by no means monopolized political power.

The state's legislative promotion of agricultural development took many different forms. Individual bank charters often created branch offices in plantation areas, required a certain proportion of mortgage loans, and specified the geographical distribution of loans around the state. Certain general laws (such as the election of domicil and the ban on usury) were also expected to encourage lending to agriculture. And the granting of banking privileges to promote internal improvement projects obviously encouraged agriculture wherever the projects improved access to markets. But the major policy device for promoting agriculture was the property bank, and the fact that Louisiana's three property banks received 86 per cent of the state's total bond subsidies indicates the importance attached to them. According to Fritz Redlich, Louisiana was the first state to develop the property bank idea, beginning with the Consolidated Association of Planters in 1827. The innovation here was the combination of a plantation bank and a commercial bank in one institution, and later on the use of the state's credit to help raise the bank's specie capital. Finally, the new institution as developed in Louisiana "migrated" to several other Southern states.[24]

Although generally accurate, Redlich's description does not sufficiently recognize the property bank's rapid evolution from a nearly pure "plantation bank" to a hybrid, more urban-oriented mortgage and commercial bank. The Consolidated Association was initially conceived as a simple planters' bank: only planters were eligible to become stockholders, the bulk of the lending was to be on mortgage security, and discounts of commercial paper were to be based primarily on the bank's profits as they slowly accumulated in future years. This policy soon changed. Edmund Forstall (later a staunch advocate of the mixed form of mortgage-commercial banking) resigned as controller of the Association in 1829 because he felt that the bank had already extended its discounting operations beyond the intent of its charter. But the trend toward more commercial lending (discounts) relative to mortgage lending continued after his departure. The next step was the inclusion of urban property in the mortgage lending category. When the Union and Citizens Banks were set up, their charters permitted at least half of their mortgages to apply to property in New Orleans or its suburbs. The final blow to agricultural interests came in 1836, when the charter of the Consolidated Association itself was amended to allow one-third of its capital to be secured by mortgages on urban property.[25]

During this process of "urbanization" the property banks continued to be highly regarded in Louisiana's banking policy, and their advantages were gradually seen to be independent of their agricultural origins. They were especially praised as agents for importing capital. A property bank could borrow funds out of state by selling its state-endorsed bonds, usually at rates as low as 5 per cent; these funds were then loaned out locally at the 6 to 8 per cent allowed by the bank's charter. This arrangement was clearly less expensive than importing capital through external sales of ordinary bank stocks, which would mean paying out annual profits of 8 or 9 per cent to foreign lenders.* Moreover, bor-

---

* Obviously, the property banks were not the only institutions that could borrow inexpensively abroad and relend at a profit. The Bank of Louisiana did exactly the same. However, few other banks had the essential backing in state bonds to operate on the scale of the property banks.

rowing to promote a property bank that could begin such profitable operations at once was thought safer than importing capital for canal or railroad projects that might not earn profits for many years.[26]

In addition to its broad developmental objectives in promoting banks the state of Louisiana had some more immediate, practical, and selfish goals in mind. Most obviously, she used various banks as fiscal agents for receiving taxes and disbursing expenditures. The banks were willing to perform these services without charge, since they could profit handsomely from the use of the government deposit balances remaining in their hands.[27] More important than routine fiscal services were the ways in which banks supported the state's budget. As a stockholder in several banks, the state received a portion of their profits; and on at least two occasions it fought the banks in court, once to claim its maximum share of profits and once to avoid sharing in bank losses. These profits, and the mandatory bonuses paid by the banks toward public projects, helped the state keep taxes down.[28]

The banks were also instrumental in financing government deficits. In the earlier years (1812-29), before wide capital markets existed for the sale of government securities, Louisiana turned automatically to the banks for her borrowing. During the financially difficult years of 1813, 1814, and 1821, she authorized bank loans totaling $120,000. Again, from 1825 to 1829, state borrowing also averaged over $30,000 per year. Out of debt in the early 1830's, the state had to turn to the banks again after 1837; and its debt of $75,000 at the end of 1838 soared to $1.1 million by the end of 1841. Especially during these last years of financial crisis, the state was only able to negotiate such enormous loans because the various bank charters specifically guaranteed it special borrowing privileges—altogether, $2 million.* Indications are that in most of these deficit financing transactions the banks served as true financial intermediaries (retaining the state's paper in their own portfolios) and not merely as loan brokers. They were thus effectively "monetizing" the public debt by issuing their own monetary liabilities as they purchased it.[29]

---

* The state's eventual debt to the banks of $1.1 million was actually at the effective limit of its compulsory borrowing powers, since some of the $2 million privilege applied to banks then in no condition to lend.

The Bank Act of 1842

The Panic of 1837 marked the beginning of a major shift in Louisiana's policy toward banking. For the next decade policy responded less to the demands of a young, credit-thirsty developing region and more to the economic frustrations and financial difficulties that engulfed the state between 1837 and 1843. The shift from an expansive, easy credit policy to a more restrictive sound money policy was most noticeable in the famous Louisiana Bank Act of 1842.

The Bank Act has been accorded an honored place in the history of American banking legislation. *The Banker's Magazine* predicted in November 1877 that it would "always remain among the most enlightened pieces of banking legislation to be found on the statute books of any country." And William Graham Sumner wrote in 1896:

It leaves the impression of a schoolmaster who, having got tired of confusion, insubordination, and misbehavior, takes in hand the duty of restoring order, and distributes punishments, corrections, and new orders in the most peremptory manner. ... It obviously proceeded from very mature study of the principles and practice of banking, and may justly be regarded as one of the most ingenious and intelligent acts in the history of legislation about banking.

Modern historians have echoed these praises. Fritz Redlich devotes a full chapter of his *Molding of American Banking* (1951) to the intellectual background of the Act. He considers its major contribution to be its emphasis on fixed specie reserves, and on "liquidity and elasticity, the prerequisites of what came to be considered sound banking in modern times." In 1957 Bray Hammond called the Act "in substance the wisest adaptation of practice to environment in any banking law I know."[30] Virtually all of this praise is based on one small section of the Bank Act. Sumner did give a balanced though perfunctory summary of all 27 sections, but other commentators have focused entirely on the single section that prescribes certain "fundamental rules" of banking operation.

According to the fundamental rules, each bank's accounts and operations were divided into two distinct categories, along lines that correspond very roughly to "commercial" and "investment" banking in more recent terminology. The first category (commercial) included the cash assets: the bank's specie, and its "movement" or "loans on deposits," which were defined as commercial paper payable within ninety days. Offsetting these assets were the bank's cash liabilities in notes and deposits. In the second category (investment banking) were the "dead weight" assets or "loans on capital," defined as "accommodations on personal security, or on mortgage, loans on stock by the property banks, and all other investments of whatever nature not realizable in ninety days." Corresponding to these less liquid assets were the bank's capital and surplus accounts, and other liabilities.[31]

The practical significance of this twofold division arose from another of the fundamental rules: "No bank shall increase the investment in its 'dead weight' so long as the whole of its cash liabilities shall not be represented by one third of the amount of such responsibilities in specie, and at least two thirds in satisfactory paper, payable in full at maturity and within ninety days." Here is the object of all the praise, particularly that of Hammond and Redlich. The specie reserves behind both notes and deposits and the rapid "movement" of the loan portfolio ensured liquidity; reliance on short-term commercial paper ensured an "elastic" money supply that would automatically respond to the needs of trade.[32]

In its broad reserve requirement and its adherence to the "commercial loan" and "elasticity" doctrines, the Act was far ahead of its time. Through subsequent federal legislation, these ideas eventually came to dominate American banking practice. The National Banking Act of 1863 set up specie reserve requirements, and the Federal Reserve Act of 1913 attempted to create an elastic money supply based on commercial loans. Hammond suggested that these measures, as well as the earlier banking laws of Massachusetts and New York, were directly modeled on Louisiana's law, and several writers have made similar claims.[33]

The national reputation of the Act really began fifteen years after its adoption. New Orleans banks had survived the financial crisis of 1857 with conspicuously greater success than those in other states. This success was widely attributed to the high reserve requirements of 1842, and the example was soon cited during debates over banking legislation in New York and Massachusetts. The Act's influence on the reserve requirement provisions of the National Bank Act of 1863 appears equally clear. Samuel Hooper, a Boston merchant and banker, was so much impressed with the Louisiana law that he made it the central example in a tract on specie reserves written in 1860. He was also an influential legislator; and through him the Louisiana reserve requirements found their way into the Massachusetts Bank Law of 1858, and from there into the National Bank Act, passed while Hooper was a member of the Congressional banking committee. Any influence of the Louisiana law on the Federal Reserve Act, however, was presumably indirect and by way of the National Bank Act. It should also be noted that only the reserve requirement of the Louisiana Act was passed on, and even that imperfectly; the Act's novel emphasis on short-term commercial loans was overlooked.[34]

Despite the high praise and influence attributed to the fundamental rules of the Bank Act of 1842, we must recognize that they are inadequate in the light of modern economic theory. Indeed, much of the praise is itself based on obsolete theories of "sound banking." As Hammond has suggested, the use of an automatic reserve mechanism to control the money supply would be archaic in the light of modern central banking policies that rely on discretionary controls.[35]

But the problem with the Act's "commercial loan" and "elasticity" doctrines is more fundamental. Although lending only on short-term commercial paper might seem to ensure the liquidity of an individual bank, it could not do so for the whole community of banks. What appears sound to the individual banker in prosperous times may not prove to be sound for the banking system as a whole when a financial crisis occurs. As Paul Trescott reminds us: "The bank's efforts to contract [i.e., to liquidate loans] would set off a paradoxical result. Reducing the quantity of money and the flow of spending would reduce the ability of debtors to pay off their loans and possibly undermine their solvency and that of their creditor banks. The dangerous fallacy of composition involved in 'self-liquidating' loans was demonstrated periodically in American financial panics." During the collapse of cotton prices in 1837 and the ensuing financial panic the widespread bankruptcy or illiquidity of established merchants stabbed at the heart of the supposedly sound commercial loan doctrine.

Moreover, even if the commercial loan requirement did create an elastic money supply it would still have been undesirable: monetary expansion in a commercial boom and monetary contraction in a crisis merely accentuated the cyclical instability of the Louisiana economy.[36]

As indicated, virtually all the previous analysis of the Bank Act of 1842 has focused only on the fundamental rules contained in its first section. This narrow focus may be adequate if one is concerned with the intellectual history of banking theories or the origin of federal banking legislation. But it is entirely inadequate, and even misleading, if one is interested specifically in the development of Louisiana's banking policy. In this respect, the traditional focus produces a remarkably truncated and unhistorical interpretation of the origins, content, and practical significance of the Act.

Previous discussions of the Bank Act's origins have simply declared that its "author" was Edmund J. Forstall, prominent planter and New Orleans businessman. There is indeed little doubt that Forstall wrote and promoted the fundamental rules dividing assets into "movement" and "dead weight" and providing for mixed reserves in specie and short-term commercial paper. Redlich has carefully traced the development of Forstall's argument, beginning most notably with his 1837 *Report on the Banking Situation of the Monied Institutions of New Orleans* (prepared for the legislature's Joint Committee of Finance of which Forstall was co-chairman). Not really an original thinker, Forstall developed his proposals from contemporary tracts on banking (particularly Gallatin's *Considerations on the Currency and Banking System of the United States*, 1831), from his knowledge of the practices of the great European banks, and most of all, from his twenty years of active experience in four of the New Orleans banks.[37]

The simple explanation that Forstall "authored" the Bank Act of 1842 breaks down when one considers its legislative history. Debate began in a special session of December 1837, climaxing in Governor White's veto of a banking bill in March 1838; and it continued in each legislature over the next five years. During this period both Whigs and Democrats were evolving tighter party organizations. The spectrum of banking ideologies included pro-bank Whigs at one extreme and "hard money" Democrats at the other, but a mixture of opinions completely confused partisan alignments in the middle.[38]

The Bank Act that finally emerged from this political thicket was not entirely the work of Edmund Forstall or of any other one man; nor did it consistently bear the stamp of either political party. It did not reflect the "politics of consensus" either; and the conflicts and debates preceding it seem to have followed the lines of economic interest and ideology more than those of political affiliation. The resulting law was a compromise, containing provisions that would appeal to each interest necessary to accumulate majority support in both houses of the legislature. The process of conflict and compromise is clearly evident in the Louisiana legislative journals, particularly in the sessions of 1838 and 1842. And by identifying the major objectives and issues in this process, indicating where the Act of 1842 stood in each case, I will attempt to outline the extent to which the Act went beyond Forstall's fundamental rules.

Paraphrasing the popular interpretation of the New Deal, one might describe the broad objectives of the Bank Act of 1842 as resumption, relief, and reform. The first two were relatively short-range responses to the atmosphere of financial crisis in which the law was written. Moreover, these two goals were often in conflict: giving generous relief to burdened debtors by granting delays in repayment made it more difficult for the banks to prepare for a resumption of specie payments. The reform objective was partly an extension of the goal of resumption—it provided safeguards to prevent future suspensions—and partly an attempt to eliminate certain "abuses" in bank administration.

The first major legislative goal, resumption of specie payments, was generally accepted, but conflicts arose over timing and approach. Those who believed most strongly in a specie-based money supply urged immediate resumption as the only cure—a sort of "tight money" policy that would force prices down to "normal" levels (and would probably bring economic recession as well, though this was not always recognized). They were opposed by those who favored setting a more remote date for resumption, chiefly in order to avoid the forced liquidation of debts, which might bankrupt debtors and shortchange creditors. It was hoped that a few extra months or years would provide relief: debtors could accumulate earnings from several crops; the nation as a whole might act to end the suspension (some hoped that a national bank would appear); and business "confidence" might gradually return, providing the necessary basis for a credit system.

By the time the Act of 1842 was passed, the arguments for delay had lost much of their appeal. Because of depressed cotton and sugar prices (partly a result of the suspension itself), additional crops did little to retire past debts. Realistic political assessments showed that a national bank might never appear, and several other states had already resumed specie payments, reducing the risks of "specie raids" if Louisiana should resume. Finally, the prolonged suspensions had clearly undermined confidence instead of calming fears. The Bank Act set September 30, 1842, as the date of resumption; this was soon amended to December 5, when complete resumption did occur (though not without problems).

In order to provide a stable, controlled currency during the suspension, and in order to permit the banks to accumulate the specie reserves needed for resumption, all of the bank bills provided for the issue of a type of "postnote"—in this case paper currency that could be redeemed in specie only after the anticipated date of resumption. The fact that these postnotes were not immediately convertible to specie made them an attractive liability to banks with inadequate reserves, and several banks began to consider expanded lending. But postnotes also lacked the "natural" restraint of specie convertibility, and their issue had to be strictly limited by law. The Act of 1842 limited the total issue of old notes and postnotes to twice a bank's specie reserve; the other half of the backing was to consist of state bonds or mortgages.* Thus the issue of postnotes provided some immediate financial relief (expanded credit) while hopefully preparing the way for a timely resumption of sound money backed by specie.[39]

In 1842 the desire to resume specie payments was frustrated by another problem arising out of the prolonged suspension. At least five New Orleans banks (the Exchange, Atchafalaya, Orleans, Carrollton, and Improvement Banks) were apparently insolvent, with no prospects of ever resuming profitable operations. But their note

---

* The use of securities (bonds or mortgages) as backing for currency, and their deposit with public officials, closely followed the "free banking" practice that began in New York in 1838 and came to Louisiana in 1853.

issues made up about 35 per cent of the total for all the banks.[40] In these "weak" banks circulation (and loans) had expanded, whereas the "strong" banks had sharply contracted their own circulation (and loans) and had resorted to passing out the depreciated notes of the weak banks. How could the insolvent banks be liquidated and their currency withdrawn without disrupting the money supply and forcing huge losses on their stockholders? As a solution, the Bank Act provided that strong banks would receive (but not redistribute) the notes of the "weak" banks at par. In return, the strong banks would receive assets from the portfolios of the weak banks equivalent in value to the amount of such banknotes that they accepted. The surviving banks were thus required by the state to participate in a sort of currency insurance scheme vaguely similar to the federal deposit insurance program of 1933 (but without government backing).*

Linking the fates of the strong and weak banks was hard enough on the survivors of the panic. But the Bank Act put the strong banks under a still greater strain. Pursuing its second major objective, relief to burdened debtors, the Act provided that anyone indebted to one of the liquidating banks would not have to pay immediately but could extend his loan up to six years (paying 10 per cent immediately, and 15 per cent each year). The surviving banks thus acquired very illiquid assets along with greatly enlarged cash liabilities. By attempting to achieve without compromise the conflicting goals of sound money (resumption) and easy credit (relief), the Bank Act threatened the liquidity and even the survival of the banks.

Particular attention was paid to relieving the agricultural sector. In each bill, the rural interests fought for guarantees of their

---

* The "weak" banks also had to be persuaded to liquidate. Besides threatening legal sanctions against them, the legislature offered several incentives to make their liquidation more attractive—higher interest-rate limits on their remaining portfolios, elimination of all required bonus payments to the state, and elimination of the obligation to complete improvement projects. Most of the details of the liquidation of banks were worked out in the supplemental act of March 14, 1842. Some of the younger surviving ("strong") banks also benefited from a provision of the act of March 14, 1839, which allowed them to reduce their nominal capital to the amount actually paid in. By raising the debt/capital ratio ("leverage") this provision weakened the protection of the bank's note and deposit holders. Senate objections killed the provision in the 1842 debates.

continued access to bank credit during this period of reduced lending. The 1838 bill provided that 40 per cent of all new loans (up to one-half of a bank's capital) must go to rural borrowers, who would not even need city endorsements. Objection to this "agrarian" proposal was one of the main reasons for Governor White's veto of the bill. The final Act of 1842 contained a milder clause requiring the banks to fulfill the rural loan requirements of their original charters. Various bills also restricted the power of the banks to close their branch offices; and the 1842 law required the prior consent of the legislature.

In addition to the immediate goals of resumption and relief, the Bank Act of 1842 and the years of debate that preceded it reflected concern for long-range reforms of the banking system. The purpose behind many reform proposals was to ensure the continuation of a "sound," specie-based money supply after resumption. Forstall's fundamental rules had this goal, and it was also to be one of the responsibilities of the new Board of Currency created by the Act. But even the reforms actually adopted were by no means unanimously supported. Forstall's rules were criticized as "rigid and inflexible," and the Board as unnecessary and meddlesome. Apparently, few people shared Forstall's concern for reserves behind deposits; and even fewer seem to have appreciated the value of the commercial paper requirement, which did not appear in Forstall's own 1838 proposals.[41]

A popular alternative proposal for guaranteeing the specie convertibility of the money supply involved two simple reforms: frequent publicizing of the financial condition of the banks, and weekly settlements in specie of any balances that accumulated between the banks as they received each other's notes during the routine course of business. Publicity, it was believed, would compel the banks to hold sufficient reserves to maintain the confidence of their noteholders and depositors. Regular specie settlements would force each bank to redeem its notes and would thus prevent an overexpansion of the currency. These two reforms appeared in all the bank bills, in the Act of March 14, 1839, and in the Act of 1842. They seem to have been particularly favored by bankers and merchant groups as a less rigid approach to specie payments than Forstall's fundamental rules on specie reserves and commercial loans.

Despite its popularity, the settlement rule was no more a fool-proof regulator of the money supply than was Forstall's commercial-paper rule. If a bank attempted to expand its money issues much more rapidly than its neighbors, it would soon be restrained by adverse settlement balances as other banks received its notes more rapidly than it received theirs. But if all the banks expanded their issues together at about the same rate, as was likely during a boom period, settlement of specie balances would do little to prevent inflationary money issues.

Several other reforms were also designed to guarantee sound money by preserving bank solvency. The banks were to circulate blacklists of their delinquent debtors in order to identify poor credit risks. Loans with a bank's own stock as collateral were restricted. Dividends were prohibited during periods of suspended specie payments in order to prevent unwise drains on a bank's capital. "Speculation" by the banks in cotton, sugar, other commodities, and corporate stocks was outlawed.

Besides the objective of ensuring sound money, Louisiana's bank reforms had the simpler, moralistic goal of reforming bank administration in order to prevent or punish frauds and "abuses." Several rules were intended to prevent the control of a bank by a small faction. Wide stock ownership was required (50 people with at least 30 shares each), strict limits were placed on the use of proxies, and all bank directors were required to remain in the state and to attend meetings regularly. Those who blamed the financial crisis and specie suspension on the moral irresponsibility of bank managers, rather than on impersonal economic causes, emphasized this last set of reforms above the others.

It should be apparent from the preceding discussion that the Bank Act of 1842 was not a single-minded, detached reform law, as many admiring historians have claimed. In light of modern economic theory it is clear that Forstall's fundamental rules did not provide an automatic mechanism to guarantee sound money. The act as a whole was neither the exclusive brainchild of Edmund Forstall nor the reasoned product of a consensus among the business and political community. Instead, it reflected a series of political and economic compromises, negotiated with great difficulty over five years of continual debate. Essentially, the act was a short-term response to immediate and severe financial crisis. The broad range of its objectives and the variety of its provisions for surveillance and regulation of the banks make it a striking example of vigorous state intervention in economic affairs; but the more radical proposals that did not appear in the final law are equal testimony to the continued power of Louisiana's merchant and banking interests.

Reaction, Restriction, and the Slow Relaxation of State Policy, 1841-1861

From one perspective the Bank Act of 1842 climaxed five years of efforts to rescue Louisiana's financial system from irresponsibility. But from another viewpoint the Act presided over a year of financial chaos and introduced a period of restrictive, antibank policy.

The legislators' awareness of the need to agree on some compromise bank bill did not assure the bill a warm reception once passed, and the Act brought angry denunciations and active resistance from a surprisingly large number of merchants and bankers. The cashier of the City Bank wrote to one of his branches: "We have fallen on evil times, and our Legislature are doing every thing in their power to hasten the ruin of the state." And Thomas Morgan of the New Orleans Collector's office reported to Secretary of the Treasury Forward: "Fears are entertained that [the Act's] consequences will be most disastrous both to the Banks and the public. Whether all or any of the Banks will accept of such important alterations in their charters is considered as extremely uncertain, and if not they will be forced into liquidation."[42]

The strongest complaints were directed at the Act's short-run provisions for resumption and relief. Because of the early resumption date, banks would have to liquidate their loans rapidly in order to raise specie reserves. But how could this be done, since the Act also granted liberal delays to the banks' debtors? Strong banks objected vigorously to the requirement that they support the note issues and absorb the portfolios of weaker banks, claiming that this would drag all the banks into bankruptcy together. Many of the lesser reform proposals also irritated the bankers. In the face of their loud protests and their threats to delay the Act's implementation by lengthy lawsuits, the legislature gave in.

On March 7, 1842, an amendment to the original Act softened many of the clauses that had been most sharply attacked, and delayed both resumption and the weekly settlement of interbank balances for three months. The stronger banks soon accepted the amended bill; the weaker banks entered liquidation proceedings either voluntarily or by court action.[43]

With all this controversy surrounding the passage of the Bank Act, it is hardly surprising that the financial community felt uncertain and began a cautious contraction of credit. Credit had become extremely scarce and costly even by January 1842, while the Act was still taking shape. Now, the tight credit market continued into October, severely depressing the state's economy. The Act's immediate psychological and political impact was partly responsible for this enduring crisis, but the Act itself contributed to the problem in several other ways.[44]

The weak and strong banks of New Orleans were forced to work closely together in supporting all outstanding note issues. But as long as interbank specie settlements were deferred there was no clear basis for their dealings. Although the banks met many times (with the help of the Board of Currency established to administer the Bank Act), they were unable to agree on a procedure for interbank settlements that all could accept. Each breakdown in these negotiations soon led to another financial crisis—the worst occurring in May, when the strong banks suddenly announced their resumption of specie payments six months ahead of the deadline set by the amended Bank Act. This premature return to the specie standard was no occasion for public celebration, since it was mainly a self-serving maneuver enabling the strong banks to sever all ties with the weak banks and withdraw support of their banknotes. By withdrawing support, they hoped to force their weaker rivals to accept a strict procedure for interbank specie settlements.

Owing to this power play by the stronger banks, noteholders throughout Louisiana suddenly found 35 per cent of their banknotes (those issued by the weak banks) inconvertible and depreciated. The New Orleans *Price Current* calmly described the riotous response to this derangement of the currency:

A material depreciation of this paper [of the weak banks and the municipalities] was the immediate and natural result of the resumption of specie payments on the part of the banks. The loss, of course, falls heavily upon the bill holders, particularly the poorer classes, and the excitement broke forth, yesterday, in an insane attack upon a note broker's office by a mob, which caused all other brokers to close their doors.

Lacking sufficient reserves, the banks had to suspend again within seven weeks.[45]

The Bank Act did more than disrupt the money supply. By forcing the banks to liquidate their portfolios in order to accumulate large specie reserves, it tightened credit and depressed the economy. Here again, the twin goals of sound money and easy credit conflicted. Opinions varied on the wisdom of such a rapid and disruptive readjustment of money and prices to previous levels. Those who believed most strongly in the specie standard generally accepted economic contraction as the price of prompt resumption. Supporters of easy credit, however, argued that a more gradual resumption under less rigid rules might have done less damage to the economy. In my view, some deflation of prices and a return to some sort of specie standard were inevitable; but the rigid rules of the Bank Act made the process unnecessarily harsh.

The political impact of the Bank Act was perhaps as important as its immediate financial impact. Although both parties had shaped its contents, it was popularly identified with the Whigs, who controlled both the governorship and the legislature. During the subsequent financial crisis the Democrats took full advantage of this impression. The state elections of July 1842 swept into office an antibank Democratic governor and legislative majority, and contemporary commentators considered the banking problem the decisive issue of the campaign. The prolonged financial crisis and the Bank Act thus ushered in several years of very unsympathetic public policy toward banks.[46]

The banking policies advocated by the Democrats after 1842 arose from a complex mixture of ideological commitments and practical concerns. The years of financial crisis had convinced many men that specie was the only legitimate money, and that the banks were hotbeds of speculation, corrupt mismanagement, deception, and disaster. Converted to this hard money ideology, many Democratic "reformers" fought for the complete liquidation and abolition of all banks. Solomon Downs, as chairman of the Senate Finance Committee, led the way in enacting such ideas into law. On a more practical level, the Democrats spoke for a good many Louisianans—planters, farmers, and others—who were heavily burdened by bank debts. And laws compelling the banks to be generous to their debtors found many supporters. Louisiana also had a bankrupt state treasury and a huge (and partly delinquent) state debt. To avoid assessing higher taxes to finance the debt, it was necessary to find some way of reducing, eliminating, or delaying its burdens. Such a "repudiationist" fiscal policy, as its opponents described it, was easier to rationalize because much of the debt had originally been incurred to subsidize the hated banks, and most of the state bonds were held by "foreigners." These antibank repudiationist attitudes most completely dominated the legislative scene in 1843-45, gradually softening later in the decade.[47]

Democratic political pressure on the surviving banks was severe in 1843. The Board of Currency was transformed into a partisan machine consisting of the Secretary of State and the State Treasurer. Governor Mouton named antibank men to the state directorships on the boards of the property banks. Special efforts were made to force the Union Bank into liquidation, despite its apparent solvency and against the wishes of its stockholders. The same hostility to banks pervaded the Constitutional Convention of 1845, whose delegates reaffirmed their faith in what one of them called the "good old system of hard money." The final version of the Constitution declared: "No corporate body shall be hereafter created, renewed, or extended with banking or discounting privileges." Existing banks were only saved, for the duration of their charters, by the belief that immediate abolition would violate the Federal Constitution (regarding the charters as contract). Louisiana's General Incorporation Act of 1848 revealed a similar desire to eliminate banking. Flatly prohibiting all conceivable forms of banking activity, it also indicated a distaste for speculative or financial occupations in general by denying incorporation to "commission business, brokerage, stock jobbing, factors, and exchange businesses of any kind."[48]

After the economic dislocations of 1837-43 the state government faced both a deficit budget and several maturing short-term debts to the banks (resulting from previous deficits). In such straits it could hardly afford to assume responsibility for the $18 million of state bonds previously issued on behalf of the banks. As the banks failed or fell behind on their bond payments, the Democratic legislature at first contemplated the outright repudiation of its obligations to foreign bondholders. This goal was indirectly achieved in an act of April 5, 1843, which permitted the banks to accept state bonds at par value in payment of debts owed to them. The bonds, generally in arrears on both interest and principal, had market values as low as 30 per cent of par; thus the state was encouraging its citizens to buy its bonds back from foreign bondholders at 30 to 60 cents on the dollar in order to repay their bank debts at the same bargain rates. It was a classic case of relieving debtors (the state and those indebted to the banks) at the expense of both foreign creditors and bank stockholders.[49]

Acting for the European bondholders, Baring Brothers of London and Hope & Co. of Amsterdam employed such New Orleans agents as Edmund Forstall in a vigorous propaganda and lobbying campaign to force Louisiana to redeem her debts at full value. In 1844 the state settled its short-term bank debts by cashing in its bank stocks, drawing on sinking fund accounts and permitting some banks to close unprofitable rural branch offices. By 1847 even the huge bond issues of the property banks had been repaid, refinanced, or renegotiated with the bondholders, and the repudiationist Act of 1843 had been repealed. To prevent the recurrence of such a fiscal crisis the Constitution of 1845 prohibited any future debt issues totaling over $100,000 without prior approval in a general election and specific provision for taxes sufficient to repay the debt.[50]

The strenuous effort involved in reducing the state debt by some $6.5 million betwen 1843 and 1850 was viewed as a matter of honor by Edmund Forstall and his contemporaries. To a modern economist it might appear as a case of "tight" fiscal policy, which implies heavy taxation and a depressed demand for goods and services. But the transactions were usually not this straightforward, for the state went to great lengths to avoid taxation and even to avoid direct state payments on bonds. Once again, much of the burden fell on the banks. When the state raided its sinking fund bank accounts or sold its bank stocks, the banks often had to pay funds out of specie reserves. Losing their specie to the foreign bondholders, they were forced to reduce their notes and deposits by tightening their loans and discounts. Thus the main impact of the state's debt-retirement policies came from monetary contraction rather than from a direct tax drag on the level of spending. In a sense, the banks were forced to meet the state's debt (originally incurred on their behalf) by "taxing" their stockholders and their debtors, who were denied credit or renewals.[51]

As the Louisiana economy gradually recovered from depression and the state government from its fiscal crisis, the public policy began to swing toward a position less antagonistic to banking. By 1850 it was widely believed that the Constitution of 1845 had been too restrictive, both in its attempt to eliminate banking entirely and in its severe limitations on the use of state (deficit) financing to promote internal improvements. New Orleans needed more banking facilities, not fewer, in order to finance her expanding trade. A campaign to promote a railroad network out of New Orleans had already begun, and its backers quickly recognized the potential value of a banking system large enough to absorb some of the new railroad securities. It was also observed, with some irony, that instead of eliminating all banks the Constitution of 1845 had actually given the few surviving chartered banks a privileged monopoly. Their exceptional profit rates (15 to 25 per cent per annum) provided further evidence of an unsatisfied demand for banking facilities.[52]

The first sign of change was the passage (March 1852) of an act to renew the charter of the Citizens Bank. Enough Whigs had won legislative seats in the elections of November 1851 to pass the bill over the veto of Democratic Governor Joseph Walker. The act was not entirely expansionary, however, since it also sought to relieve the state of a nagging fiscal problem. The Citizens Bank had been in liquidation since October 1842, and its assets had diminished to the point where it could no longer afford to pay the interest on its state-endorsed bonds. By restoring the bank to active and profitable operation, the state avoided assuming these bond obligations. Nonetheless, the rechartering was a major expansion of banking facilities.[53]

The Constitutional Convention of 1852 provided the occasion for a full discussion and reevaluation of state banking and fiscal policy. Responding to the public desire for expanded trade and new railroad construction, or at least recognizing that the demand for expanded banking could not be ignored, many Democrats had abandoned their all-out opposition to banking. Now, they generally favored a system of "free banking" with charters "democratically" available to any enterprising citizen. But the Whigs, with a small majority in the convention, successfully blocked all attacks on the older special-charter approach; and in the end the legislature was allowed to create new banks by either method. In order to ensure a sound money convertible into specie, the new constitution gave noteholders a priority claim over other bank creditors, authorized the state to register all banknotes and to require "ample security," and denied the legislature any power to sanction or forgive a suspension of specie payments (as it had done in 1839 and 1842).[54]

A further reminder of the previous financial crisis appeared in the debates over limitations on the state debt. The government was permitted to issue up to $8 million of state bonds to finance internal improvements (but not banks). However, each project had to be approved by popular referendum, taxes sufficient to repay the debt had to be assessed, and the state could only provide 20 per cent of the capital for a given project. It should be noted that the constitution did not prevent banks from investing in these improvement bonds; although banking and public works could not be directly joined in a single enterprise, the banks could at least help to finance the projects.[55]

In 1853, following the lead of the new constitution, the legislature established a "general system of free banking" that was modeled primarily after the familiar Free Banking Act of New York but had several conservative features more in line with Louisiana experience. The most debated question in the free bank bill was the proper method of ensuring the soundness of the new banknotes that would be issued. The Bank Act of 1842 had required the banks to maintain reserves of specie and commercial paper. Free banking laws in other states required instead that a bank keep its reserves in the form of government bonds deposited with the state auditor, and Louisiana's Free Bank Act followed this tradition. Proponents of the arrangement believed that the public was better protected by state-held securities than by any assets (e.g., specie or commercial paper) left under the bankers' control.

Clearly, the old Democratic distrust of a banker's integrity had not entirely disappeared.[56]

The crucial assumption of the bond-security plan was that the bonds could be sold by the state in time of need and the specie proceeds used to redeem notes. This idea was sharply attacked. *DeBow's Review* published an influential series of articles arguing that backing banknotes with government bonds would only pile credit on credit, perpetuating government debt, encouraging extravagance in government spending, and permitting an inflationary spiral of money and credit. In a general financial crisis even government bonds would only be marketable at "terrible sacrifices"; hence the banknotes would only be partly secured. The only true guarantee of a safe, convertible note issue would be mandatory specie reserves, like those required by the Louisiana Act of 1842 and the British Bullion Act of 1844.[57]

Edmund Forstall also urged that a specie-reserve rule be incorporated in the Free Bank Act; and during the final days of debate in the legislature he was invited to give his expert testimony in answer to the many private bankers (potential free bankers under the new law) and others opposed to the specie requirement. Yet Forstall did not oppose the traditional bond-security scheme, as *DeBow's* had. In fact, he wrote enthusiastically to Baring Brothers that this would strengthen the bond market and thus benefit Europeans who held other Louisiana bonds.[58]

The Free Bank Act that emerged from this debate combined some elements of both views. Banknotes were backed by government bonds held by the state auditor. In addition, free bankers were required to hold specie reserves equal to at least one-third of "all other cash liabilities" (notably deposits) and specie or short-term commercial paper equal to the remainder. Thus the reserve requirements of the Bank Act of 1842 had been retained only for deposits, and note liabilities were no longer backed by specie. Louisiana was not as clear about its banking principles as most historians have claimed.

Even before the constitutional convention of 1852, James Robb and other New Orleans commercial leaders had sought a free banking system to help finance railroad construction. And in 1854 the Free Bank Act was expanded so that the banks could assist two major railroad projects: the New Orleans, Jackson, and Great

Northern; and the New Orleans, Opelousas, and Great Western. The free banks were allowed to buy bonds issued by the city of New Orleans, which used its receipts to purchase the stock of the railroads. By 1857 the four free banks together held over $2 million of these bonds, providing about 15 per cent of the capital for the two railroad companies. Once again the banks had become important agents of economic development.[59]

By the end of the 1850's Louisiana's banking policy showed the cumulative effects of years of varied experience. From the expansionary days before 1837, only a shadow remained in the surviving chartered banks. From the years of financial crisis came the renunciation of state subsidies for banks embodied in the 1852 constitution, as well as a fixation on guaranteeing the soundness of banknotes. From the antibank period of the 1840's came strict regulations, stiff penalties, a lingering fondness for hard money, and a distrust of banks. Finally the free banking system blended opposition to monopoly privilege with the desire of the 1850's for expanded banking capacity. Thus Louisiana still wrestled with the old dilemma: how to combine sound money and easy credit.

CHAPTER FIVE

Sources of Financial Fluctuations

No ECONOMIC weakness of nineteenth-century America has generated more complaint by contemporaries or criticism by historians than her vulnerability to periodic financial "panics." Such sensational and ill-defined terms as "wildcat banking" and "rag money" are used to describe panics, which are attributed to the chicanery or bad judgment of individual bankers and the "over-speculation" of their "credit-thirsty" customers. The following excerpts from Bunner's *History of Louisiana* (1861) are typical of contemporary rhetoric:

[1824] The flourishing condition of agriculture and commerce, and the immense profits realized from these sources, excited at this time a general spirit of overtrading.

[1827] Money obtained thus easily [from new property banks] was spent with the same freedom, without a thought of being called upon for its re-imbursement. This inflated state of the currency . . . aggravated the financial crisis which took place ten years after.

[1833] The abundance of paper money gave rise, also, to other speculating companies. . . . By this stock-jobbing system the real estate was inflated to an exhorbitant nominal value.

[1835] The mania of speculation had now seized on all minds and turned all heads. . . . The general assembly of this year and the last followed in the steps of the most reckless of their predecessors, and even showed still greater facility in granting bank charters. It really seemed possessed by what Jefferson called the bancomania.

[1836] To make the existing state of things in the end still worse, the banks were profuse in their discounts, and did not scruple to issue paper to five times the amount of their available funds.

[1837] Usurers were now the only class that prospered, and they reaped a rich harvest from the calamities of others.

Unfortunately, most discussions take a similar attitude, and the more impersonal structural and systematic aspects of financial instability are usually ignored.

Modern economic theory has explored the complex interaction between the "monetary" (financial) sector of the economy and the "real" sector (the actual production and consumption of goods and services). "General equilibrium" models (e.g., the Hicksian IS-LM model found in most macroeconomics textbooks) give an integrated overview of this interaction, but their static framework is of limited use to a historian, especially in studying fluctuations. Our purpose will be better served by simpler models that distinguish two separate phases of the interaction: the effects of the real economy on money and finance, and the effects of money and finance on the real economy. The determination of the money supply, and the behavior of other financial variables are considered in this chapter, with particular attention to the causes of their fluctuations. In Chapter Six, the fluctuations of the real economy will be examined, with attention to the causal role of financial factors in these changes. In both chapters I will concentrate on the years 1837-42, the period of greatest fluctuation in antebellum Louisiana, and secondarily on the crisis of 1857. Financial problems were evident in both periods.

Modern Theories of Financial Fluctuations

The initial step toward "explaining" the behavior of the money supply and other financial variables in antebellum Louisiana is to examine the various modern theories on the subject, with particular concern for their historical applicability. For convenience in discussion, I will arbitrarily distinguish three broad theoretical schools: the "central banking" school, the Friedman school, and the "financial intermediary" school.

The central banking theory, the most conventional of the three, is commonly found in textbooks on money and banking.* It is

* Any of the popular texts could serve as the source for this "school" (e.g. Chandler, *Economics of Money and Banking*). Obviously, the textbook writers have deliberately simplified their theories for didactic purposes and are personally well aware of the qualifications and elaborations that could be

chiefly concerned with the quantity of money, especially money created by commercial banks, but it also considers such other variables as interest rates and the quality of credit provided by banks or other financial institutions.* Variation in the money supply is analyzed in terms of responses by commercial banks to policy controls exercised by a central bank. The basic concepts are the quantity of legally defined reserve assets held by the commercial banks and the required ratio between these reserves and a bank's monetary (demand deposit) liabilities. By controlling the total volume of reserves and specifying the reserve ratio, a central bank can control the money created by the commercial banks.

This process of money creation is usually treated quite mechanistically. With a legal reserve ratio of one-third, for example, an additional $1 million of reserves made available by the central bank will automatically cause the commercial banks to create $3 million of new money. Some textbooks may mention that a banker's fluctuating desires for excess reserves above the legally required levels can subvert central bank controls; and they may recognize the public's freedom to choose between bank deposits and other types of money (e.g., currency or coin), or between demand deposits and time deposits (usually not considered part of the money supply at all). But the money supply is still assumed to be under perfect control, and the public's freedom of choice is effectively ignored by the assumption that people will always desire bank money and other assets in rigidly fixed proportions.[1]

The most notable application of the central banking theory to American history is Bray Hammond's *Banks and Politics in America from the Revolution to the Civil War*. This work's great influence on other historians is quite remarkable when one considers how poorly Hammond's model fits the historical circumstances. In fact, the book can be read as an extended criticism of early American banking for its failure to conform to his theory. (Only

---

applied. But their textbooks have educated many historians of banking. Hence the central banking model is more clearly visible in financial histories than in the serious scholarship of monetary theorists.

* The emphasis on credit quality is largely derived from the so-called real-bills theory of bank credit, which holds that proper banking requires lending against short-term, "self-liquidating" commercial paper. Since the real-bills theory is now considered fallacious, credit quality is no longer an important part of the central banking theory.

Nicholas Biddle and the second B.U.S. are praised.[2]) Hammond
seems to argue essentially as follows: America had no central bank
to control the total money supply; therefore, the money supply
responded to cyclical variations in the real economy, and monetary instability accentuated the booms and busts. But a close examination shows that Hammond offers no theoretical basis for his
second statement. If a central bank did not control the money
supply, a central banking theory obviously cannot explain either
the variations in the money supply or the impact of such variations on the rest of the economy. And Hammond offers no clear
alternative theory to fill this gap.*

The theory developed by Milton Friedman and several of his
students seems to explain the behavior of the money supply in
terms more relevant to the nineteenth century. Compared to the
central banking theory, the Friedman school focuses even more
exclusively on the money supply, essentially ignoring the behavior of interest rates, credit quality, or other financial variables.
This narrow focus results from Friedman's belief in a direct causal
linkage between the money supply and aggregate spending or
money income (discussed further below).[3]

Even if one does not accept Friedman's larger theory, it does
offer a useful framework for explaining the movement of the
money supply. And George Macesich has elaborated a variant
that is directly applicable to the early nineteenth-century monetary system. In his model, a money supply is composed of all spe-
cie, banknotes, and bank deposits held by the public ($M = S_p + N_p + D_p$). "High-powered" money consists of all specie outside
the government treasury and is held by either the banks or the
public ($H = S = S_b + S_p$). The behavior of the money supply is
then "explained" by the behavior of three other variables: the
total supply of specie (S), the preference of the public for specie
as compared to bank money (S_p/M), and the bank's reserve ratio
($S_b/[N_p + D_p]$). The money supply rises directly in response to an
increase in the supply of specie. When the public increases its
preference for specie, the banks lose some of their high-powered

---

* An analogy may help to clarify my argument. We might explain the interior
temperature of a house in terms of the operations of a thermostat-controlled
heating system. But this "thermostat" theory would tell us nothing about either
temperature or fuel consumption in a house that lacked a thermostat.

specie reserves and are forced to contract the supply of bank money by a multiple of the amount of specie they surrender to the public; a rise in S_p/M therefore implies a decline in the total money supply. Likewise, a rise in any banker's reserve ratio means that each dollar of specie reserves will support a smaller amount of banknotes and deposits, again implying a decline in the money supply.[4]

Since this model is based on an algebraic identity it is logically impeccable. However, its historical usefulness now depends in turn on how one accounts for the observed historical fluctuations of the three new variables. At this point, the Friedman school offers no coherent theory but adopts an eclectic and often impressionistic approach, combining bits of classical economic theory (e.g., the Ricardian price-specie-flow mechanism) with ad hoc references to a variety of exogenous factors (politics, harvest failures, changing expectations, and so on). Many of the school's specific interpretations of statistics are questionable, but the eclectic approach seems unavoidable. Sooner or later, statistical precision and theoretical rigor must make allowance for the unexplained and the particular. With respect to antebellum finance, the Friedman model is more useful than the central banking model in two respects. First, it pays explicit attention to the variation of the public's relative preference for bank money and specie (in a panic for example). Second, it focuses on the banker's desired reserve ratio rather than the legal ratio. Friedman's suppression of the distinction between time and demand deposits (by counting them both in the money supply) does no harm for this early period because separate data are not available anyway.[5]

The Friedman model is quite adequate for exploring the determinants of the money supply. But some crucial aspects of the historical experience appear to involve not only money but the larger financial system. In this context, a third theoretical approach is useful: that of the "financial intermediary" school, which has recently begun to broaden monetary theory into financial theory. The works of such economists as Tobin, Gurley and Shaw, and Goldsmith develop the theory of asset choice ("portfolio balance") and relate debt, credit, and the volume and rate of issue of all financial assets to income and its growth. Indirect finance and the role of nonbank financial intermediaries (e.g., savings and loan associations, credit unions, and life insurance companies) have been particularly stressed by this school. In the nineteenth century such financial institutions played a minor role compared to commercial banks. But the financial-intermediary approach is nonetheless relevant to nineteenth-century experience, since it abandons a narrow concern with money and banks alone for a broader concern with liquidity and the general process of finance, whether direct or indirect.

Hyman Minsky has applied this financial theory to the relation between financial fluctuations and major economic cycles, and his simple model can easily be modified and applied to the antebellum economy. Sustained economic expansion, or the upward phase of a "long-swing" cycle, generates patterns in the financial sector that tend to increase the instability of the "real" economy's response to exogenous shocks. Deferring connections with the real economy for the moment, let us examine the behavior of Minsky's three financial variables: the debt/income ratio, the behavior of prices of financial assets, and the ratio of "ultimate liquidity" to aggregate income.[6]

During a long period of expansion, many economic units finance their increased spending by issuing securities, some of which are in turn purchased by financial intermediaries who are expanding their own issues to savers. Typically, debt grows faster than income. In the open economy of antebellum Louisiana some of these securities were also sold outside the state, thus affecting exchange rates and the balance of payments.[7]

The market prices of financial assets rise as buyers come to expect the capital gains associated with growth; this "purely speculative" price rise is most characteristic of the stock market and real estate. In antebellum Louisiana real estate speculation would be more important and the stock market less important than in today's economy. Our model might also allow for speculation in commodity inventories (e.g., cotton), especially since claims on these inventories were important assets to the commercial banks and merchants.

Minsky defines his third variable, ultimate liquidity, as "assets whose nominal value is essentially fixed and which are not the liabilities of any private unit within the economy. The ultimately liquid assets carry no default risk, and as they are essentially fixed in market value, they are always available to meet payment commitments."[8] Today, ultimate liquidity would include the nation's supply of specie, treasury currency, and the federal debt. In the nineteenth century it would include only specie, since government bonds (often held abroad) were not beyond the risk of default or depreciation in an open economy.* In Minsky's closed economic model, ultimate liquidity does not grow as rapidly as a booming economy, which will thus have a shrinking ratio of ultimate reserves. In the open economy of antebellum Louisiana specie imports during the boom years might partially avert this shrinkage, whereas specie exports would aggravate it.

Financial Fluctuations in Louisiana

Attempts to apply the above theories to the financial history of antebellum Louisiana often fail for lack of quantitative evidence. There are no meaningful statistics pertaining to the financial crisis during the war of 1812, the national "panic" of 1819, or the minor crisis of 1825. Since qualitative evidence for these same periods is also fragmentary and unrevealing at the state level, no attempt will be made to analyze these early fluctuations. Even for the period after 1830, there are no data on the total supply of specie in the state, so that in terms of the Friedman theory neither S nor S_p/M can be measured. In the following discussion, I will rely on some inferences and some qualitative evidence to fill the statistical gaps and "explain" the variations observed in the data.

The central banking theory is most obviously applicable to the behavior of the second Bank of the United States under Nicholas Biddle. By contracting the volume of specie reserves available to the state banks, the B.U.S. could pressure the state banks to reduce their note and deposit liabilities, their loans, and their discounts. It did just this to the Louisiana banks in 1832 and 1834.

---

* Presumably Minsky counts only federal bonds as ultimately liquid partly because of the federal government's power to monetize its debt. On this basis the debts of antebellum state governments were also ultimate liquidity. Louisiana could, and often did, monetize its debts by requiring state-chartered banks to buy them. As noted in the text, this argument is not relevant for an open state (or federal) economy with external debts. But during the years when the suspension of specie payments insulated the state economy from fixed external financial claims, state government bonds could be considered ultimate liquidity within the state.

There were, of course, other factors influencing the financial environment in those years, such as large exports of specie to Europe and the anxieties created by the "bank war" between Jackson and Biddle; but the B.U.S. action seems to have been the main cause of the financial contractions.[9]

Some scholars have used an inverted form of the central banking theory to explain the monetary expansion preceding the panic of 1837. According to this view, the B.U.S. was no longer able to exert a restraining influence on the state banks after the removal of federal deposits in 1833-34, or certainly after the expiration of its federal charter in 1836. Left to themselves, the state bankers expanded their note and deposit issues while permitting their specie reserve ratios to decline, and this inflationary expansion set the stage for the ensuing liquidity crisis. This interpretation was also popular among antebellum Louisianans, particularly those who favored the idea of a "national bank" along B.U.S. lines.[10]

Despite its popularity, this explanation of the origins of the 1837 panic is a weak one. As we have seen, the absence of a central bank does not imply any specific ratio of specie reserves and certainly indicates nothing about the probable volume of specie available to the state banks. Worse still, the one empirical prediction that the theory does offer—that the antebellum reserve ratio would fall after the removal of B.U.S. influence—is not supported by the available evidence for Louisiana or the nation as a whole.[11]

If one does choose to explain the behavior of the money supply in terms of legal reserve ratios, a better case might be made for a capital/notes ratio than for the conventional specie/notes or specie/(notes + deposits) ratio. As Hammond himself has pointed out, nineteenth-century laws more often limited money issues to a multiple of bank capital. Taking this legal viewpoint, contemporary Louisianans, and other Americans, often explained the expansion of the money supply as a straightforward result of the chartering of new state banks. Referring specifically to Louisiana, they pointed to the rapid chartering of new banks in 1831-36, which raised the aggregate paid-in capital to over $36 million (it had been only $4.6 million in 1830). But this explanation, too, is oversimplified. Even during the optimistic years of rapid expansion, the money supply did not quite keep up with the ceiling set by the growth of bank caiptal; in fact, the money/capital ratio fell from .71 in 1830 to .50 in 1837. More important, this "capital ceiling" explanation does not at all apply to the years of crisis and depression, when the banks contracted their money issues far below the limits set by their capital.[12]

It should be apparent that the central banking theory and its variants are poorly suited to explaining Louisiana's financial fluctuations. In a disguised institutional form, however, this theory does have an unexpected application, for it sheds light on antebellum efforts to limit the money supply during periods of suspended specie payments. I will develop this point more fully in my broader discussion of suspension.

The Friedman school offers a potentially more complete framework for analyzing the fluctuations in Louisiana's money supply. But because of lack of statistical evidence on all but the bank-money variables (bank money, $D + N$, and the reserve ratio $S_b/D + N$), most of the conclusions must be rough guesses based on qualitative evidence.

The first variable to be examined is the total quantity of specie available to Louisiana and her banks ($S_p + S_b$). I have chosen to examine the variation of the total U.S. specie supply and then to consider any reasons for believing that Louisiana's fluctuation might have deviated from the national pattern. Available data on U.S. exports and imports of specie seem to indicate a rough correspondence with the fluctuations of the real economy—net specie imports during booms, and a tendency toward net exports during depressions. This pattern is most visible in the 1820's and 1830's. (It completely disappears in the 1850's because of the large exports of California gold.) There were continuing net imports from 1832 to 1838, with especially large balances in 1834, 1836, and 1838; and the period 1839-46 saw continuous exports (except for a large net import of $20 million in 1843). During the years 1832-46, then, specie flows generally accentuated the financial instability of the economy, enlarging the monetary base in years of expansion and contracting it in years of retardation.[13]

Lacking any direct evidence on the flows of specie in and out of Louisiana, we must assume that they roughly paralleled the national flows. Scattered evidence does permit some hypotheses about possible deviations from the national trend, however. There are two reasons for suspecting that Louisiana received a dispro-portionate share of the specie flowing into America between 1833 and 1837. First, the heavy sales of Louisiana bonds in Europe brought in much specie to serve as capital for the New Orleans banks. (Only part of the specie actually remained in the banks, of course; the rest gradually diffused throughout the economy.) Second, New Orleans was a major port of entry for America's im-ported silver, and the sharp jump in silver imports from Mexico in 1834-35 may have temporarily expanded Louisiana's supply of specie. And there is direct evidence that the New Orleans banks arranged for large imports ($1.65 million) of specie from Cuba and Mexico in the fall of 1836.[14] Louisiana could also gain or lose specie relative to the national trend through flows of specie to or from other states. These flows arose spontaneously when there was an imbalance in interregional payments. They also occurred as a result of deliberate bank transactions, such as seasonal adjust-ments in the domestic exchange market or attempts to increase reserves. On occasion the federal government also initiated inter-regional flows (see Chapter Three).

Considering all these factors, what is the best estimate of Lou-isiana's specie supply between 1832 and 1843? In 1833-34 Lou-isiana probably accumulated specie even faster than the rest of the nation because of her heavy silver imports. In 1835-36 foreign sales of bank bonds continued this rapid expansion. And in 1837-38, while the nation as a whole was still importing specie, Lou-isiana's specie expansion was relatively slower because the federal government transferred some $4 million out of the state (not all in specie, however). Nicholas Biddle's financing of Southern cot-ton exports in 1838-39 probably left less of the export earnings (and specie) in the South than would have remained there if the cotton trade had been financed, as usual, by Southern factors and bankers. There is no clear evidence on what happened to Lou-isiana's total specie supply during the suspension of 1839-42, and the national flows will have to remain our best estimate for those years.

The second variable in the Friedman school's explanation of monetary fluctuation is S_p/M, the fraction of the money supply that the public chooses to hold in specie. Here again, statistics are lacking. But the lack is probably less damaging, since this variable probably fluctuated less violently than the specie supply. Examination of the ratio at the national level indicates that it was generally fairly stable except after a suspension of specie payments. During the suspension period bank money was not convertible into specie, which was temporarily at a premium and hoarded by both banks and individuals; hence many people could not immediately achieve the higher S_p/M ratio that they desired. Only after the resumption of specie payments did the ratio reflect a stronger desire for specie and a stronger distrust of bank money. In the case of Louisiana, there is clear evidence of a desire for specie during the periods of suspension. A distrust of paper money was expressed everywhere, and after 1842 "hard money" politicians dominated the state government for a few years. The sharp rise in bank reserve ratios $(S_b/D + N)$ after 1843 is indirect evidence of the public preference for a higher ratio. A milder version of the same response occurred after the crisis of 1857.[15]

Good statistics are available for the third variable in the Friedman model, the reserve ratio of the banks (see Tables C.1 and C.2). The data reveal a slight reduction in the reserve ratio sometime after June 1835, though the figure for that date may have been abnormally high owing to "Biddle's panic" in 1834. In any case, the slight decline is not sufficient to account for the monetary expansion and price inflation that preceded the crisis of 1837. The correspondence of New Orleans bankers with the Secretary of the Treasury, together with the joint effort of the same bankers to import specie in the fall of 1836, indicates that they were not entirely satisfied with the lower reserve ratio, although at that time they were unwilling to raise it by reducing their loans and monetary liabilities rather than increasing their specie.[16]

The financial crisis struck in March 1837, marked by the failure of several large New Orleans merchant firms, and the banks immediately sought to raise their reserve ratios. In their scramble for greater liquidity, they granted no new loans and pressed their borrowers to repay existing loans as promptly as possible (which would eliminate an equal amount of note or deposit liabilities). But the entire community had joined in this scramble for liquidity (i.e., specie), and the public was trying to acquire specie by converting notes and deposits. The public "won" the scramble: the banks saw their reserve ratio fall from .168 to .139 between January and May. During the brief crisis of October 1857 the banks had a similar experience when their specie declined faster than their notes and deposits.[17]

Once the scramble for liquidity ended in the suspension of specie payments, the specie reserve ratio lost some of its immediate importance. Bank money was not convertible into specie, and the expansion or contraction of notes and deposits could proceed unhindered. But most bankers, anticipating the eventual resumption of specie payments, tried to maintain or rebuild their reserves during suspension. During the short suspension between May and December, 1837, the aggregate reserve ratio of the banks did rise somewhat (from .139 to .182). During the long suspension of 1839-42, however, this policy was less successful, in part because of conflicts between the stronger and weaker banks. The ratio drifted irregularly downward from .307 in October 1839 to a low point of .190 in April 1841, then drifted upward to about .3 at the time of resumption (see Table C.2).

The really big shifts in the reserve ratio typically came just after a resumption of specie payments. Since bank money and specie were once again convertible at par, the public stopped hoarding specie and deposited it in the banks. And the bankers, eager to maintain public confidence in their note and deposit liabilities, did not immediately use the new specie reserves to support expanded lending. The most striking rise in the reserve ratio came after the resumption of December 1842: over $3 million dollars of specie flowed into the banks, and the ratio jumped from .278 (September 1842) to .693 (January 1843). A similar sharp rise occurred after the panic of 1857; and a slightly milder rise at the end of 1847 was probably connected with the British financial crisis of that year. There was no substantial inflow of specie to the banks after the resumption of December 1838, presumably because people were still uncertain about financial conditions at that time.

The abnormally high reserve ratios of 1843 through 1845 deserve some special comment. Even after the success of the resumption was beyond doubt, the banks did not begin to lower their reserve ratios by expanding credit. By the beginning of 1844, in fact, the aggregate ratio had reached 96 per cent. Apparently, bankers were still concerned over the public's distrust of bank money. In addition, they were probably responding to the evident desire of the legislature and the Democratic Party for the liquidation of all banks. A forced liquidation would require much higher reserve ratios and a much higher proportion of cash assets than those needed to conduct ordinary banking operations. As the prospect of immediate liquidation receded after 1845, the banks gradually lowered their reserve ratios to more normal levels.[18]

The financial implications of the Friedman model for Louisiana may be briefly summarized as follows. In general, it appears that each of the three variables behind the money supply moved so as to accentuate the cyclical fluctuations of the money supply. The total supply of specie rose substantially during the boom years, peaked in 1838, and gradually declined during the years of depression, reducing the financial base available to the economy at the time of resumption (the year 1843 is an important exception to this pattern). The public's specie/money ratio (S_p/M) rose sharply in the early stages of financial crisis, forcing a sharp contraction in bank money. It remained roughly stable during the subsequent suspension of specie payments and fell suddenly after the resumption, permitting an expansion of the total money supply. Finally, the bank reserve ratio $(S_b/[D + N])$ rose sharply at the time of resumption, delaying the expansion of bank money that might otherwise have occurred.

Our third model of financial fluctuations is that offered by Hyman Minsky, which goes beyond money to consider finance, debt, and credit in general. This model's three key variables—ratio of debt to income, behavior of asset prices, and ratio of ultimate liquidity to total income—may each be applied to the Louisiana experience.

The fragmentary statistics available for Louisiana prior to the panic of 1837 seem to fit Minsky's hypothesis of a rising debt/income ratio during periods of sustained economic expansion. Ideally, we would want data on total issues of primary and indirect securities during those years; but such data simply do not exist. However, we do have statistics on bank loans, bank purchases of the securities of merchants and planters, and changes in the debt of the state government. From 1830 to 1837, while Louisiana's money income was rising by 77 per cent, the volume of bank loans increased by 770 per cent. The last two years of expansion,

1835-37, show a similar pattern; while money income expanded by 16 per cent, bank loans expanded by 58 per cent. During these same years, the state government rapidly expanded its borrowing to subsidize banks and internal improvement projects. Qualitative evidence about other types of debt strongly supports this statistical pattern. Planters borrowed heavily in order to expand their production by buying more land and slaves. Granting and receiving a greatly expanded amount of trade credit, the New Orleans factors raised their debt/capital ratios and left themselves much more vulnerable to failure in case of reduced earnings. In significant contrast with this period, the years before the panic of 1857 showed no indication of a substantial rise in the debt/income ratio.[19]

Minsky's second variable is the behavior of asset prices. It was widely believed among antebellum Louisianans, and has been repeatedly asserted by later historians, that rampant speculation had forced up the prices of land and other assets before the panic of 1837. As early as 1832, one observer commented on the chartering of the Union Bank: "It will materially assist in keeping up the bubble of the real estate mania, at present prevailing here, in a style only equaled by the previous Law's Mississippi Scheme." Similar remarks pervade the chronicle of the contemporary Louisiana historian E. Bunner.[20]

Despite the wide acceptance of this view, there are serious problems in distinguishing "speculative" changes from other price changes. In fact, Lance Davis has recently questioned whether the term "speculation" can have any "operational" meaning for an economic historian, since evidence of the motivations or "innermost thoughts" of the asset buyers is not generally available. Nathan Rosenberg and J. R. T. Hughes have also questioned the vague uses of the terms "speculation" and "overspeculation" in historical literature, and have shown the inadequacy of using these terms to explain economic fluctuations. It seems to me that the Minsky model goes a long way toward answering these criticisms. It relates "speculative" rises in asset prices to expectations ("innermost thoughts") of future rapid economic growth; and Minsky shows clearly how such expectations would lead to a revision of the calculated rate of return on assets. For historical purposes, any substantial price rise that cannot be explained by changes in current conditions of supply and demand—by changes in the current productive value of the asset—would be prima facie evidence of speculation.[21]

In the case of Louisiana before 1837, we have ample qualitative evidence indicating a widespread expectation of sustained economic growth and a rapid rise in the prices of certain assets beyond any reasonable rise in their immediate productive value. The most dramatic examples cited by contemporaries usually involved real estate on the suburban fringes of New Orleans, much of it swampy land. One source for 1832 mentions a plantation that had sold a few years earlier for $90,000, had been transferred recently for $480,000, and was about to be subdivided and sold for a total of $1 million. Obviously, these prices were based on the expectation of a rapid rise in the population of New Orleans, which was in turn based on the expectation of sustained growth in the New Orleans economy. There are also frequent references to rising prices for plantation land and slaves. Rather than reflecting pure speculation, these increases may have been in part a response to the high prices received for cotton in the mid-1830's. Although most of the evidence of speculation refers to real estate, there is some indication of speculation in stocks and securities. One sober example comes from the New Orleans *Price Current* (July 3, 1835):

Stocks—the attention of a portion of our community appears to be wholly engrossed with this topic. Hardly anything else is talked of, and the excitement that prevails is very great. In addition to the many banking institutions, railroads, insurance companies, etc., that were already in full and successful operation, and the stocks of which stand deservedly very high, our Legislature at its last sitting granted charters, exceedingly liberal in their provisions, to several new ones, the subscription books of which were opened much about the same time. Such a large amount of stock being thrown into the market at once, was calculated to produce the impression that it could hardly all be immediately taken; but the avidity evinced to obtain shares, and the high premium paid since the books of some of them have closed, in order to obtain them, show these impressions to have been entirely groundless.

For the period prior to the panic of 1857, there is little evidence of a speculative rise in asset prices.[22]

Minsky's third key variable is the ratio of ultimate liquidity to total income. In the open economy of nineteenth-century Louisiana, this was essentially the quantity of specie within the state as compared to the total income; and the specie supply has already been considered in our discussion of the Friedman model. In his closed model, Minsky hypothesizes that the specie/income ratio will decline during periods of sustained economic expansion. But we have seen that the opposite was true in Louisiana where the supply of specie almost certainly grew faster than total income in 1830-37.[23]

On the whole, our application of Minsky's financial model suggests the same conclusion we drew from Friedman's monetary model: that the financial variables expanded in a potentially disruptive way during boom years and contracted when the economy contracted. The one element favoring financial stability was the continuing expansion of Louisiana's supply of specie (ultimate liquidity) until 1838.

The Financial System During Suspension

In our discussion of Louisiana's money supply, the period of suspended specie payments is a special case that does not really fit any of the three models we have used. The central banking theory, with its emphasis on reserves and reserve ratios, is obviously irrelevant in a period when specie is no longer the banker's reserve asset. The Friedman model may tell us something about the public's desired specie/money ratio (S_p/M) or the banker's desired reserve ratio ($S_b/[D + N]$); but during suspension the supply and allocation of specie no longer determined the actual ratios. The Minsky model does not focus on the behavior of the money supply at all.

The explanations offered by most antebellum Louisianans are equally unhelpful. Believing in the specie standard and believing that all other types of money (particularly banknotes and deposits) ought to be convertible into specie, they viewed the suspension of specie payments simply as a failure of the monetary system. Theirs was a postmortem examination of a deceased specie standard; one did not listen for the heartbeat of a corpse, and they had no reason to examine the functioning of the economy during suspension. Moreover, contemporary explanations of the suspension were characteristically framed in moral terms. Indignant at the breakdown of the specie standard, they threw the blame on the evil and immoral behavior of individual bankers—the granting of unsound loans, the "overextension" of credit, "kiting," and other frauds. Unfortunately, most historians of the antebellum panics have also assumed this righteous indignation. They have similarly explained the suspensions in moral terms with vague economic content; and they have been similarly indifferent to the problem of explaining the behavior of the money supply during suspension. Typically, a historian will briefly refer to the depreciation of bank monies and other currency and attribute it to the "over issue" of these monies.[24]

A fresh treatment of the economic significance of suspension must have two basic considerations: the effects of suspension on Louisiana's financial relations with the outside world, and the conditions of money and credit within the state during suspension. The second consideration includes the initial impact of the suspension itself, the problems of living with suspended specie payments for a period of time, and the problems of resuming payments.

Before suspension, Louisiana and the rest of the nation had been operating under the international specie standard, which provided a system of fixed exchange rates—or at least, exchange rates that fluctuated within the narrow limits of the "gold points" defined by the cost of physically transferring specie. Suspension introduced a system of freely fluctuating exchange rates between countries and even between states and cities within the United States. As long as she held to the gold standard, Louisiana would have to cope with losses of specie resulting from deficits in her external balance of payments; and she was particularly vulnerable to "specie raids" launched from states that had previously suspended. Suspension did stop the drain on her specie reserves. On the other hand, suspension, combined with the failure of so many trading firms, almost completely disrupted the mechanism of international and interregional payments. With many bills of exchange under protest and the value of others uncertain, a high rate of interest was charged on all exchange transactions to compensate for the risk of default. Nor could payments easily be made in banknotes or deposits, since bank money was no longer on a par with specie and the depreciation varied from bank to bank. (This disruption helps to explain why Louisiana banks exported cotton on their own account in 1838 and 1839.)[25]

The effect of suspension on external financial relations, then, was largely disruptive. But it did prevent a further involuntary outflow of specie to other states or nations. And the freely fluctuating exchange rates that accompanied it allowed a more expansionary domestic monetary policy, since the state did not have to worry about its balance of payments.

By eliminating specie reserves and convertibility at par between all types of money, suspension removed the "natural regulator" of Louisiana's internal monetary system. Each bank was left free to expand or contract its own note and deposit liabilities. A responsible banker, of course, would limit his expansion, keeping in mind the necessity for a future resumption of specie payments; but nothing restrained the irresponsible. Lacking both a gold standard and a central bank, Louisiana sought other means of controlling her money supply. The state legislature attempted to define rules for the banks, but was largely unsuccessful: suspension had been in effect for over two years before the legislature and the governor agreed on the first banking directives. Most of the burden of control, therefore, was left to the banks themselves. Voluntary cooperation was achieved through a Board of Presidents on which each bank had one vote; and the threat of informal sanctions by the other banks was often sufficient to bring reluctant members into line behind a majority decision. The Board thus performed some of the essential functions of a modern central bank.[26]

The initial impact of suspension on monetary and credit conditions within Louisiana was distinctly favorable. During the two months between the initial crisis in March 1837 and the suspension on May 13, the New Orleans banks had been forced to contract their loans because their specie reserves were shrinking rapidly. This contraction only added to the difficulties already created by the general financial crisis. The banks had attempted, apparently unsuccessfully, to provide some relief to their borrowers by agreeing to renew existing loans on the basis of a 10 per cent reduction each 60 days. But several banks soon became unwilling to continue with this agreement, fearing specie losses to the public or to other banks that contracted more rapidly. Suspension removed this fear and enabled the banks to extend greater relief to needy borrowers. In fact, the banks justified suspension to the public on precisely this basis:

> The unlimited resources of our country, and particularly of Louisiana, will enable the banks of this state to resume their specie payments at an early period with perfect safety, and in the meantime measures will be adopted, to prevent an injudicious extension of circulation and to inform the public by monthly publications of the relative position of the banks. By adopting this step [suspension] they can at once extend their facilities so as to afford efficient and immediate relief—check the continuance of the numerous failures—restore confidence in the community—create a resumption of business transactions in the way of purchases and sales, and prevent the ruinous sacrifices that are daily [occurring] under the unexampled pressure that now exists, and at the same time retaining at their command the necessary specie to facilitate the minor transactions of the community and to enable them to resume their general payments at the earliest possible period.[27]

Only by the suspension of specie payments could the banks begin to cope with the extreme conflict between "easy credit" and "sound money" that the panic had imposed on the economy.

Suspension was also in the banks' own interest, since it eased the conflict between their two objectives of liquidity and solvency. Under the specie standard they had been forced to scramble for liquidity by rapidly contracting their loans. But this contraction often placed an unmanageable burden upon their debtors; and the resulting defaults and bankruptcies only reduced the total value of bank assets, undermining the solvency of the banks. Suspension temporarily relieved the banks of their concern for liquidity and enabled them to take measures to protect their solvency (i.e., the long-term value of their assets). They granted extensions and delays to hard-pressed debtors, and at the same time sought to improve the collateral behind their loans by shifting from personal security to mortgage security on land or slaves. At the outset, then, suspension both strengthened the solvency of the banks and permitted them to extend financial relief.[28]

Although suspension was at first clearly beneficial, it posed severe long-term problems. Essentially, some agency had to control both the quantity and the composition of the money supply. Controlling the quantity of money was actually the easier problem to solve. The banks themselves were generally unwilling to issue many notes and deposits during suspension, since they could anticipate an eventual resumption of payments and wanted to maintain specie reserves to meet it. They were also conscious of the strong public opposition to suspension, which might lead to legal penalties or the forfeiture of their charters. It is not surprising, therefore, that the banks generally cooperated willingly, through the Board of Presidents, to limit their individual issues of currency. Naturally, there was a good deal of hard bargaining over the particular formula for establishing quotas; but once set the quotas were generally obeyed. The quota formulas adopted in 1837 and 1839 began with a standard percentage of capital as the basic limitation on note issue. This percentage was then modified, through compromise and bargaining, to take account of the unequal liquid holdings of the various banks and to allow slightly higher quotas to the smaller banks.[29]

Although actual quotas for note issues were easily arranged, there was constant disagreement on the appropriate method for switching from the existing level of issues to the quota limitations. Some banks were over their quotas and were expected to contract gradually to reach the level set by the agreements; others whose note issues were below their quotas were expected to expand at the same rate to replace the currency withdrawn by the contracting banks. The basic difficulty here was establishing rules for equitable settlement between expanding and contracting banks. The strong banks, who had the largest reserves of specie and liquid assets and usually had a circulation far below their quota limitations, generally wanted strict and frequent settlements. They were reluctant to expand their own issues; and they did not want to receive the notes of the weak banks at par because this would require them to accept some of the more questionable short-term assets of the weak banks.[30]

Conflicts over the rules of interbank settlement were the major reason for the periodic breakdowns of bank cooperation between 1837 and 1843. Dissatisfied banks demanded revision or stricter enforcement of the rules and threatened to withdraw from the agreements. Sometimes a few strong banks simply resumed specie payments on their own initiative, embarrassing the rest of the banks and disrupting monetary arrangements entirely. The most damaging instance of premature resumption occurred in May 1842; it lasted only two weeks, but entirely disrupted the monetary system, depleted the reserves of the banks, and inaugurated six months of severe contraction in Louisiana finance. The cost of such disagreement was high for the banks as well as the community, since a rapid contraction of their loans always threatened their solvency.[81]

Considering the potential conflicts of interest between the banks, their partial success in cooperatively regulating the money supply between 1837 and 1842 was quite remarkable. During the first period of suspension (May 13, 1837, to December 24, 1838) some sort of voluntary agreement seems to have been operative almost from the start. And the agreement to resume set forth continuing arrangements for interbank settlements. During the longer suspension that began in October 1839, agreements seem to have been operative up to December 1841. The banks were obviously conscious of what they called their "solidarity" during suspension, whereby any damage to the reputation or credit rating of one bank meant potential damage to all. While the banks cooperated, the public benefited from a limited money supply (often too limited if the strong banks were unwilling to expand their circulation) with all banks accepting each other's notes at face value. Even so, a minority of Louisianans objected—and their argument seems strong in retrospect—that voluntary cooperation by all the banks was not beneficial to the community in the long run. If it led to the gradual replacement of the notes of weak banks by those of strong banks the public would indeed hold a sounder money supply; but in the process the strong banks would unavoidably absorb many of the weaker banks' illiquid assets.[82]

In any event, the weak banks failed and went into liquidation under the Bank Act of 1842, and their circulation rapidly depreciated in value. Rather than diluting the portfolios of the strong banks in an attempt to support the weak banks, might Louisiana have done better by letting the weak banks fail at an earlier date? The initial contraction of money and credit would certainly have been much more severe, but the final difficulties arising from the confused settlement situation of 1842 might have been alleviated or perhaps avoided altogether. Even if true, this retrospective criticism is somewhat unfair, since it rules out the solution that a majority of Louisianans had hoped to achieve: the survival (through cooperation and mutual support) of all their banks.

As suggested by the above discussion, the problems of controlling the quantity of money and controlling its composition, or quality, were sometimes interrelated. Suspension of specie payments, by removing the basis of monetary convertibility, created a variety of problems for the banks and the public. In large part these were problems involving the composition and relative value of various types of bank money. Uncertainty about the relative value of different banknotes created problems with bank deposits as well. Cautious bankers often refused to accept on deposit any money other than specie or their own notes; and deposit accounts were refused, or were closed out if the holder sought to withdraw more specie than he had deposited.[33]

Once the discipline of specie convertibility was ended by suspension, further problems were created by the proliferation of a variety of nonbank money issues. The most important of these fiat issues were the large sums issued by the three municipal governments of New Orleans as a cheap form of deficit financing and also as a partial replacement for the contracted bank currency. Secured by state bonds or mortgages against municipally owned real estate, these municipal notes were received on deposit and paid out at par by the banks. Several hundred thousand dollars' worth were issued, in denominations as small as twenty cents; and they gradually began to play the major role in the routine business transactions of New Orleans, whose people withdrew their specie into private hoards. After the sudden resumption of specie payments by some banks in May 1842, municipal notes depreciated rapidly because they were not acceptable at par value with specie. The results, as reported by *Price Current*, were heavy losses for those who held New Orleans notes, especially among the poorer classes. There were riots, and at least one broker's office was attacked by an angry mob. After the first resumption of December 1838 the banks had arranged to replace municipal notes with their own circulation by purchasing long-term city bonds in the same amount. It is not known whether similar arrangements were made after the difficulties of 1842.[34]

In addition to the municipal notes, there were numerous other private money issues during the period of suspension. In the early days of suspension in 1837, the banks had attempted to limit this by continuing to redeem their own small-denomination notes in specie. But the resulting drain of specie soon forced them to halt even these payments. The New Orleans *Commercial Bulletin* predicted the damage that this action would cause:

Citizens will be bothered in the market, merchants in the payment of small dray charges, mechanics in the settlement with their workmen, and last though not least, the whole city in the procurement of the savory lunch and delicious julep. The result of all which will be that we shall be flooded with individual tickets imposed upon the community at every turn, and with a strong probability of their never being redeemed. Issues of this kind have already commenced, and might no doubt be serviceable if restrained to a few who are perfectly solvent, but there is no limit to their issue, and every cabaret keeper who can raise a dollar to begin upon will have his individual circulation.

This prediction was aptly confirmed by a New Orleans housewife:

The Second Municipality has issued paper notes as small as twenty cents, but as yet they will not pass. The old negro market women don't understand them and they will take nothing but silver. But the wise ones say that soon there will be no silver and then they must take the small notes or let their vegetables spoil on their hands. . . . All sorts of little miserable notes are in circulation now. Any sort of a grog shop keeper issues his bond and some of them pass at market. A piece of silver of any size is quite a curiosity now. I have kept a little to pay my post office bill but it is almost like drawing blood to part from it for anything else. As for their pitiful little notes I hate the sight of them and always part with them as soon as possible.[35]

The difficulties of controlling the money supply during suspension were great enough, but the problem of resuming payments was worse. Since 1837 Louisiana's money supply had been evolving away from its former specie base; and when resumption came, under the auspices of the Bank Act of 1842, the results were traumatic.

The actual decision to resume payments was a complex one. Differing attitudes toward the importance of specie backing, together with the unequal strength of the banks, caused many disagreements over the timing and the procedures for resumption. Edmund Forstall, as president of the Citizens Bank, consistently fought hardest for an early resumption based on strict settlements between the banks (in specie if possible), and urged that the banks be required to accumulate at least minimal specie reserves well in advance. On the other side, the leaders of the weaker banks bargained for delays in resumption and for interbank settlement procedures that would minimize the demand for specie. The New Orleans merchant community, whose viewpoint was well represented among the bank presidents, was ambivalent, wanting a prompt return to a specie currency and normal procedures for domestic and foreign exchange, but also wanting to avoid severe contractions of credit or pressure on borrowers—again, it was the problem of sound money and easy credit.[36]

The successful resumption of December 5, 1842, was achieved under terms set by the Bank Act of February 1842 and supplementary laws passed during that year. The immediate, short-run effect of the Act was unambiguous. As early as January 1842 the banks and their rural branches began to contract credit in an effort to build up ample reserves before the date of resumption. And immediately after the Act was passed liquidation proceedings were begun for the four weakest banks (Exchange, Improvement, Atchafalaya, and Bank of Orleans). The remaining notes of these banks quickly vanished from circulation, further contracting the money supply.[37]

It is clear that the Bank Act both effected resumption and led to the sharp contraction of money and credit. It is not clear whether contraction was the inevitable byproduct of resumption or merely of the particular way in which the Bank Act accomplished resumption. The sharp arguments of contemporary Louisianans illustrate the main issues.

Those who defended the Bank Act generally preferred a money supply composed of or rigidly backed by specie. To them, the contraction of money toward its specie basis was thus both necessary and desirable. Edmund Forstall articulated this viewpoint: "The law of 1842 has done its work nobly. By forcing with its Iron Rules accountability it has swept away as by magic the trash under which the wealth of this state was actually smothering. As confidence has been returning the metallics have been seen creeping out of every corner, and never at any epoch have our banks witnessed such an accumulation of gold and silver in their vaults." Forstall probably influenced the Board of Currency, which expressed the same viewpoint in its 1843 Report:

New Orleans the Emporium of the Great West is no longer stained with the obloquy of using false measures of value. Exchanges of commodities, be the amount what it may, are now regulated by the Constitutional Standard! Depreciated paper money forced into liquidation by an Iron Rule, and driven out of circulation as currency, has been immediately replaced by the metallics, and the empty vaults of our banks . . . are already replenished, despite the prophecies of theorists, and designing men. . . . In fine our banking system, struck to the heart by depreciated paper money, was expiring under the weight of bankruptcy. The more it had been useful whilst regulated in its oscillations, by gold or silver, the more it had become dangerous, deprived of its natural regulator. Thanks to the energetic measures of the last legislature, this system, inherent to our natural industry, may now be considered as saved.[38]

Critics of the Bank Act, including many bankers and merchants, held a quite different view, blaming its provisions for the financial difficulties of 1842. In the words of Robert Palfrey, cashier of the City Bank: "Our country is blessed by providence and cursed by legislation. . . . The Bank Bill does the work of destruction admirably well, and if it continues six months longer it will ruin every one, both in the city and country."[39] Such critics accepted the specie standard and the eventual necessity for resumption, but were less convinced of the necessity for rigid specie reserves. They believed (incorrectly) that regular settlements between the banks would probably ensure convertibility just as effectively (see pp. 125-26). And since bank money could be safely controlled without rigid specie backing, resumption should have been accomplished at a more deliberate pace, avoiding unnecessary contractions of credit. The legislature should simply have set a date for resumption and left the banks to prepare themselves. Instead, the Bank Act imposed its "iron rules": separating bank assets into "movement" and "dead weight," forcing the banks to grant delays to many of their debtors, yet not recognizing such dead-weight loans as proper backing for bank money. These rules, with the required reserve ratios, had forced the banks into unnecessarily harsh contraction or into liquidation.[40]

Was the financial crisis of 1842 "necessary," then? To some extent, it was. If we accept the necessity for returning to the specie standard at par, as all contemporaries did, then the temporary devaluation of the money supply permitted by suspension had to be corrected, and some degree of painful readjustment was unavoidable (as it was in Britain during the 1920's, to recall a more recent controversy). The failure of the weak banks was probably also unavoidable, since they had not managed to achieve much liquidity or strength during suspension. Finally, a longer delay of resumption would probably have accomplished little. In the early days of suspension, delays in repayment saved many debtors and bankers from insolvency, and it was hoped that each season's crops would enable more debtors to meet their obligations. But after four seasons these hopes remained unfulfilled, and by 1842 time alone had lost its healing powers.[41]

Even when all these points have been conceded to Forstall's argument for the "necessity" of contraction, however, the key point remains. Forstall's "iron rules," embodied in the Bank Act, compelled the surviving banks to increase their liquidity (especially in specie) and contract their credit to an excessive degree. Without these restraints, in my judgment, most banks could have resumed payments while providing a more adequate supply of money and a more flexible allocation of credit.

Compared to the financial crisis of 1837-42, the "panic" of 1857 was both brief and mild, at least in Louisiana. After a month of tight money and credit, three of New Orleans' five free banks and the much larger Citizens Bank suspended specie payments on October 14;* all of them had resumed by November 18. The other banks survived the demands of their customers, remained on a specie basis, and held to a severe contraction of credit until late November. Within three months financial markets were back to normal. This disturbance, such as it was, occurred largely because the markets for domestic and foreign exchange had been disrupted by the commercial crisis and failures centering in New York. Internally, Louisiana had not been under the financial strains that had precipitated the panic of 1837. Reserve ratios were high (36 per cent in August 1857, compared to a national average of 13 per cent), and since 1842 the Louisiana economy had not expanded nearly as rapidly as it had in the 1830's. Thus Minsky's two symptoms of financial instability, a rising debt/income ratio and speculative rises in stocks and real estate prices, did not precede the 1857 crisis.[42]

* The Citizens Bank suspended payments only on its deposits, and continued to redeem its notes.

Many Louisianans attributed the relative mildness of the 1857 crisis to the "sound" banking system that had been established by the Bank Act of 1842. The same conclusion was drawn by other Americans of the day, who soon came to consider the Louisiana Act as a model for reform in other states. Historians, too, have generally accepted this legalistic explanation of Louisiana's particular good fortune.[43]

However appealing, the popular explanation is greatly oversimplified. The rules of the Bank Act undoubtedly did contribute to the financial stability of the old chartered banks by requiring them to maintain ample specie reserves, which raised public confidence in their ability to remain on a specie basis. In fact, the original act had been strengthened by a law of 1857 imposing a $100 fine on any bank director who approved expanded loans while his bank was deficient in reserves. A similar specie reserve requirement applied to the deposit liabilities of the free banks; but their notes (27 per cent of the state's banknotes) were backed instead by state bonds, which were illiquid in time of crisis. Thus the famous rules of 1842 did not apply fully to Louisiana's free banks in 1857. More important, they did not even ensure the soundness of the chartered banks. The Citizens Bank was able to avoid total suspension (notes as well as deposits) only because of an extraordinary act of "solidarity": on the urging of the governor and the Board of Currency, the other three chartered banks lent her a total of $400,000 in specie.[44]

It is more likely that the panic touched New Orleans lightly because its seasonal timing favored her more than other financial centers. October was the bare beginning of the shipping season in the Gulf States, and there was a correspondingly light demand for credit; few merchants, factors, or bankers were yet heavily extended or vulnerable to default in case of credit contraction. The Bank Act seems to have contributed more indirectly, by stunting economic growth in the preceding years and thus leaving Louisiana's financial system less vulnerable to collapse than it had been in the 1830's. The framers of the Act had intended to do just this, and we may grant their success; but their policies had other effects, especially in the real economy of which the financial sector was only a part.

CHAPTER SIX

Banking, Stability, and Development

THE PRECEDING chapter explored the determinants of monetary and financial fluctuations, one side of the two-way relationship between the financial and "real" sectors of the economy. This chapter will consider the other side: the extent to which the behavior of money and finance caused cycles and fluctuations in the larger economy. Since we will eventually conclude that the antebellum banking system was indeed a substantial cause of economic instability, we must weigh the disadvantages of that instability against the contributions that Louisiana's banking system made to her growth and development, as described in earlier chapters. The concluding section of this chapter will evaluate these contributions against the explicit norm of an ideal, or optimal, Louisiana economy.

Financial Theories of Economic Fluctuations

One of the easiest ways to see the need for an explicit theoretical discussion of the relationship between finance and the real economy in Louisiana is to review the opinions offered by contemporary observers and by most historians. According to these writers, the state's troubles began long before the panic of 1837, as "overtrading and extravagance" led to a dangerously weak, "speculative" economy. Sometimes this view implies an "overconsumption" theory, with "extravagant" imports causing a deficit in the balance of trade. More often, the "artificial" boom of the 1830's is blamed on "overinvestment" in real estate, slaves, and internal improvements. This investment had been encouraged by financial misdeeds—above all, by the expansion of Louisiana's banking capital to an amount far in excess of the legitimate needs of trade. The bonds sold abroad by the state to raise this capital financed a deficit in the balance of trade (caused by extravagant imports, of course) and merely postponed the day of judgment when that deficit would lead to specie exports. Finally, inflationary expansion of the currency debased sound values, raised prices (even of exports sold in world markets!) and further raised the optimistic expectations of the boom period.[1]

According to the usual historical interpretation, then, the panic and suspension of 1837 were merely the bursting of the bubble, the collapse of an artificially inflated situation. A wide variety of specific factors are cited as immediate causes of this inevitable collapse. Many have simply accepted Nicholas Biddle's self-serving explanation, which blamed Jackson's specie circular and the distribution of the federal surplus. Others have noted foreign causes, such as a decline in the price of cotton, or the credit restrictions initiated by the Bank of England. And still others have pointed to a change in public expectations: "When conservative people, aroused at the overtrading and speculation that prevailed, demanded specie instead of banknotes, the crash came." As suggested by this comment, and indeed by the term "panic" itself, the banks have received much of the blame for the collapse. They had overextended themselves in two ways: by creating an excessive quantity of credit relative to their capital or specie reserves, and by permitting a lower quality of credit in the form of long-term and speculative loans.[2]

Traditional explanations for the depression stage that followed the panic have also emphasized financial causes. The suspension of specie payments has received most of the blame, presumably because the depreciation of inconvertible bank and paper money disrupted and "demoralized" spending and payments. The proper cure, from this standpoint, was a prompt resumption of specie payments, although the depression might continue even after resumption while the economy gradually worked off its burden of debt and default. Some historians have suggested that the prolonged depression had real as well as financial causes. But most often they have simply implied that the boom period had to be matched by a bust while the economy caught up to its overinvestment or while foreigners recovered enough confidence to resume their lending.[3]

Economic analysis would reveal many flaws or gaps in the implicit theories behind these traditional historical explanations. Hughes and Rosenberg have exposed three of the more common deficiencies. The first problem in most cases is that such key terms as "excessive credit," "overspeculation" and "overinvestment" have been implicitly defined in a tautological way. Thus excessive credit, by hindsight, becomes any credit transaction in which the borrower later defaulted, and overspeculation or overinvestment is any future-oriented venture that proved unprofitable. In other times and places, the same practices were "sound." Any cyclical theories built on such definitions are obviously invalid. Another common problem is the tendency of many commentators to rely on strained analogies, such as the law of gravity ("what goes up must come down") or the bursting of a bubble, to explain the upper turning point of the cycle between boom and depression. High or rising investment stimulates income and spending, leading to higher real output and eventually to inflation; it cannot of itself produce a decline in income and output. The third problem is a tendency to overemphasize the panic phase of the cycle, which predisposes historians to explain the fluctuations in purely monetary or financial terms. A complete explanation of economic fluctuations would have to relate any financial changes to variations in some form of demand for real output—consumption, investment, government spending, or net exports—and would explain variations in real output for all phases of the cycle. The argument would have to offer quantitative evidence, with particular attention to the timing of various financial and real changes.[4]

Hughes and Rosenberg follow up their criticisms in an interesting way. Having attacked the purely financial explanations of antebellum fluctuations, they nearly go to the other extreme of adopting a purely real model. Their nearest statement of their own framework is that fluctuations resulted from "justifiable (i.e., initially profitable) expansions blocked by structural maladjustments." But the evidence they assemble seems designed to test a simple Keynesian accelerator-multiplier model. They conclude that changes in the rate of investment in internal improvements (particularly railroads and roads) accentuated upward and downward trends but did not account for the turning points in the antebellum cycle. And they end on a questioning note. "Where, precisely, did the variations in aggregate demand originate in the

American economy? Where were the origins of the American Cycle? The answer remains clouded in obscurity."[5]

Fortunately, recent economic theory has ended its fixation on models in which self-generating business cycles are derived from accelerator-multiplier interactions. These "first-generation" Keynesian models have been replaced by models that contain several interacting economic sectors and allow for the influence of exogenous "shocks" on the system. For our purposes the most useful extension has been the recognition of the financial sector either as a source of exogenous shocks or an integral part of the total economy. To maintain continuity with the theoretical framework of the previous chapter, I will pursue this point in terms of the Friedman, central-banking, and financial-intermediary models.

Friedman's sophisticated quantity theory certainly makes money an important variable in the economic system; in fact, it gives money the primary role in explaining fluctuations of aggregate spending in the real economy. As noted earlier, this model also offers a useful classification system to account for the changes in the quantity of money. But it has a major drawback for both historical and policy applications: by positing a direct causal connection between money supply and total spending (or money income), it bypasses all the important economic processes through which the financial and real sectors interact. Friedman offers no explicit discussion of the varying demand for money, interest rates, allocation of credit, monetary effects on particular types of spending (investment versus consumption, etc.), or the dynamics of these and other factors. All such matters must appear as *obiter dicta*, filling out what would otherwise be a very flimsy skeleton of theory and statistical evidence.[6]

The central-banking theory is not as explicit or useful as Friedman's model for explaining variations in the money supply in a world without central banks; but it is far more applicable to the relationship between money and the real economy. Suppose there has been a contraction of the money supply, leading to higher interest rates and a tighter rationing of bank credit. Through competition and arbitrage these tight credit conditions are spread throughout the economy, though some sectors are usually squeezed harder than others. Potential borrowers have to reduce their spending on investment or consumption (or government purchases); and these initial reductions of spending (and income) are magnified by negative multiplier effects as reduced incomes steadily force reduced consumption and corresponding reductions in income and output throughout the economy. Negative accelerator effects may also reinforce the decline, since the slowdown in consumer-goods output causes cutbacks in investment spending. The process works equally well in reverse, and an expansion of the money supply will lead to an expansion of total spending, income, and output.* This basic model can be expanded to take account of foreign trade and finance. With an economy on fixed exchange rates (as it would be under a specie standard) a persistent deficit in the balance of payments will restrict domestic spending as the loss of specie reserves to foreigners forces domestic contraction. Tight money and credit would tend to alleviate the deficit because high interest rates would attract foreign capital. Alternatively, the restriction on spending can be eliminated by changing from fixed to fluctuating exchange rates (for example, by suspending specie payments).

Two major limitations of the central banking model, however, restrict its application to financial and economic fluctuations in antebellum Louisiana. First, it is essentially static, indicating the equilibrium tendency of an economy rather than describing a state of dynamic disequilibrium. Yet the financial system of the nineteenth century often acted on the real economy through just such dynamically unstable situations—the traditional booms and panics. Second, the central banking theory is a "flow" model in which the financial sector affects the real sector by acting directly on income and spending flows. The model makes no provision for the indirect impact of the financial sector through changes in the value of real capital, financial assets, and debts, all of which react on spending.

The financial intermediary theory provides a useful complement to the central banking theory. Whereas the latter seems best suited to explain the relation between financial and real sectors during

* This brief exposition of a linear causal sequence omits the two-way interaction and feedback between the financial and real sectors that is depicted in the Hicksian IS-LM model. It also omits such esoterica as the impact of monetarily induced price changes on the real sector via Pigou or "real balance" effects (see p. 169).

times of stability or gradual change, the former focuses more on the period of dynamic instability. The work of Minsky and of James Duesenberry will be used to illustrate this third approach.

Minsky explicitly designed his model to explain major depressions rather than smaller and more frequent "business cycle" fluctuations. He argues that severe depressions arise from a major financial crisis, which ordinarily can only occur after a "long swing" expansion (perhaps encompassing several minor cycles). During sustained expansion, Minsky's three key variables—the debt/income ratio, the prices of real estate and stocks, and the ultimate liquidity/income ratio—all increase in such fashion as to increase the instability of the real economy in response to any exogenous shock. A higher debt/income ratio increases the risk that even a slight decline in income will force some borrowers to default on their debts. If their creditors have similarly high obligations, a spiral of defaulted debts may begin, forcing many people to reduce their spending. And if some of the defaulters are financial intermediaries, as is likely, their insolvency will destroy many liquid assets (bank deposits, savings accounts, etc.), forcing still sharper reductions in spending. A decline in income is also likely to halt and reverse the speculative rise in real estate and stock prices, which had been based on expectations of sustained growth. This capital loss, by reducing the net worth of owners (i.e., assets minus liabilities), may induce further defaults and reductions in spending. Finally, the proportion of ultimately liquid assets (those immune from capital loss or default) sets a lower limit on the collapse of asset values. The smaller the base of ultimate liquidity relative to income, the more severe a financial and economic crisis will be.

Duesenberry, whose model of economic fluctuations has many characteristics in common with Minsky's, suggests that the nineteenth-century economy had a basically stable equilibrium growth path, from which it was frequently displaced by exogenous shocks.* Variations in the financial sector could provide such

---

* By making the financial sector endogenous (responsive to income changes), with its systematic tendency to instability, Minsky has at least shifted the emphasis from a stable model subject to occasional shocks toward an inherently unstable model. Yet the mechanisms of his and Duesenberry's models are nearly identical.

shocks through sudden shifts to tight money and credit, or through financial crisis. Duesenberry also clarifies the adverse financial and economic effects of price deflation, an important phenomenon in the highly competitive and open nineteenth-century economy. Since deflation raises the real value (that is, purchasing power) of both assets and debts, the private sector as a whole will be wealthier after deflation. According to the usual argument of neoclassical economics (the "real balance" effect), this new wealth would permit an increase in spending and income. Duesenberry challenges this assumption. The enhanced value of assets, he says, is likely to produce only small and gradual increases in spending and income. But the increased real value of debts is likely to produce much more striking reductions in the same variables because of bankruptcies and insolvency among financial intermediaries. Thus price deflation may make the private sector wealthier in real terms, but it is still likely to reduce total spending and income.[7]

Financial Aspects of Economic Fluctuations in Louisiana

The first prerequisite for any complete application of an economic theory is the availability of quantitative evidence. For antebellum Louisiana, the data are insufficient to permit any rigorous analysis. But they are sufficient to contribute to a less rigorous, historical "explanation," and to raise some disturbing questions. In Appendix B, I have assembled figures on Louisiana's money and real income from 1823-24 to the Civil War (see Table B.4). The "great depression" of 1837-42 is barely visible, except for a 22 per cent decline in money income during 1841-42; and the "panic" of 1857 was accompanied by a strong rise in both money and real income. By contrast, declines of over 20 per cent in money income appear in 1831, 1835, and 1841, years not usually associated with financial crises. In addition, the familiar major panics and crises show up far more clearly in the declining prices of cotton, sugar, and other commodities than in the variations of commodity output—the opposite of what one would expect in a modern model of depressions.

These strange statistics obviously require explanation. First, my data apply almost exclusively to agriculture and trade in agricultural products. Hence they cannot reveal any depression that was concentrated in other sectors of the economy, such as investment or retail trade. This prominence of the agricultural sector in the data also accounts for the declining income in noncrisis years, since other evidence suggests that these were years of poor cotton or sugar crops caused by floods and other disasters. Second, even stable income figures disguise some important changes. For example, a very pronounced drop in cotton prices during the crisis of 1837-43 was offset by unusually large crops; but planters certainly viewed this price decline as the portent of a depressed market and lower incomes in the future.[8]

The planters had reason to worry about falling prices. The Southern economy, depending as it did on slave labor, responded differently to short-term depression in demand than the free-labor economy of Northern manufacturing. In the South labor was a fixed expense, and excess field hands could not be "laid off" to reduce output.* The planter would only "shut down his plant" when market prices for cotton fell so far that he could not even cover the relatively small variable costs of harvesting his crop. For this reason, a depression in Louisiana agriculture resulted in severe price declines rather than reduced output and "Keynesian" unemployment. In fact, given a series of good harvest yields, total output could (and did) actually increase during a depression, forcing prices even lower.[9]

Fortunately, the Louisiana income data can be supplemented by qualitative evidence and fragmentary statistics. From these, it is clear that the financial crisis of 1837-42 was quite genuine, and that it had significant effects on the real economy in Louisiana, just as the theories we have discussed would predict.

The initial exogenous shock that triggered the downward spiral in 1837 is impossible to identify with any certainty. In my judgment Peter Temin has made the best case for a foreign disturbance: the declining cotton prices and restriction of credit in Great Britain, which resulted from a foreign-exchange deficit caused mainly by a succession of poor British grain harvests.[10] But we must keep in mind that the precise, immediate shock was quite unimportant in itself. The unstable dynamic response of the Amer-

* There were some alternative uses for slave labor, such as the rental of slaves to others; but these were strictly limited, especially when there was a generally depressed demand for labor.

ican economy, and particularly of its financial sector, would probably have magnified any initial disturbance into a prolonged and
severe decline.

The available historical evidence, carefully considered, does
reveal the kind of downward spiral in the financial and real economy that the Minsky and Duesenberry models have led us to expect. Newspapers and other primary sources testify to the occur-
rence of a debt-default spiral among Louisiana's merchants, planters, and bankers, the collapse of one rendering the next insolvent
and leading to further defaults. We have similar evidence of a
collapse of speculation, and of sharp price reductions in real estate
and stocks. Tightened credit shows up partly as a rise in open-
market interest rates (on good collateral) to 24-36 per cent annually, and partly as a parsimonious rationing of bank credit. The
money supply (or rather, its bank-money component) also contracted sharply, although most of this decline occurred in the later
stages of the crisis (which does not fit Friedman's theory that
changes in the money supply initiate changes in the real economy).
The money supply fell by 58 per cent between October 1836 and
October 1839; it then recovered to 80 per cent of its volume, but
fell by another 80 per cent between April 1841 and June 1842.[11]

The bulk of contemporary testimony confirms that this disruption of the financial system led to a depression in the real
economy. In March 1837, even before suspension, *Price Current*
remarked: "The present very critical state of money affairs has
cast a gloom over everything, and almost paralyzed commercial
operations. In general, people seem more desirous of curtailing
their business than of contracting further responsibilities in any
shape, recent months having made them distrustful of the future."
And on February 19, 1842, during a sharp decline: "Business in
all its branches continues to be seriously affected by the great
scarcity and the unsettled state of the currency question." These
comments do not really reveal the full range of the financial crises,
since they concentrate on the commercial sector. The correspondence of a Natchez banker provides further details that undoubtedly applied to New Orleans as well:

With cash, negroes and plantations and city property can be purchased
50 per cent cheaper than last fall. Some of the new houses that have
been erected last year are offered for less than the cost of building alone.

Nearly all our merchants have ceased to meet their engagements, not being able to make collections, and having large stocks of goods on hand. Mechanics are discharging their hands because they cannot make collections to pay them. Our commission merchants are in great difficulty and not one of them can get through the season without extraordinary help from the Banks, and the Banks themselves will have great difficulty in sustaining them and themselves. You will say this is a melancholy state of things, and so it is, but it will deter people from making new engagements, and another good crop will remedy the difficulty to a great extent, and I hope things will be permanently improved by it. Provisions are the only things that continue at high prices . . . but the prices must decline—it is inevitable. At Vicksburg they are even worse off than here. No one pretends to pay at all, and property which has been selling at New York prices cannot now be sold at all.[12]

The most severe economic impacts obviously came during the initial period of sharp contraction prior to suspension and in 1842 just prior to resumption. The economy was not equally depressed during the intervening five years, as shown by the income statistics in Appendix B. Nor did the depression strike the various industries with equal severity. Cotton and sugar were produced and sold as usual, and in even greater quantity, although they brought less income to the planters, merchants, and tradesmen. With the conclusion of the boom in urban and plantation real estate, related investment activities undoubtedly suffered sharp declines; these included construction, the draining and clearing of land, and the activities of the foundries and machine shops (the "mechanics" in the Natchez letter) who manufactured and repaired heavy plantation equipment such as sugar refining machinery. Finally, a general decline in incomes and liquidity certainly imposed harsh depression on wholesale and retail trade. Shopkeepers who had to cope with depreciated money and delinquent debtors were often less than eager to sell on credit to those customers who were still willing to buy.[18]

By contrast, the available data show that the brief panic of 1857 had a limited economic impact in Louisiana. The severe financial crisis in New York (September-October) forced the banks of that city to curtail their normal purchases of bills of exchange from Southern merchants and bankers. With their Northern credits cut off, the Southerners in turn were unable to finance cotton purchases. The price of cotton in New Orleans dropped sharply, and the market was virtually shut down for a month or two; but by early 1858 finances and the cotton market had both returned to normal. The crisis did contribute to the failure of 58 New Orleans merchant firms in late 1857, and of 45 others in 1858; but these were nothing when compared to the 1,321 failures in New York or the 376 in Boston. True, even a few mercantile failures put pressure on the liquidity of the New Orleans banks. But the banks had sufficient reserves to sustain themselves; and since they took advantage of temporary suspension and cooperative action to entrench themselves more deeply, the spiral of default and contraction was broken.[14]

The temporary depression of the cotton market in 1857 was quite damaging to the income of Louisiana's planters. And some historians have exaggerated the loss by accepting at face value the testimony of angry Southerners who used the crisis of 1857 to justify their advocacy of Southern commercial and financial "independence" from New York. When Senator J. H. Hammond of South Carolina claimed that the panic had cost Southern planters $35 million, he implicitly assumed that without the panic the South's entire cotton crop would have sold at the September prices of 16 cents or more per pound. But these early-season prices had reflected erroneous expectations of a small crop: the 1857-58 crop was actually 5 per cent greater than the year before, and in Louisiana it increased by 17 per cent. A more reasonable counterfactual hypothesis might be that without the panic cotton prices would have averaged the same as in the previous season (12.4 cents, versus the actual average of 11.2 cents in 1857-58). This assumption would imply a loss of about 10 per cent of the year's crop—$17 million for the South as a whole and about $2 million for Louisiana.[15]

From the theoretical and historical analysis in this and the preceding chapter, we can conclude that the financial system did play a causative role in major fluctuations in the real economy of antebellum Louisiana, most notably during the crisis of 1837-42. The inflationary expansion of the money supply during the 1830's was not simply a mechanical result of the rapid chartering of new banks or of "wildcat" bank lending. Instead, the foreign sale of bank stocks merged with broader economic currents to enlarge the supply of specie reserves in Louisiana; meanwhile, the public and the banks were willing to accept lower reserve ratios, enlarging the money supply even further. The expectations of continued growth (or inflation) encouraged speculative rises in the prices of stocks and real estate. And the long period of continued expansion raised debt/income ratios to a high level. The expansion of all these financial variables left the system unusually vulnerable to a shock from abroad.

Once the panic struck, Louisiana suffered a dynamic downward spiral of money and credit. Suspension of specie payments brought some temporary relief, but the failure of the weaker banks and the scramble for liquidity and specie nevertheless imposed many hardships: monetary contraction, price deflation, rising debt burdens, and probably some (Keynesian) reductions in income or employment in certain sectors of the economy. The Bank Act of 1842 brought an end to suspension, purged the banking system, and imposed a rigid set of rules that both reflected and aggravated the conflict between sound money and easy credit. Contrary to prevailing opinion, these rules could not and did not singlehandedly prevent any future financial crisis. The panic of 1857 was indeed shorter and milder than the crisis of 1837-42; but this time the external shock had come in the slack season, and it fell on an economy and financial system that had not experienced the strains generated by several preceding years of rapid expansion.

The Optimal Structure of the Louisiana Economy

We have seen that Louisiana's banking system allocated the great bulk of its credit to market-oriented agriculture (mainly cotton and sugar plantations), to New Orleans trade and commerce, and to internal improvements (mainly for New Orleans). Very little bank credit went to diversified and subsistence farming, or to manufacturing. The remainder of this chapter will consider whether this pattern of financial allocation encouraged an efficient use of the state's resources—that is, whether it followed the "optimum" path of economic development for the Louisiana economy.

In much of the literature on economic development it is taken as a first principle that development means industrialization. Historians have accepted this conception of economic progress for a century in their debates over "industrial revolution."* Economists may substitute terms like "big push," "take-off," or "linkages," but they still imply clearly that to develop is to industrialize. The severe problems of modern "underdeveloped" countries that depend heavily on a few agricultural exports for their incomes have reinforced this presumption. However, the actual history of economic development is not all one-sided on the question of industrialization. Economists are increasingly emphasizing, for example, that measures to improve the efficiency and productivity of agriculture are as important as the development of new industries. In the highly developed nations some regions have specialized in agriculture. And a few nations have "developed" (that is, reached high levels of per capita income) and yet remain substantially agricultural: Denmark, New Zealand, Canada, or even the United States in the nineteenth century.

A broader criterion for economic development encompasses both industry and agriculture: the principle of specialization and "division of labor" through access to larger markets. A region, or even a nation in a freely trading world market, prospers and develops by concentrating on those activities in which it has a "comparative advantage," whether manufacturing, agriculture, commerce, finance, or some combination of these. In the context of economic development, "comparative advantage" is not a static condition, and a region may alter its pattern of specialization in response to long-run shifts in its dynamic comparative advantage. Shifts of this kind could arise from many changes relative to conditions in other regions: changes in the cost of land, labor, and capital; in transportation, technology, and labor productivity; or in the pattern of domestic and foreign demand for different commodities.

Many historians have criticized the South, and Louisiana in particular, for their lack of economic "diversification." But diversification can take many forms. Perhaps the simplest diversification is the initiation of new industries or activities that have become

---

* Several historians have emphasized the harshness of the industrial revolution, and especially the sacrifices allegedly imposed on the working classes. But even these critics have accepted the "necessity" of industrialization, merely arguing that "progress" might have been accomplished less painfully by other means than laissez faire capitalism.

profitable as a result of changes in factor costs, technology, or demand. This form is essentially the pursuit of a dynamic comparative advantage, as discussed above. Examples might be the development of a Southern textile or iron industry, or of mechanized cotton-picking.* Another form of diversification represents a compromise with the pursuit of dynamic comparative advantage. Broadly speaking, productivity and incomes are increased as an economy moves away from the primitive diversification of self-sufficiency and limited markets toward specialization and larger markets. Under such conditions, diversification can easily mean partially sacrificing the most profitable and productive activity in favor of a less productive alternative. However, such a course might be chosen in order to reduce the economic risks associated with the most profitable activity. Southern planters who reduced cotton or sugar production in order to become more self-sufficient in foodstuffs or other supplies probably made this compromise with comparative advantage.†

Clearly, we cannot say that any and every form of industrialization or diversification would have represented progress in antebellum Louisiana. A further distinction in perspectives is necessary. First, we must evaluate the economic structure from the perspective of a decision-maker within the antebellum economy, whether an actual historical participant or a hypothetical "rational" economic planner. From this decision-maker's perspective, many things must be taken as given: slavery; the Southern political and social structure; Southern culture; the supply of capital, resources, skills, and technology; and so on. Economic decisions in antebellum Louisiana were made within this matrix of given conditions, perhaps changing some of them in marginal ways. After this analysis is made, we can evaluate the economic structure from the broader perspective of the total society, with the

---

* By mentioning these examples of modern Southern industries, I do not mean to imply any judgment about their potential place in the antebellum economy. Their profitability in 1960, or even in 1870, does not prove that they should have been initiated before 1860.

† The current intensive research on the antebellum plantation economy leaves this question in some doubt. Planters produced more of their own food than we had previously suspected, but we know too little to estimate the quantity of potential cotton or sugar that was sacrificed in producing food. See Gallman, "Self-Sufficiency in the Cotton Economy of the Antebellum South."

advantages of historical and economic hindsight. We may then contemplate altering some of the conditions that Louisianans took as given. We might ask, for example, whether the South would have developed more effectively without slavery. Because of its greater range of assumptions, this second inquiry is a more difficult type of counterfactual history than an evaluation of decisions by individuals or groups, and it requires correspondingly more ambitious and more self-conscious theories.[16] Fortunately, it is not as important in evaluating the performance of the banking and financial community, which is our purpose.

We turn first to the narrower question: Did the bankers and other Louisiana entrepreneurs fail to pursue the best opportunities for the economic development of their society that existed within their inherited legal and institutional structure? Notice that we are asking not merely whether they maximized their own private profits and income, but whether they maximized the income of their entire society.

In recent years historians have sharply criticized the "backward" and "stagnant" economy of the antebellum South, implicitly assuming that the South should have industrialized, or at least should have diversified beyond its cash-crop agriculture and specialized commerce. Eugene Genovese, who has presented the most elaborate and persuasive argument, claims that the South lacked "an adequate rate of material growth," that it did not keep up with the North in population, manufacturing, transportation, urbanization, or even agricultural development. The basic cause of this stagnation was slavery—not merely as a system of labor, but as the determinant of a unique class structure and culture. The "dominant slaveholding class" could only preserve its own power, prestige, and prosperity by opposing all efforts toward "modernization" of the economy and the society. Even the slaveholders' own plantation agriculture revealed this in the low productivity of its labor, in its soil exhaustion, and in its lack of crop diversification or agricultural reform.[17]

There is abundant evidence to contradict Genovese's assertion that slaveholding planters dominated the Louisiana economy and kept other economic interests strictly subservient to the plantation economy. The planters themselves repeatedly complained that merchants and bankers exerted "monopoly" power and restricted

the planters' access to credit. Rural political initiatives to overcome this disadvantage through property banks or branch banks
met with limited success. The slaveholders, then, could not dictate
the course of Louisiana's economic development. However, the
conflicts between planters and merchants and bankers did not pre-
clude a larger community of interest in the prosperity of the commercial and agricultural economy that they built and dominated
together.

One cannot simply assume a priori, as Genovese and others
commonly do, that the South, and Louisiana in particular, should
have been substantially more industrialized by 1860. It is at least
conceivable that heavy investments in slaves, plantations, and
New Orleans commerce were in fact a rational pursuit of the
state's comparative advantage. This presumption is strengthened
if we acknowledge that Louisiana's planters and merchants earned
substantial profits on their investments; and the best available evidence suggests that they did. Conrad and Meyer have found that
the production of cotton with slave labor was profitable for the
great majority of planters, and especially so for those in the recently settled and more fertile lands toward the Mississippi.[18] The
behavior of Louisiana planters, who persisted in expanding their
holdings, tends to confirm this; and contemporary newspapers
and documents consistently affirm the profitability of producing
both sugar and cotton by plantation slavery. Richard Easterlin
estimates Louisiana's agricultural income per worker in 1840 (including slaves as workers) at $251, third highest in the nation; its
nonagricultural income per worker in the same year was $913,
highest in the nation.[19]

Proving that plantation agriculture and commerce were highly
profitable to planters and merchants does not prove that they
brought prosperity to the whole society. But even here the preliminary indications are positive: Easterlin's statistics indicate that
Louisiana's per capita income (including slaves) was about 44 per
cent above the national average in 1840 (second in the nation) and
15 per cent above the national average in 1860. But per capita incomes are obviously misleading where the income distribution is
grossly unequal, as it was in the South. The slaves obviously did
not share in the "average" prosperity, and the share going to
small farmers, urban workers, and other classes is similarly un-

certain. If any classes were poor (relative to their counterparts in free states), however, it was not because of the unproductivity of their state's economy but because of the way the system (including the tax structure) distributed income.[20]

Although Louisiana's economy was clearly not "backward" in the profitability of its investments or the level of its income, it was apparently "stagnant." In 1840-60, while the national economy raised its per capita income by 33 per cent, Louisiana's rose by only 6.5 per cent. This estimate (from Easterlin) is roughly confirmed by the specific statistics of sugar, cotton, and New Orleans commerce. Contemporary observers noticed the disparity, and many accused their fellow Louisianans of complacency and lack of enterprise. Men like J. D. B. DeBow (editor of *DeBow's Review*) advocated greater investment in manufacturing, particularly in New Orleans but possibly also in cotton mills or sugar refineries scattered around the state. Several historians have echoed these accusations of complacency and accepted the prescription of industrialization. But neither they nor their sources offer any real evidence that expanded manufacturing would actually have been more profitable for antebellum Louisiana than its existing use of resources.[21]

It is clear that Louisiana's decision-makers were not absolutely unsympathetic toward manufacturing, for they did establish local manufacturing and utilize industrial technology where it was profitable within the framework of their predominantly agricultural-commercial economy.* Let us develop one example at length. In 1838 (the only year for which complete data exist) Louisiana led the entire nation in the industrial use of steam engine power. Over half of this was used by sugar planters in refining raw sugar, with the remainder mainly in steam-powered cotton presses (mostly in New Orleans) and saw mills. The steam engines for these operations were not manufactured in Louisiana but were imported from England (or later, and less expensively, from West-

---

* The bulk of the manufacturing was concentrated in the New Orleans area. Among the leading industrial products (as measured by capital invested) were bricks, lumber, ships, furniture, clothing, shoes, flour, and bread; by 1860 metals, machinery, and cotton goods were important. Census data show a total capital in manufacturing of $6.4 million in 1840, $5 million in 1850, and $7.2 million in 1860; but the categories and coverage are not consistent. *USBC*: [1], pp. 241-49; [2], III, 196-204. *USC*, [42].

ern cities). This practice was probably consistent with Louisiana's comparative advantage at the time: it cost her less to buy the engines with her export earnings than to build them. By the 1840's, however, a growing demand for the repair and replacement of machines already in use helped stimulate the growth of a substantial foundry and machine-shop business in New Orleans. And once established, the new shops found additional business opportunities, such as the repair of steam boats operating in the port of New Orleans, or the construction of equipment for other local industries.[22]

The accusation of complacency was also directed against Louisiana entrepreneurs because they failed to develop an adequate transportation system; and again, some historians have echoed the contemporary critics. It would seem that a prevailing belief in the inevitable supremacy of Mississippi river transport did sometimes restrain popular enthusiasm for railroad construction. And Genovese argues that the planters actively opposed railroads, fearing that small farmers in the interior would acquire greater economic and political power when they reached new markets.* However, Merl Reed's comprehensive study of railroad development in antebellum Louisiana leaves the strong impression that there was if anything an excess of railroad enterprise, leading to the construction (or attempted construction) of many totally uneconomical lines. In 1842-52, when railroad enterprise was apparently lacking, there was also no complacent indifference to railroads; but the Bank Act of 1842 and the Constitution of 1845 had severely restricted banking, government subsidy of improvements, and the chartering of new corporations.[23]

Our discussion seems to justify the general conclusion that Louisiana bankers, planters, merchants, and other entrepreneurs made fairly rational private and political economic decisions within the context of their resources and economic structure. Their emphasis on market-oriented plantation agriculture and New Orleans

---

* Genovese, pp. 25, 164-65 (Genovese contradicts himself on p. 184). In fact planters were no more united on the railroad question than other classes. Those who had good access to water transport showed little enthusiasm for railroads; those who were not so well located, such as the wealthy planters of the Feliciana parishes in Louisiana, strongly supported railroads for their own area and opposed or ignored those located elsewhere. See Reed, *New Orleans and the Railroads*, Chapters 4 and 8.

commerce followed the state's comparative advantage. Manufacturing, transportation, and similar activities were often pursued vigorously and profitably where they complemented or strengthened the prevailing agriculture and commerce.

Stanley Engerman has vigorously upheld the economic rationality of the antebellum Southern entrepreneurs who defended their economy of cotton, commerce, and plantation slavery. He suggests that they could easily have responded to any subsequent changes in their comparative advantage—by developing textiles or other industries, by expanding railroads, or by increasing expenditures on education. But these changes could quite properly wait until diversification became socially profitable.[24]

Engerman's argument is implicitly based on a neoclassical comparative-static model in which relative prices and costs adjust smoothly and continuously over time, and in which future economic conditions are not influenced by past conditions except through market forces. These special assumptions are not always fulfilled, which raises the possibility that some types of "premature" diversification would be rational. Today's educational expenditures will help to determine tomorrow's labor skills, and even tomorrow's supply of teachers and demand for education. Today's technology and investment in research set limits on tomorrow's technological alternatives. And today's urbanization influences tomorrow's concentrations of industry and commerce. Thus Douglass North has validly criticized the antebellum Southern economy for underinvesting in education and urban development; that kind of diversification could not "wait."[25]

A consideration of technology, education, and urbanization moves us beyond the perspective of the individual decision-maker and toward the broader evaluation of Louisiana's economic structure. Genovese has also offered one of the most comprehensive critiques of the Southern economy from this perspective. He specifically criticizes the historians and "bourgeois economists" who take an existing economic structure as given and judge the rationality of private or governmental resource allocation within that context. An economic system is interdependent. In Louisiana, for example, the cash-crop export economy limited the demand for domestic industry, which limited urbanization and transportation change, which limited the diversification of agriculture, and so on.

Piecemeal changes in such a system may have very limited potential, and even a series of individually "rational" decisions will perpetuate a stagnant economy. Genovese's response is to consider not piecemeal adjustment but global change—thoroughgoing revolution. Comparing the antebellum South as it actually was to a hypothetical South (slaveless, industrialized, urbanized, and with a different class structure) clearly reveals the stagnation and "internal contradictions" of Southern society.

Genovese's approach makes fine retrospective prophecy and gives a useful perspective on the total pattern of Southern development. But it is much less relevant to the historical evaluation of more limited and partial changes within the Southern economy. Although all things are potentially variable for the culture as a whole, many things are perforce "given" for the individual participant. Individual businessmen, planters, or politicians, caught in the web of conditions that the culture imposed, could hardly contemplate or implement Genovese's revolutionary alternative. Specifically, Louisiana's decisions on the allocation of finance were made in the context of a predominantly agricultural and commercial economy. From this limited perspective, diversification toward manufacturing before 1860 offered a very limited prospect of greater social returns; in fact, it would probably have lowered the productivity and living standards of Louisiana citizens. The actual benefit of greater railroad investment was at least doubtful. On the other hand, the long-run returns to investment in education, town development, and technology (agricultural as well as industrial) were probably underestimated.

As prophets or planners of their total economy, Louisiana's financiers failed, for they undertook no economic revolutions. But in their more human roles as entrepreneurs of limited vision and power, facing the constraints of an existing economic and social structure, they chose reasonably well. It seems unlikely that the slight preferences exercised by Louisiana banks for lending to New Orleans trade, internal improvements, and commercial agriculture took the economy far off its optimum development path.

Appendixes

Money and Banking Transactions

BANKING HISTORIANS have been very ready to project modern monetary theories into the past, and have often gained sharpened insights into past banking practices by doing so. But the projection has been misleading when modern institutional and behavioral assumptions fail to fit past reality. In this case, the composition of the money supply in the antebellum economy requires us to alter our model of bank lending and money creation. This appendix will compare certain structural characteristics of modern and antebellum banking: composition of the money supply, lending procedures, reserve assets, and reserve ratios. I will then review the basic transactions occurring within these structural frameworks (or models). Finally, I will suggest some limitations and modifications of the models, and some historical lessons to be learned from them.

Composition of the Money Supply. Today's money supply has two categories: demand deposits, which are liabilities of the commercial banks; and paper currency and token coins, which are liabilities of the government. In the antebellum money supply, demand deposits and banknote currency were the liabilities of the commercial banks; the rest of the money supply was specie, which was sometimes a government liability (when minted into coins) and sometimes a commodity (as bullion). It will instantly be recognized that we are here comparing two historical models, not two literal historical realities. For the sake of convenience and clarity, I have "consolidated" the Federal Reserve and the Treasury, treating all modern currency as government issue. Similarly, I have ignored parts of the real antebellum money supply, such as treasury notes, private and municipal notes, and the existence of token coins as well as full-bodied coins and bullion. Bimetallism also contributes little to the analysis, since we are not concerned with the exact composition of the "specie" supply.

The most fundamental difference between modern and antebellum money supplies is the status of paper currency. Modern currency is a liability of the government, that is, a "rival" of bank liabilities (deposits). Antebellum currency was a bank liability, and from the banker's viewpoint a close substitute for bank deposits. This circumstance has obvious effects on the nature of bank transactions that have not been adequately considered by economic historians. We must recognize that antebellum banknote currency was not homogeneous, as modern paper currency is in practice. The notes of one bank were not the same as those of another, even when both were nominally redeemable in specie. For our purposes, the importance of this characteristic is that a banker distingiushed between his own banknotes and the notes of other banks. I will specifically assume that he considered the notes of other banks as a sort of secondary specie reserve, since they could (he thought) be converted into specie on demand.

Bank Lending. Today's bankers "finance" a loan (i.e., any purchase of an earning asset) by creating a liability in the form of a demand deposit for the borrower. The antebellum banker had a wider range of choices, owing to the different money supply with which he dealt: he could create a demand deposit liability; he could issue banknote liabilities; he could pay out the notes of other banks to his customers; or he could pay out specie. Banking historians have gone to great lengths to reveal loan-created deposits where contemporaries sometimes did not recognize them. But they have paid too little attention to the other forms of loan financing, which are not rational within the modern banking model. In particular, the antebellum custom of issuing banknote currency for loans simultaneously expanded money and credit, and also had implications for the nature of bank deposits.

Reserve Assets and Reserve Ratios. The volume of credit or money (notes and demand deposits) created by banks can be effectively limited by the existence of some specified reserve asset and a reserve ratio relating that asset to the monetary liabilities created. If $A =$ the volume of specified reserve assets in existence, and $M =$ the monetary liability, then by defining a minimum reserve ratio ($R = A/M$) we can determine the maximum amount of monetary liability ($M = A/R$). With fractional reserves, changes in the volume of reserves will allow magnified changes in the maximum volume of monetary liabilities. For example, if the reserve ratio were 20 per cent, an additional $1 million of reserves would permit the banks to create an additional $5 million of money in the form of demand deposits or notes.

Modern reserve assets include the deposits of the commercial banks with the Federal Reserve and the currency or coin held as "vault cash"; all are liabilities of the government. The modern reserve ratio is fixed by a legally authorized government agency, the Federal Reserve. Through its open market operations in government bonds, the Federal Reserve can also create or destroy bank reserves, thus controlling the total supply available to the banks. Modern reserve controls exist so that the government may control the supply of money and credit according to its macroeconomic policy; their purpose is certainly not to guarantee the convertibility of bank deposits into other types of money.

The ultimate antebellum reserve asset was specie—that is, gold or silver in both coins and bullion. But in periods of financial "normalcy" certain other assets were often counted as "specie funds": the notes of specie-paying banks, interbank deposits, and even bills of exchange approaching maturity in the hands of distant banks, which could be expected to generate interbank deposits when repaid. Our attention here will be confined to specie and the notes of specie-paying banks. Antebellum reserve ratios were rarely established by law before 1837, and thereafter the legal ratios usually applied only to banknote liabilities (Louisiana was the prominent exception after 1842); but responsible bankers informally maintained their own reserves behind both notes and deposits. The only function of reserve controls in the antebellum era was to preserve the liquidity of a bank's asset portfolio, to ensure the convertibility of notes or deposits into specie on demand.

Modern reserve assets are subject to a variety of exogenous influences, such as international gold flows, but the Federal Reserve system can take deliberate actions to offset these influences and thus control the total volume of reserves available to the banks. The volume of antebellum reserve assets was not subject to any such control. One major source of change arose from the fact that the reserve asset, specie, was also part of the money supply; any increased public demand for specie, either for use in transactions or for hoarding, deprived the banks of reserves. The second major exogenous factor was the balance of payments, since any deficit threatened to drain specie reserves to foreign countries.

It is common in modern banking theory to recognize that reserve ratios may differ for different banks and for different types of liabilities (time deposits and demand deposits, for example). Such variations were even more prevalent in the antebellum period, since each banker could decide for himself whenever there were no legal ratios. The possibility of different reserve ratios for banknotes and deposits also existed. In order to simplify the discussion, however, I have omitted all these differences in reserve ratios from the following analysis.

The Simple Mechanics of Bank Transactions. From the preceding comparisons of antebellum and modern banking, we can now analyze the set of elementary banking transactions within the antebellum structure. They may be depicted as in Table A.1 considering the funds in-

TABLE A.I

The Set of Basic Bank Transactions

Transaction (A)	Change in assets	Change in liabilities	Complementary transaction (B)[a]
1A. Specie loan	−$100 specie +$100 loan	none	1B. Loan repaid in specie
2A. Loan credited to deposit account	+$100 loan	+$100 deposit	2B. Loan repaid from deposit account
3A. Loan of notes	+$100 loan	+$100 notes	3B. Loan repaid in Bank's own notes
4A. Loan of "specie funds"	−$100 s.f. +$100 loans	none	4B. Loan repaid in specie funds
5A. Deposit of notes	none	+$100 deposits −$100 notes	5B. Depositor withdraws cash in banknotes
6A. Deposit of specie funds	+$100 s.f.	+$100 deposits	6B. Depositor withdraws cash in specie funds
7A. Deposit of specie	+$100 specie	+$100 deposits	7B. Depositor withdraws specie
8A. Issue of notes to purchase specie[b]	+$100 specie	+$100 notes	8B. Bank redeems its own notes in specie
9A. Banks swap note issues[c]	+$100 s.f.	+$100 notes	9B. Banks settle their accumulated notes with each other
10A. Another bank redeems its notes in specie	+$100 specie −$100 s.f.	none	10B. Bank redeems notes of another bank in specie[d]

[a] Assets and Liabilities have the same entries, but with plus and minus signs reversed.
[b] Bank wants to increase its specie reserves and banknote circulation. Customer must find banknote paper more convenient than specie.
[c] Perhaps geographically, to circulate notes at a distance and thus delay their redemption.
[d] It is unlikely that banks did this to any great extent.

volved to be $100 in each case. For every transaction (A), there is an opposite or complementary transaction (B) in which the payments and receipts are reversed.

Four types of money are involved in the ten transactions: demand deposits, the bank's own notes, notes of other banks (listed as "specie funds" in the table), and specie. The first two types are liabilities of the bank whose transactions are examined; the other two are assets to the particular bank but liabilities of somebody else, either another bank or the government (except for specie as a commodity). Each transaction produces particular changes (+ or −) in the assets and liabilities shown on the bank's balance sheet. Transactions 1A-4A are "loan" transactions, where purchases of any earning asset (here simply labeled "loan") are "financed" respectively by a particular type of money. Transactions 5A-10A are "money conversion" transactions, representing each of the six possible pairings of the four types of money, with the bank simply exchanging one type for the other. The complementary transactions portrayed (1B-10B) simply reverse the plus and minus signs in the assets and liabilities.

By comparison, the modern banking system operates more simply. With only two types of money, bank deposits and government currency, a modern banker can perform only three of the ten transactions; and equating modern government currency with antebellum "specie funds," we find that the possibilities are transactions 2, 4, and 6. (If we equate today's government currency with antebellum specie, the possible set is 2, 1, and 7.) Clearly, modern banking theory, with its implicit institutional assumptions, is inadequate to explain antebellum banking. A model of three dimensions cannot explain a world of ten dimensions.

Of the four alternative loan transactions, the antebellum banker ordinarily preferred lending his own notes (3A) or deposits (2A) to depleting his reserves of specie or specie funds (just as a modern banker prefers to give his borrowers deposit balances rather than currency). But if the notes of other banks depreciated, they were often loaned out (4A) in preference to the bank's own more valuable liabilities. On the other hand, the banker preferred to have his customers repay their loans in specie (1B) or in the undepreciated notes of other banks (4B), since he did not want to contract his own liabilities (2B or 3B). All loans augmented the money supply, just as they do today; loans repaid reduced the money supply.

The choice between currency and deposits was largely up to a bank's customers, as it is today; but the monetary significance of the choice was entirely different. The modern customer who switches from deposits to currency is switching from bank money to government money. He creates a "cash drain" of reserves from the banks and forces them to contract credit because of this loss of reserves. The antebellum customer who shifted from deposits to banknote currency (5B) had no such effect, since both were bank liabilities. The same equivalence of banknotes and deposits undermined any meaningful distinction between "loan-created" and "lodged" deposits, a distinction much emphasized in modern theory and in most histories of banking. If a banker made a loan by issuing his own notes (3A), the borrower or a subsequent recipient of the notes might choose to deposit them in the original bank (5A) or in another bank (6A). These were all very common transactions in the antebellum era. Would the deposit of loan-created banknotes then be considered a lodged or a loan-created deposit? This ambiguity has been overlooked by modern theorists because it does not exist in the modern banking system, which has only one type of bank money (deposits). Modern theory is inadequate to describe historical reality.

Through Transactions 6A-9A, a bank could obtain specie or specie funds in exchange for its own liabilities; only a fraction of these new reserves would be required to back the new liabilities, and the remainder was available to back further expansion of money and credit. But observe that a "lodged" deposit of the bank's own notes (5A), unlike a deposit of specie or specie funds, did not create excess reserves. The only other way for the antebellum banking system to expand reserves was to liquidate some of its earning assets (1B, 4B).* The reverse transactions (6B-9B, 1A, 4A) could cause a shortage of reserves, through cash drains or through lending out reserves.

Modern theorists and banking historians have emphasized the danger of "pyramiding" reserves through interbank deposits. An alternative version of pyramiding in the antebellum era has gone virtually unnoticed: the acceptance of notes of other banks as reserve "specie funds." If many banks tried simultaneously to convert these banknote reserves into specie reserves (10-A), they immediately discovered (as with interbank deposits in later years) that there was not enough specie to go around. When the pyramid collapsed, leaving specie as the only acceptable reserve, the banks were forced to either contract their credit severely or suspend specie payments. Suspension, in turn, not only broke the mechanical link between specie and other types of money (Transactions 7, 8, and 10) but also inhibited all the routine mechanisms of exchanging any one type of money for another (Transactions 5, 6, and 9 as well), since the relative values of banknotes or deposits of different banks were unstable. Money completely lost its usual convertibility.

The above comparative models could be expanded in several ways. Time deposits could easily be considered; but these functioned about the same in antebellum days, so little would be gained. A more useful addition to the antebellum model would allow for different reserve ratios behind notes and deposits. But the results would be quite analogous to those observed in the modern system for shifts between city and country banks or between time and demand deposits.

* A modern bank has both monetary reserves (vault cash) and non-monetary reserves (deposits at the Federal Reserve). The Federal Reserve can conduct a great variety of transactions to increase its reserve deposits, but all of them appear to the commercial bank as either the sale of an earning asset or the receipt of a lodged deposit. The bank can also obtain reserves through an inflow of currency from the public. In the antebellum system, all reserves were simultaneously part of the money supply.

APPENDIX B

Estimation of Louisiana Income, 1823–1860

IT IS HIGHLY desirable to have some estimate of aggregate output and income for Louisiana during the antebellum period. Naturally, no such data can be found in the primary sources. We must rely on some type of "synthetic" estimate, based as closely as possible on available and relatively trustworthy evidence.

Recent work by Robert Gallman has provided very careful estimates of U.S. commodity output and gross national product in real terms (adjusted for changing price levels). These estimates begin with 1834 and are based largely on data from the decennial censuses and their manuscript sources.[1] Richard Easterlin has extended Gallman's work to a regional and even state-level breakdown of income per capita, but only for the years 1840 and 1860 of the antebellum period. He estimates Louisiana's per capita income in 1840 at $113. Unfortunately, his data do not give a separate figure for the state in 1860. But he does conclude that the per capita income of the "West South-Central" states (Louisiana and Arkansas) was 144 per cent of the U.S. average in 1840 and 115 per cent of the U.S. average in 1860; and he cites Gallman's evidence to suggest that U.S. real income grew by one-third during the interval. Together, these data imply that Louisiana-Arkansas real income grew by about 6.5 per cent. If we further assume (arbitrarily but not unreasonably) that the two states grew at about the same rate per capita, we can estimate Louisiana income at $120 per capita in 1860 (in 1840 dollars).[2]

I have experimented with the possibility of extending the Gallman-Easterlin approach to derive Louisiana income for other years, particularly 1830 and 1850. This idea has been abandoned for two main reasons. First, the published census materials for other years are not as complete and not comparable with Easterlin's sources. Second, the effort involved in correlating them would still provide only four scattered estimates for the entire antebellum period. The alternative is to construct a less comprehensive aggregate statistic, and I have been able to do so for all the years from 1823-24 to 1859-60. The usefulness of such annual data, especially for the study of short-term economic fluctuations, surely compensates for a less comprehensive coverage. My basic approach is to estimate a major portion of Louisiana aggregate income by summing the value added to production by three of the state's major industries: cotton, sugar, and commercial operations. These estimates are first made in current prices and then deflated with appropriate price indexes to obtain the final "real income" measures. Three different "deflation" procedures have been used, and the results are compared.

Adequacy of Coverage. Reliance on just three "industries" for estimating aggregate state income gives a better coverage than one might expect, since Louisiana concentrated heavily on these activities. It should also be noted that I will take the total value of production for cotton and sugar, making none of the usual deductions for "purchases of intermediate materials" from other industries. Thus I have indirectly included the incomes earned by those who supplied cotton and sugar planters with these intermediate goods or services—food and clothing for slaves or work animals, livestock, farm equipment, annual land maintenance, hired craftsmen, etc. To the extent that these intermediate goods and services were obtained from outside Louisiana I have overestimated the state's income.

A comparison of my results with those of Easterlin (and with his major source, Ezra Seaman) provides a check on the coverage, at least for the year 1840.[3] My estimate of agricultural production (cotton plus sugar) accounts for over 80 per cent of Seaman's estimate for all Louisiana agriculture. My estimated total income of $23 million, including the value added by trade, is about 60 per cent of Easterlin's $40 million estimate.* Of course, I have omitted many activities entirely, such as manufacturing (which Seaman estimated as $2.6 million). The $5 million given for value added by trade and commerce is also far below Seaman's figure of $13.7 million, and is arrived at by a completely different approach. Other significant income-producing activities are omitted from the Easterlin and Seaman calculations, as they are from ours: finance, insurance, real estate, personal and professional services, and goverment. In a modern calculation of aggregate income these would be counted. Of these excluded activities, the government at least was relatively large. Recent estimates of per capita expenditures (by census

---

* Easterlin's figure of $113 per capita, with a population of 352,411 in 1840, gives the total income of $40 million.

regions) for federal, state, and local governments suggest an estimate
of $3.3 million for Louisiana in 1840.[4]

It is clear that my estimate of aggregate income is far from complete.
However, it is sufficiently comprehensive to give a meaningful indication of year-to-year variations and long-run trends in the state's economy. And it is quite likely that the omitted activities, with the partial
exception of government, fluctuated and grew roughly in line with the
three major activities studied here.

The Basic Sector Estimates. The estimates for value of sugar and
cotton production (Tables B.1 and B.2) are fairly straightforward. Data
on Louisiana's production of cotton in bales per year (annually from
1800) were found in Watkins, pp. 190-200. Prices, in cents per pound
(annually from 1802), are from Gray, II, 1027. To connect these data
we need evidence on the average weight of cotton bales, which showed
an upward trend over the years and also varied from one state to another. Gray also states (II, 705) that bales in Louisiana were generally
packed heavier than those in the older cotton states to the east. Lacking data on Louisiana, I have used the national average weight for each
year, computed from production data (beginning 1822-23) found in
Matthew Hammond, I, 357.[5]

Data on Louisiana sugar production (in hogsheads or pounds), sugar
prices in New Orleans, and total value of production were found in
Gray, II, 1033-34. Prior to 1834-35 the value of product was estimated
by using annual average data to approximate seasonal averages and
assuming that the average hogshead of sugar weighed 1,000 pounds.

The statistics for value added by trade and commerce (Table B.3)
were obtained in the most rudimentary way: by taking 10 per cent of
the value of all produce arriving in New Orleans each year.[6] This is
simply an educated guess at the average percentage earned by merchants and shippers, based mainly on evidence about the marketing of
cotton and sugar. Sitterson, in his thorough study of the sugar industry
(*Sugar Country*, p. 191), estimated that freight and marketing costs for
sugar going through New Orleans in the 1840's and 1850's were about
at this level; and similar estimates for cotton marketing are provided
by Gray (II, 715-16) and North (*Economic Growth*, p. 115). Gray arrives
at a figure of about $4 per bale, which would be 10 per cent for a
400-pound bale with cotton prices at ten cents per pound. (See Table
B.1.) As this figure implies, one might wish to estimate trade earnings
from data on the physical volume of trade rather than its dollar value.
Moreover, commercial charges did not always vary with agricultural
prices, as my estimate does. Yet data based on physical volume alone,

such as tonnage of shipping, would be equally misleading, since many commercial charges were based on market values.[7]

Deflation Procedures. Three different estimates of "real" (constant-dollar) income have been computed, using different methods of adjusting for changing prices. Two of these simply involve "deflating" the total value added in current dollars by different price indexes. The third involves a calculation of the real values for each separate sector, before aggregation. A comparison of the three results is provided in Table B.4.

The first method is to adjust the nominal value-added figures with a cost-of-living index. I have used an index (provided by George R. Taylor) listing the New Orleans prices of goods received from other states. This index includes flour, tobacco, pork, whiskey, bacon, and some thirty other common products. It specifically excludes cotton and sugar, Louisiana's two main products, which were sold primarily outside the state; their prices heavily influenced Louisiana's income, but not her cost of living.

The second method is to adjust the nominal income figures with another of Taylor's indexes, this time of wholesale prices for all commodities traded at New Orleans. Cotton and sugar receive heavy weights in this index; the resulting "real" income figures are therefore more suggestive of the trends in Louisiana's productive powers than of the trends in her income or standard of living.

The third method is based on a recent suggestion by Paul David that one might estimate the "real" income contribution of each sector or industry separately by deflating its nominal value-added figures with an index of its own commodity prices (see Tables B.1-B.3). Here, I have

TABLE B.1

Cotton Production

Year	Bales produced	Price per lb.	Year	Bales produced	Price per lb.
1801-02	3,500		1812-13	10,160	
1802-03	5,000	14.7¢	1813-14	15,221	15.5¢
1803-04	4,741	15.0	1814-15	20,021	16.9
1804-05	6,000	19.6	1815-16	35,557	27.3
1805-06	7,000	23.3	1816-17	35,000	25.4
1806-07	4,500	21.8	1817-18	39,212	29.8
1807-08	5,239	16.4	1818-19	52,000	21.5
1808-09	7,800	13.6	1819-20	48,000	14.3
1809-10	8,000	13.6	1820-21	54,500	15.2
1810-11	6,220	14.7	1821-22	69,221	17.4
1811-12	7,135	8.9			

TABLE B.I

Cotton Production (continued)

Year	Bales produced	Weight of bale (lbs.)	Pounds produced (millions)	Price per lb.	Total value ($ millions)	"Real" value ($ millions)[a]
1822-23	55,000	298	16.4	11.5¢	1.88	1.92
1823-24	80,159	282	22.6	14.5	3.28	2.64
1824-25	101,133	287	29.0	17.9	5.20	3.39
1825-26	138,177	312	43.1	11.9	5.13	5.04
1826-27	121,795	331	40.3	9.3	3.75	4.72
1827-28	100,748	334	33.6	9.7	3.26	3.93
1828-29	95,000	341	32.4	9.8	3.18	3.79
1829-30	106,207	339	36.0	8.9	3.20	4.21
1830-31	117,743	341	40.2	8.4	3.37	4.70
1831-32	89,062	360	32.1	9.0	2.89	3.76
1832-33	121,580	350	42.6	10.0	4.26	4.98
1833-34	156,857	363	56.9	11.2	6.38	6.66
1834-35	186,238	367	68.3	15.5	10.59	7.99
1835-36	164,617	372	61.2	15.2	9.31	7.16
1836-37	243,774	378	92.1	13.3	12.26	10.78
1837-38	291,748	378	110.3	9.0	9.93	12.91
1838-39	241,871	383	92.6	12.4	11.49	10.83
1839-40	411,224	383	157.5	7.9	12.44	18.43
1840-41	350,812	393	137.9	9.1	12.55	16.13
1841-42	299,840	396	118.7	7.8	9.26	13.89
1842-43	456,858	408	186.4	5.7	10.62	21.81
1843-44	373,786	412	154.0	7.5	11.55	18.02
1844-45	339,524	414	165.4	5.5	9.10	19.35
1845-46	445,783	411	183.2	6.8	12.46	21.43
1846-47	303,571	431	130.8	9.9	12.95	15.30
1847-48	467,626	417	195.0	7.0	13.65	22.82
1848-49	437,518	436	190.8	5.8	11.06	22.32
1849-50	178,737	429	76.7	10.8	8.28	8.97
1850-51	250,465	416	104.2	11.7	12.19	12.19
1851-52	412,829	428	176.7	7.4	13.08	20.67
1852-53	447,298	438	195.9	9.1	17.83	22.92
1853-54	322,596	433	139.7	8.8	12.29	16.34
1854-55	305,911	434	132.8	8.4	11.15	15.54
1855-56	450,347	444	200.0	9.1	18.20	23.40
1856-57	323,953	465	150.6	12.4	18.68	17.62
1857-58	379,816	466	177.0	11.2	19.82	20.71
1858-59	500,218	471	235.6	11.5	27.09	27.57
1859-60	777,738	468	364.0	10.8	39.31	42.59

SOURCES: See text discussion.

[a] The real value was determined by valuing each year's production at the 1850–51 price of 11.7¢ per pound.

TABLE B.2

Sugar Production

Year	Output (1,000 hogs-heads)	Price per hogshead	Price per lb.[a]	Total value ($ millions)[b]	"Real" value ($ millions)[c]
1823-24	30		7.125¢	2.138	1.80
1824-25	32		6.25	2.000	1.92
1825-26	30		6.375	1.910	1.80
1826-27	32		6.375	2.040	1.92
1827-28	30		6.375	1.910	1.80
1828-29	45		6.375	2.870	2.71
1829-30	71		7.0	4.970	4.25
1830-31	88		5.125	4.510	5.31
1831-32	48		5.5	2.640	2.87
1832-33	70		6.25	4.375	4.21
1833-34	75		5.875	4.410	4.50
1834-35	100	$60	7.25	6.000	6.00
1835-36	30	90	8.625	2.700	1.80
1836-37	70	60	5.5	4.200	4.20
1837-38	65	62.50	6.375	4.063	3.91
1838-39	70	62.50	6.125	4.375	4.21
1839-40	115	50	4.0	5.750	6.93
1840-41	87	55	5.625	4.785	5.20
1841-42	90	40	4.125	3.600	5.40
1842-43	140	42.50	4.5	5.950	8.38
1843-44	100	60	5.75	6.000	6.00
1844-45	200	45	6.875	9.000	12.00
1845-46	186	55	6.375	10.266	11.16
1846-47	140	70	6.75	9.800	8.37
1847-48	240	40	4.25	9.600	14.33
1848-49	220	40	4.75	8.800	13.20
1849-50	248	50	5.25	12.396	14.93
1850-51	211	60	5.875	12.678	12.68
1851-52	238	50	5.125	11.827	14.25
1852-53	322	48	4.375	15.453	19.32
1853-54	449	35	4.25	15.726	27.11
1854-55	347	52	6.125	18.025	20.72
1855-56	231	70	8.875	16.200	13.85
1856-57	73	110	10.25	8.137	4.45
1857-58	280	64	7.125	17.901	16.73
1858-59	362	69	7.125	24.998	21.74
1859-60	222	82	8.125	18.191	13.28

[a] These data are actually given by calendar year, but they are listed with the closest marketing season. Thus the 1824 price is shown for the 1823–24 marketing season.
[b] For the years 1823–24 to 1833–34, I assume that each hogshead weighed 1,000 pounds.
[c] Real value based on the 1850–51 price of 6¢ per pound or $60 per hogshead.

TABLE B.3

Income from Louisiana Commerce
(*in $1,000's*)

Year	Income in current prices	Real income from trade[a]	Year	Income in current prices	Real income from trade
1823-24	1,506	1,320	1842-43	5,378	7,910
1824-25	1,904	1,500	1843-44	6,009	7,610
1825-26	2,045	1,930	1844-45	5,720	8,060
1826-27	2,173	2,390	1845-46	7,719	9,900
1827-28	2,289	2,490	1846-47	9,003	9,580
1828-29	2,076	2,230	1847-48	7,978	10,640
1829-30	2,207	2,570	1848-49	8,199	11,230
1830-31	2,604	3,140	1849-50	9,690	9,890
1831-32	2,181	2,510	1850-51	19,692	19,690
1832-33	2,824	3,040	1851-52	10,805	13,180
1833-34	2,982	2,980	1852-53	13,423	14,750
1834-35	3,757	3,210	1853-54	11,534	12,670
1835-36	3,924	2,970	1854-55	11,711	11,950
1836-37	4,352	3,660	1855-56	14,426	13,360
1837-38	4,563	4,430	1856-57	15,816	11,540
1838-39	4,226	3,460	1857-58	16,716	14,930
1839-40	4,976	5,180	1858-59	17,295	15,870
1840-41	4,982	5,240	1859-60	18,521	17,470
1841-42	4,572	5,440			

[a] Income adjusted with index figures based on the average wholesale price of all commodities sold through New Orleans each year; 1850–51 = 100. Prices obtained from Cole, *Wholesale Commodity Prices*, p. 179. For index figures, see Table B.4, column 5.

adjusted the value of cotton and sugar production with indexes of cotton and sugar prices, and the trade and commerce estimates with Taylor's all-commodity index, each index being expressed in terms of the same base year (1850-51). For the trade and commerce sector this gives the same result as the all-commodity method. For cotton and sugar, it is precisely equivalent to multiplying each year's physical production by the 1850-51 price for that commodity—that is, it completely eliminates any variation in planters' incomes that arose from price variations. This canceling of relative price changes may be reasonable for a closed economy where rising prices to one man are rising costs to another. It seems much less reasonable for an open economy, where changes in the price received for exports are a major source of the variation in real aggregate income. I am therefore somewhat skeptical, in retrospect, of the usefulness of this approach for antebellum Louisiana.[8]

An impressionistic comparison of the three deflated indexes with each

TABLE B.4

Comparison of Deflation Estimates
(all monetary values in $ millions)

Year	Income in current prices	Cost of living estimate		All–commodity estimate		Sum of deflated sector incomes
		Index[a]	Real income	Index[a]	Real income	
1823-24	6.93	91.9	7.54	114	6.08	5.76
1824-25	9.10	95.5	9.53	127	7.17	6.81
1825-26	9.08	94.6	9.60	106	8.57	8.77
1826-27	7.96	88.4	9.00	91	8.75	9.03
1827-28	7.46	86.8	8.59	92	8.11	8.22
1828-29	8.13	95.2	8.54	93	8.74	8.73
1829-30	10.38	83.9	12.37	86	12.07	11.03
1830-31	10.48	87.6	11.96	83	12.63	13.15
1831-32	7.71	92.4	8.34	87	8.86	9.14
1832-33	11.46	94.0	12.19	93	12.32	12.23
1833-34	13.77	97.3	14.15	100	13.77	14.14
1834-35	20.35	109.2	18.64	117	17.39	17.20
1835-36	15.93	126.8	12.56	132	12.07	11.93
1836-37	20.81	124.8	16.67	119	17.49	18.64
1837-38	18.55	116.0	15.99	103	18.01	21.25
1838-39	20.10	143.2	14.04	122	16.48	18.50
1839-40	23.17	116.9	19.82	96	24.14	30.54
1840-41	22.32	104.6	21.34	95	23.49	26.57
1841-42	17.43	90.5	19.26	84	20.75	24.73
1842-43	21.95	73.5	29.86	68	32.28	38.10
1843-44	23.56	75.8	31.08	79	29.82	31.63
1844-45	23.82	79.3	30.04	71	33.55	39.41
1845-46	30.45	83.0	36.69	78	39.04	42.49
1846-47	31.75	90.2	35.20	94	33.78	33.25
1847-48	31.23	85.2	36.25	75	41.64	47.49
1848-49	28.06	86.7	32.36	73	38.44	46.75
1849-50	30.37	95.5	31.80	98	30.99	33.79
1850-51	44.56	100.0	44.56	100	44.56	44.56
1851-52	35.72	91.4	39.08	82	43.56	48.10
1852-53	46.70	101.0	46.24	91	51.32	56.99
1853-54	39.55	113.9	34.72	91	43.46	56.12
1854-55	40.89	131.4	31.12	98	41.72	48.21
1855-56	48.83	128.4	38.03	108	45.21	50.61
1856-57	42.64	142.8	29.86	137	31.12	33.61
1857-58	54.44	114.8	47.42	112	48.61	52.37
1858-59	69.39	113.5	61.14	109	63.66	65.18
1859-60	76.02	113.4	67.04	106	71.72	73.34

SOURCES: The income in current prices and the sum of deflated sector incomes are the totals of the figures given in Tables B.1 to B.3.

[a] For all index figures, 1850–51 = 100.

other, with the original data in current prices, and with other economic time series suggests several things. The three approaches yield broadly similar results—as seen by comparing their peaks and troughs, for example. None of them corresponds very closely with the familiar chronology of national business cycles, nor even with the qualitative evidence on fluctuations in the Louisiana economy. And the growth rate of total income between 1840 and 1860 is over 50 per cent higher than Easterlin's data would imply. Despite these several incongruities I am still inclined to "believe the numbers." For most purposes, the cost of living approach has proved the most useful.

Statistical Data

TABLE C.I

Partial Balance Sheet, for all Chartered Banks of Louisiana
(all assets and liabilities in $ millions)

			Assets		
Date	(1) No. of banks	(2) No. of banks plus branches	(3) Loans and discounts	(4) Stocks held	(5) Due from other banks
Jan. 1820	2				
Jan. 1830	3		6.80		
Jan. 1834	10		29.58	.03	1.66
June 1835	10	41	37.39	.04	2.85
Aug. 1836		45	51.23	.81	3.46
Oct. 1836	14		53.69	.95	4.07
Jan. 1837	16	47	59.27	.19	3.08
July 1837	7		30.65	.51	1.70
Dec. 1837		47	55.59	1.00	1.40
Mar. 1838	16		52.06		1.36
Dec. 1838	16		56.86		.69
Oct. 1839	16	47	49.14		.25
Jan. 1840	16		45.84	2.07	5.49
Dec. 1840	16	47	48.65		1.82
May 1841	16		48.40		2.86
Mar. 1842			23.38		
Apr. 1842			29.77		2.03
May 1842			29.16		1.98
Jan. 1843	6	28	20.42		
Jan. 1844	6	28	16.74		
Dec. 1844	6	28	18.42		
May 1845			20.31		
Apr. 1846	6	28	21.58		
Dec. 1846	6	28	22.58		
Apr. 1847	6	28	23.87		
Dec. 1847	6	28	21.48		
Jan. 1849	6	28	19.17		2.54
Jan. 1850	6	28	18.60		3.88
Dec. 1850	7	29	23.20		2.70
Dec. 1852		29	22.41		1.48
Dec. 1853		29	17.04	5.74	2.44
Dec. 1854		19	29.32	.84	2.42
Dec. 1855		19	27.14	4.19	3.15
Dec. 1856		19	27.50	2.59	6.10
Dec. 1857		19	31.20	4.79	6.42
Dec. 1858		15	23.23	5.32	3.95
Jan. 1859			30.58	5.48	9.50
Dec. 1859	12		35.07	5.84	7.31
Dec. 1861		13	26.36	5.78	
Dec. 1863		6	16.23	3.67	1.25

TABLE C.I (continued)

Date	(6) Notes of other banks	(7) Real estate	(8) Specie	(9) Specie funds	(10) Other assets	(11) Reserve ratio[a]
	Assets (continued)					
Jan. 1820			.29			.364
Jan. 1830			1.49			.180
Jan. 1834	1.13	.61		2.22	.58	.437
June 1835	.04	.08	2.82		2.53	.391
Aug. 1836	1.68	3.61	2.61		6.28	.139
Oct. 1836	1.98	4.25	3.07		6.79	.138
Jan. 1837	2.37	4.64	3.11		.52	.168
July 1837	.98	1.42	1.12		5.63	.116
Dec. 1837	4.51	5.70	2.73		1.79	.182
Mar. 1838	4.41	7.84	2.97		3.22	.233
Dec. 1838	1.72		3.99		6.06	.286
Oct. 1839	.78	7.43	2.85		7.91	.292
Jan. 1840	2.60	6.57	3.40		4.25	.245
Dec. 1840	2.58	13.19	3.16			.332
May 1841	1.36		3.41		3.01	.196
Mar. 1842		2.32	1.36		5.10	.236
Apr. 1842		2.51	2.26		12.65	.268
May 1842		5.39	1.74		12.38	.242
Jan. 1843		2.47	4.45		5.10	.693
Jan. 1844		3.02	7.89		5.10	.963
Dec. 1844		3.32	8.28		4.64	.788
May 1845		3.47	6.85		4.63	.537
Apr. 1846		3.54	6.64		4.45	.486
Dec. 1846		3.44	6.59		4.25	.460
Apr. 1847		3.13	5.72	.62	4.21	.449
Dec. 1847		2.98	7.58	.35	3.55	.613
Jan. 1849		2.72	8.15	.37	3.02	.648
Jan. 1850		2.74	6.98	.49	2.66	.526
Dec. 1850		2.63	5.75	1.24	2.93	.431
Dec. 1852		1.32	4.36	1.21	4.13	.417
Dec. 1853		1.34	5.95	1.65	1.15	.398
Dec. 1854		1.95	7.47		2.16	.399
Dec. 1855		3.32	6.57		1.99	.360
Dec. 1856		2.34	8.19		2.23	.372
Dec. 1857		2.47	6.81		1.49	.300
Dec. 1858		2.49	10.37		1.15	.648
Jan. 1859		1.28	16.06		2.68	.470
Dec. 1859		2.14	12.13		1.08	.387
Dec. 1861		2.13	13.66	6.07	1.29	.587
Dec. 1863	.45	.58	8.81	1.03	4.74	.600

[a] Ratio of specie held to circulation plus deposits (see overleaf).

TABLE C.I (concluded)

	Liabilities					
	(12)	(13)	(14)	(15) Owed to	(16) Other	(17)
Date	Capital paid in	Circula- tion	Deposits	other banks	liabili- ties[b]	Sources (see p. 205)
Jan. 1820	.92	.46	.34			1
Jan. 1830	4.67	1.30	2.02			1
Jan. 1834	23.66	4.79	4.28	1.29	1.78	2
June 1835	26.42	5.11	7.11	4.00	1.39	3, 4, 5
Aug. 1836	34.07	7.13	11.74	7.16	4.09	1, 5
Oct. 1836	34.07	8.38	13.81	8.42	4.76	6
Jan. 1837	36.77	7.72	10.78	11.90	.85	7, (4, 5)
July 1837	25.59	3.56	6.13	2.10	1.02	1
Dec. 1837	39.94	7.56	7.43	9.13	3.75	8,(5)
Mar. 1838	39.52	4.73	8.02	10.59	.90	1
Dec. 1838	40.93	6.28	7.66	8.12	3.52	1, 5
Oct. 1839	41.74	4.35	5.42	3.83	5.95	4, 5
Jan. 1840	41.74	7.00	6.86	7.34	6.81	9
Dec. 1840	41.71	6.44	3.09	7.09	7.78	4, 5
May 1841		8.85	8.50	1.91	3.31	9
Mar. 1842	20.95	2.23	3.56			10
Apr. 1842	35.45	3.71	4.74	.82	2.12	11
May 1842	35.45	3.01	4.18	.84	2.19	11
Jan. 1843	20.93	1.09	5.34			4, 5
Jan. 1844	20.05	1.72	6.47			4, 5
Dec. 1844	19.67	2.10	8.42			4, 5
May 1845	17.94	3.14	9.62			10
Apr. 1846	17.53	4.20	9.45			4, 5
Dec. 1846	17.39	3.55	10.77			4
Apr. 1847	17.09	4.75	7.98	.87	1.60	4, 5
Dec. 1847	15.58	3.71	8.65	1.29	1.34	4, 5
Jan. 1849	15.23	4.17	8.43	1.64	.91	4, 5
Jan. 1850	14.26	5.07	8.21	1.76	.45	4, 5
Dec. 1850	12.37	5.09	8.28	1.38	8.74	4, 5
Dec. 1852	12.20	3.51	6.95	.92	8.50	5
Dec. 1853	10.93	4.41	10.56	.81	8.10	5
Dec. 1854	17.36	6.97	11.74	2.02	2.35	5
Dec. 1855	20.18	6.59	11.69	1.15	2.23	5
Dec. 1856	19.03	7.22	14.75	1.69	2.30	5
Dec. 1857	21.73	9.19	13.48	.96	2.21	5
Dec. 1858	22.80	4.34	11.64	1.34		5
Jan. 1859	25.21	11.60	22.55	1.59	.46	12
Dec. 1859	24.50	11.58	19.78	1.17	2.20	13, (5)
Dec. 1861	24.63	6.18	17.06	.75	1.01	5
Dec. 1863	17.39	8.88	5.81	.35	.13	5

[b] Includes capital accounts.

SOURCES TO TABLE C.I

The sources for each year are listed in the order of primacy and presumed derivation. A source number in parentheses indicates that the source contains errors for that year.

1. *USC*, [9], p. 676.
2. *USC*, [2], No. 498, pp. 18-19.
3. *USC*, [4], pp. 66-67. This document contains variations in reporting dates from Dec. 29, 1834, to Nov. 6, 1835.
4. *USC*, [17], pp. 326-27.
5. *USC*, [42], pp. 102-3.
6. *USC*, [5], No. 65, p. 155.
7. *LS*, [22], Appendix A. My information is derived from a copy containing handwritten corrections (probably by William G. Hewes, president of the Commercial Bank of New Orleans); this version is filed in Treasury Dept., [4], No. 307. An inaccurate version of the same document appears in *USC*, [7], p. 672; its errors are repeated in Sources 4 and 5 above.
8. *USC*, [36], No. 471, pp. 56-61.
9. *USC*, [13], pp. 844-45.
10. *Ibid.*, p. 846. Data not strictly comparable.
11. *Hunt's Merchants' Magazine*, VII (1842), 78.
12. *LS*, [21], 1859, pp. 46-49.
13. *USC*, [20], pp. 165-68.

APPENDIX C

TABLE C.2

Monetary Variables during the Fluctuations of 1837-43
(all dollar values in $ millions)

Date	Loans	Specie	Circula–tion	Deposits	C + D	Reserve ratio
June 1835	37.4	2.83	5.11	7.11	12.22	.231
Aug. 1836	51.2	2.61	7.13	11.74	18.88	.138
Oct. 1836	53.7	3.07	8.38	13.81	22.19	.138
Jan. 1837	59.3	3.11	7.72	10.78	18.50	.168
May 1837	50.9	2.33	6.59	10.15	16.74	.139
Dec. 1837	55.6	2.73	7.56	7.43	14.98	.182
Mar. 1838	52.1	2.97	4.73	8.02	12.76	.233
Dec. 1838	56.9	3.99	6.28	7.66	13.94	.286
Oct. 1839	49.1	2.85	4.34	4.93	9.27	.307
Nov. 1839	48.9	2.77	5.23	5.18	10.42	.266
Dec. 1839	49.9	2.50	5.53	6.12	11.65	.215
Jan. 1840	52.0	2.53	5.80	6.05	11.85	.213
Feb. 1840	52.6	2.90	6.68	6.19	12.87	.225
Mar. 1840	52.6	3.15	6.93	6.53	13.46	.234
May 1840	50.7	3.58	7.11	7.22	14.33	.249
June 1840	48.7	3.53	6.83	6.67	13.50	.262
July 1840	48.4	3.37	6.56	6.43	12.99	.259
Aug. 1840	48.6	3.61	6.13	6.30	12.43	.291
Sept. 1840	48.5	3.53	5.78	6.04	11.82	.298
Oct. 1840	48.4	3.43	5.62	6.31	11.93	.288
Nov. 1840	48.7	3.39	5.92	6.55	12.47	.272
Dec. 1840	48.6	3.16	6.44	7.02	13.46	.235
Jan. 1841	49.2	3.22	7.37	7.27	14.64	.220
Feb. 1841	48.9	3.42	7.57	7.56	15.13	.226
Mar. 1841	49.2	3.32	8.05	8.13	16.18	.205
Apr. 1841	49.5	3.36	8.89	8.79	17.68	.190
May 1841	48.4	3.41	8.85	8.50	17.35	.196
June 1841	48.5	3.41	8.25	7.86	16.11	.211
July 1841	48.4	3.17	7.50	7.14	14.65	.217
Aug. 1841	46.0	2.91	6.82	6.31	13.13	.222
Sept. 1841	46.1	3.07	6.26	5.97	12.23	.251
Oct. 1841	45.4	3.01	6.08	6.08	12.17	.248
Dec. 1841	45.2	2.34	5.87	4.91	10.78	.217
Mar. 1842	33.3	2.30	4.03	4.82	8.85	.259
Apr. 1842	29.8	2.26	3.71	4.74	8.45	.268
May 1842	29.2	1.74	3.01	4.18	7.19	.242
June 1842	35.4	1.08	1.45	2.13	3.58	.303
July 1842	35.4	1.03	2.38	3.36	5.74	.179
Aug. 1842	34.2	.90	1.92	2.74	4.67	.194
Sept. 1842	33.2	1.21	1.73	2.62	4.35	.278
Jan. 1843	20.4	4.45	1.09	5.34	6.43	.693

SOURCES: *Hunt's Merchants' Magazine*, VII (1842), p. 361; Table C.1.

TABLE C.3

Federal Deposits in Louisiana Banks as a
Percentage of Total Louisiana Deposits

Date	Federal deposits	Sources
1833	no deposits	Figures for the years 1833-36 are from
Jan. 1834	4.6%	*USC*, [5], No. 77, pp. 3-11.
June 1835	17.3	
Oct. 1836	31.3	
Jan. 1837	40.2	*LS*, [22], Appendix A
Mar. 1837	40.0	*USC*, [6], pp. 111-13 (estimate)
July 1844	4.0	*USC*, [39], p. 12 (estimate)
Dec. 1846	2.0	*USC*, [14], No. 33, p. 3

TABLE C.4

Population Statistics

Census	Louisiana		New Orleans		U.S. (1,000's)	
	Pop.	Growth	Pop.	Growth	Pop.	Growth
1810	76,556		17,242		7,224	
1820	153,407	100%	27,176	57%	9,618	33%
1830	215,739	41	46,082	70	12,901	34
1840	352,411	63	102,193	121	17,120	33
1850	517,762	47	116,375	14	23,261	36
1860	708,002	37	168,675	45	31,513	35

SOURCES: *Historical Statistics*, pp. 7, 13; Taylor, "American Urban Growth," p. 315; U.S. Census for 1850 and 1860.

TABLE C.5

Cities and Towns of Louisiana in 1860

Town	Population	Town	Population
New Orleans	168,675	Thibodeaux	1,380
Donaldsonville	11,484	Minden	1,146
St. Landry	10,346	Opelousas	786
Algiers[a]	5,816	Providence	582
Baton Rouge	5,428	Bayou Sara	540
Jefferson[a]	5,107	Washington	536
Shreveport	2,190	Vermillionville	498
Carrollton[a]	1,756	Bastrop	481
Plaquemine	1,663	Pineville	393
Alexandria	1,461	Floyd	298
Homer	1,451	Delhi	175

SOURCE: *USBC*, [2], p. 195. [a] Suburbs of New Orleans.

Notes

Notes

Complete titles, authors' names, and publishing information will be found in the Bibliography, pp. 237-59. The following abbreviations are used in the Notes:

AL	*Acts of Louisiana*
CBC	Canal Bank Collection
CAPC	Consolidated Association of the Planters of Louisiana Collection
CBL	Citizens Bank of Louisiana
LS	Louisiana State Documents
LSB	Louisiana State Bank Collection
USBC	United States Bureau of the Census
USC	United States Congress

Each of these sources appears in the Bibliography alphabetized under its full title. Bracketed numbers following some abbreviations refer to specific items listed under that heading in the Bibliography.

Introduction

1. Even Douglass North, in his pioneering analysis of antebellum economic growth, discusses banking only as a source of cyclical instability and ignores its possible relationship to economic growth. North, pp. 184, 187-88, 199-201. See also Rightor, p. 595; Reed, "Boom or Bust," pp. 36, 48-49; Caldwell, "The New Orleans Trade Area," pp. 6-7.

2. Winston, p. 215. Even Robert Roeder, who is generally a more sophisticated observer of New Orleans merchants and bankers, adopts the stereotypes of wildcat banks and "reckless expansion." Roeder, "Merchants of Ante-Bellum New Orleans," p. 118.

3. The studies of the role of state government by Oscar and Mary Handlin, Louis Hartz, Milton Heath, James Primm, and others are discussed in Lively, "The American System: A Review Article." Wilburn's *Biddle's Bank* has extended the political analysis of that federal bank to the level of state politics. Sharp, in *The Jacksonians Versus the Banks*, has gone a step further, focusing on the politics of state-chartered banking after the panic of 1837.

4. The problems and pitfalls of implicit theorizing in conventional historical writing are aptly illustrated in Fogel, "The Specification Problem in Economic History." Particularly relevant to our discussion is Fogel's critique of Eugene Genovese's essay, "The Significance of the Slave Plantation for Southern Economic Development."

5. See Sitterson, "The McCollams," and "Financing and Marketing the Sugar Crop of the Old South."

6. Atherton, Chapter 6; Woodman, *King Cotton*, Chapter 7.

7. Woodman, *King Cotton*, Chapter 3.

Chapter One

1. E. A. Davis, pp. 62-67, 110-15.

2. See Table B.1. See also: Gray, II, 890-91, 896-98; Menn, Chapter 1.

3. Sitterson, *Sugar Country*, pp. 3-13, 28-30. Table B.2.

4. E. A. Davis, pp. 176-78. Gray, II, 811, 833, 1042. Menn, Chapters 1-2.

5. Richard A. Easterlin, "Interregional Differences in Per Capita Income, Population, and Total Income, 1840-1950," in *Trends in the American Economy*, p. 128. Towns over 10,000 were considered "urban." Taylor, "American Urban Growth," pp. 311-15.

6. E. A. Davis, pp. 64-67, 100, 107-8, 114-15. Callender, *Selections*, p. 315. Tables B.4 and C.4. Albion, *The Rise of New York Port*, p. 390.

7. Roeder, "Merchants of Ante-Bellum New Orleans." Shugg, Chapter 2. Table B.4. *USBC*, [2], III, 202-4, 729.

8. Rightor, pp. 579-83.

9. Caldwell, *Banking History*, p. 26. *Ordinance Establishing the Louisiana Bank*. The bank was eventually given until 1823 to complete its liquidation, possibly because of its weakened financial condition in 1819 (total assets: $777,883; total liabilities: $821,547). Rightor, p. 584. *AL:* 4 Leg., 1 sess. (Mar. 3, 1819), p. 48; 5 Leg., 2 sess., (Mar. 14, 1822), p. 40.

10. Rightor, p. 585. Caldwell, *Banking History*, p. 29. *Acts of the Territory of Orleans*, pp. 86-100, 164-78. *LS*, [5]: 5 Leg., 1 sess. (Feb. 19, 1820), p. 34; 7 Leg., 2 sess., pp. 48-76, 83-84. *AL*, 6 Leg., 1 sess. (Mar. 26, 1823), pp. 66-68.

11. *LS*, [5]: 1 Leg., 1 sess., Appendix; 1 Leg., 2 sess., pp. 4-6; 1 Leg., 3 sess., pp. 4-5. *AL*: 1 Leg., 2 sess., pp. 212-14, 260-62; 2 Leg., 1 sess., pp. 8-10, 36, 70-72.

12. *LS*, [5]: 1 Leg., 2 sess., pp. 67-69; 1 Leg., 3 sess., p. 9.

13. *AL*, 3 Leg., 2 sess. (Mar. 14, 1818), pp. 78-90.

14. *LS*, [5]: 4 Leg., 1 sess., p. 4; 4 Leg., 2 sess., pp. 5, 13. John Clark has informed me that there were some business failures among the leading New Orleans merchant houses in 1819 and succeeding years. These presumably reflected a liquidity crisis resulting from depressed export earnings.

15. *LS*, [5]: 4 Leg., 1 sess., p. 16. *AL*, 4 Leg., 1 sess. (Mar. 3, 1819), pp. 86-88.

16. *LS*, [5]: 4 Leg., 2 sess., pp. 5, 13; 6 Leg., 1 sess., p. 5; 6 Leg., 2 sess., p. 5; 7 Leg., 2 sess., p. 6. Watkins, p. 192.

17. *LS*, [3]. *Ibid.*, [12]. *AL*, 6 Leg., 1 sess. (Mar. 26, 1823), pp. 66-68.

18. *LS*, [5]: 6 Leg., 2 sess. (Mar. 15, 1824), pp. 11-12; 7 Leg., 1 sess., p. 4. *AL*, 6 Leg., 2 sess. (Apr. 7, 1824), pp. 92-130.

19. *LS*, [5]: 6 Leg., 2 sess., pp. 25, 39-40; 7 Leg., 1 sess., p. 52.

20. *AL*: 8 Leg., 1 sess. (Mar. 16, 1827), pp. 96-116; 8 Leg., 2 sess. (Feb. 19, 1828), pp. 30-36. *LS*, [5]: 8 Leg., 1 sess., pp. 64-66; 8 Leg., 2 sess., pp. 33-34; 9 Leg., 2 sess., pp. 69-70. Grenier, "The Early Financing of the Consolidated Association of the Planters of Louisiana."

21. For statistics, see Appendix B.

22. *LS*, [5], 10 Leg., 1 sess., pp. 21, 26, 30, 33, 36, 42, 47-48, 53, 92-95. *AL*, 10 Leg., 1 sess., pp. 26-62.

23. *LS*, [5]: 10 Leg., 3 sess., pp. 39, 65-83, 102-11; 11 Leg., 1 sess., p. 4. *AL*, 10 Leg., 3 sess., pp. 42-72. Edmund J. Forstall to Baring Brothers, Oct. 16, 1834; Baring Microfilms, frame 57217.

24. *AL*: 11 Leg., 1 sess., pp. 124-36, 151-94; 12 Leg., 2 sess., pp. 16-24. *LS*, [5], 12 Leg., 2 sess., pp. 15-35, 103-5.

25. See Table 1.1.

26. Capers, pp. 45, 64, 79-81, 159-61. Caldwell, *Banking History*, pp. 90-98. Doyle, "Greenbacks, Car Tickets, and a Pot of Gold."

27. Henry W. Huntington to William N. Mercer, Apr. 4, 1837, Mercer Papers. *Semi-Weekly Creole*, Jan. 3, 1855, p. 2. *Commercial Bulletin*, Feb. 6, 1838, and Nov. 27, 1855. For sources on legislative debates, see Chapter Four.

28. *USBC*, [3], XIX, 254. Atherton, pp. 16-17. R. M. Davis, *The Southern Planter, the Factor, and the Banker.*

29. "Descriptions of Properties Mortgaged, 1847," in *CAPC*. Roeder, "New Orleans Merchants," Chapter 4.

30. See the individual bank charters. See also *USC*: [5], No. 65, pp. 150-51; [11], pp. 721-22. *LS*, [5], 10 Leg., 2 sess., pp. 81-82, 106, 110-11.

31. *USC*: [11], p. 722; [13], p. 844. Matthias Purton to Baring Brothers, Jan. 16, 1846; Baring Microfilms, frame 59516. Roeder, "New Orleans Merchants," p. 306. City Bank, *Charter, Rules, & c.*

32. Suarez, "Bargains, Bills, and Bankruptcies." Cameron *et al.*, pp. 311-13.

33. Suarez, "Louisiana's Struggling Majority," pp. 19-20. Shugg, Chapter 5.

34. *LS*, [1], pp. 106, 127, 144, 156. The Gas Light Bank was also required, by a charter amendment of March 14, 1836 (*AL*, 12 Leg., 2 sess., pp. 182-84), to lend $50,000 for ten years to the Rome Patent Brick Manufacturing Company. But there is no evidence of the loan in the 1840 documents.

35. *LS*, [1], pp. 46, 123, 129, 144. Rightor, pp. 588-90. Gerstner, pp. 26-30.

36. Reed, *New Orleans and the Railroads*, pp. 36-40, 50-54. *LS*, [1], pp. 43, 49, 192. Odom, p. 19.

37. Roeder, "New Orleans Merchants," pp. 351-61. Reed, "Boom or Bust," pp. 48-50. Reed, "Louisiana's Transportation Revolution," pp. 9-14. Cameron *et al.*, pp. 133-43, Chapters VI, VIII.

38. *LS*, [1], pp. 46, 106, 117, 123, 127, 144, 156, 167, 186. Reed, *New Orleans and the Railroads*, p. 19.

39. *CBC*: [6], pp. 70, 314-15; [8], pp. 217-18. *LS*, [21], 1857, pp. 89, 98, 106, 136. The Consolidated Association, which owned $17,500 of the stock, was in liquidation.

40. Reed, *New Orleans and the Railroads*, pp. 83-84, Chapters VI-VII. Evans, pp. 181-86, 208. *AL*, 2 Leg., 1 sess. (Mar. 15-16, 1854), pp. 69-79, 151-52. Rightor, p. 98. *LS*, [21], 1857, pp. 106, 112, 116, 124, 128, 132. For opposition to this indirect blend of banking and railroads, see *LS*, [11].

41. *Daily Delta*, Feb. 28, 1860, p. 2. "The Banking Systems of Louisiana" (anonymous pamphlet).

Chapter Two

1. Keynes, pp. 172, 207-8. Hansen, p. 132.

2. Edward S. Shaw, "Money Supply and Stable Economic Growth," in American Assembly, pp. 49-71. Friedman, *Program for Monetary Stability,* pp. 90-92. Friedman actually allows for changing monetary velocity in his rule, and Shaw recognizes this problem in making simplifying assumptions. Thus neither of them adheres literally to the simplest rule.

3. Gurley and Shaw, "The Growth of Debt and Money in the United States."

4. Cameron, "Banking in the Early Stages of Industrialization," pp. 132-33.

5. For a glimpse of the structuralist theory and controversy, see: Seers, "A Theory of Inflation and Growth"; also the contributions by Roberto de Oliveira Campos, David Felix, and Joseph Grunwald in Hirschman, *Latin American Issues.*

6. For clear discussions of forced saving and development see: Chandler, *Central Banking,* pp. 30-35; Bruton, pp. 160-69. Some economists have argued that forced saving and investment would expand capacity (output) enough to match the larger money demand at the old price levels. Cameron accepts this view in "Banking in the Early Stages," p. 121. The flaws in the argument are pointed out in Chandler, *Central Banking,* pp. 25-27.

7. Lyon, p. 39. Peters, pp. 7, 10.

8. For an example of this view of debt, see Suarez, "Bargains, Bills, and Bankruptcies," pp. 195-97.

9. See Goldsmith, Chapter 2; Gurley and Shaw, "Financial Aspects of Economic Development," "Financial Intermediaries and the Saving-Investment Process," and "Financial Structure and Economic Development."

10. See Gurley, "Financial Structures," pp. 114-15.

11. Solow, "Technical Change." Denison, *Sources of Economic Growth.* Kuznets, pp. 22-43.

12. Lance Davis, "The Capital Markets," pp. 255-59.

13. Patrick, p. 185.

14. Lance Davis, "The Capital Markets," pp. 258-72. Cameron, "The Banker as Entrepreneur."

15. Patrick, pp. 178-81.

16. *Ibid.*

17. Chandler, *Central Banking,* pp. 2-5. Gurley, "Financial Structures," p. 107.

18. Cameron *et al.,* pp. 296-300.

19. Gurley and Shaw, "Financial Structure," p. 261.

20. *Ibid.*

21. Gurley, "Financial Structures," p. 100.

22. *Ibid.,* pp. 99-100.

23. See Tables 2.1, 5.1, and C.1. Chapters Four and Six describe state policy and financial crisis. For additional information on bank reserves see: *LS,* [21], Mar. 1855, pp. 5-6; *Price Current,* Apr. 9, 1842, p. 3.

24. *LS,* [25], p. 2. *USC,* [16], pp. 272-73. *DeBow's Review,* X (1851), 587-88.

25. Thompson, p. 44.

26. The clearest detailed account of the diversion of New Orleans trade is Porter, "An Economic View of Ante-Bellum New Orleans, 1846-1860." Other useful treatments are: Fishlow, *American Railroads*, Chapter 7; Clark, *The Grain Trade* and "The Antebellum Grain Trade."

27. Porter, "An Economic View." "The Destiny of New Orleans," in *DeBow's Review*, X (1851), 440-45.

28. Fishlow, *American Railroads*, pp. 290-94.

29. "Route of Trade Up Stream," *DeBow's Review*, XIII (1852), 101. Rightor, pp. 562-64. Porter, pp. 14-15.

30. *Daily Crescent*, July 15, 1851, p. 2. See also the sources cited in Note 24 above.

31. *Daily Crescent*, Mar. 21, 1851, p. 2.

32. Other historians share my view that lack of bank credit severely handicapped New Orleans trade. For example: Roeder, "Merchants of Ante-Bellum New Orleans," p. 121; Odom, p. 58; Caldwell, "The New Orleans Trade Area," pp. 6-7.

33. Tables 2.2, B.1, B.2, and C.4. Forstall, pp. 4-7. Reed, "Boom or Bust," pp. 35-36.

34. Roeder, "New Orleans Merchants," pp. 297-98.

35. At least two contemporary Louisianans argued that idle specie was unproductive, and that banks could mobilize it to the advantage of its owners and society. See Lyon, pp. 35-37; Peters, pp. 9-10. On the inconvenience of specie and rural hoarding of it, see the following documents, all in *LSB*, [1]: Alexander Porter to Dussuau De La Croix, Apr. 27 and July 31, 1819; Richard Eastin to Richard Relf, Mar. 1, 1820; Letterbook of St. Martinsville branch, Louisiana State Bank.

36. See Table C.1 on bank capital and Tables 3.2 and 3.3 on the location of bank stockholders.

37. Roeder, "New Orleans Merchants," p. 312. John L. Lobdell to Lewis Stirling, June 16, 1837 (Stirling Papers).

38. A vague suggestion of the forced saving idea is contained in Roeder, "Merchants of Ante-Bellum New Orleans," p. 120. But Roeder emphasizes the effects on income distribution (benefits to privileged borrowers at the expense of other consumers) rather than the effects on development.

39. Rightor, p. 568. Sitterson, *Sugar Country*, p. 204. Rothstein, "Antebellum Wheat and Cotton Exports," pp. 94-97. Roeder, "Merchants of Ante-Bellum New Orleans," p. 120. Cameron *et al.*, pp. 133,

40. Redlich, *Molding of American Banking*, I, 205-9. Roeder, "Merchants of Ante-Bellum New Orleans," p. 120. Cameron *et al.*, pp. 133, 143, Chapters 6, 8.

41. For sources on branch banking, see Chapter 2.

42. Sitterson, *Sugar Country*, pp. 155-56. Pontchartrain Minute Book, pp. 1, 60-67, 155-60, 222, 228, 231, 237. Edmund J. Forstall to Consolidated Association of Planters, Mar. 14, 1836, in *CAPC*. Evans, pp. 220-43, 248. Reed, *New Orleans and the Railroad*, Chapter 7. Odom, p. 83.

Chapter Three

1. Caldwell, *Banking History*, p. 32. North, pp. 75-76, 233. Fishlow, *American Railroads*, Chapter 7.
2. Schmidt, "Internal Commerce." North, p. 103. Gallman, "Self-Sufficiency." Lindstrom, "The Southern Grain Trade." Fishlow, "Antebellum Trade," especially Table 3, p. 360.
3. North, pp. 111-17. Kettell, p. 75. Fishlow, *American Railroads*, pp. 271-75.
4. Buck, p. 43. Jenks, p. 68.
5. *CBC*, [3], pp. 96, 257, 311. William G. Hewes to Levi Woodbury, July 11, 1836, Treasury Dept., [4], No. 221.
6. Alexander Gordon to Consolidated Association of Planters, June 1, 1835, *CAPC*, folder 21. *CBC*, [7], pp. 211-12. George Tichenor to Richard Relf, Mar. 11, 1820, *LSB*, [1], folder 2. Prime, Ward, & King to H. Lavergne, Aug. 28, 1834, *CAPC*, folder 18.
7. *CBC*, [1]. Prime, Ward, & King to H. Lavergne, Oct. 10, 1834, *CAPC*, folder 18. W. M. Martin to Richard Relf, Nov. 23, 1855, *LSB*, [1], folder 94.
8. N. N. Wilkinson to Cornelius Heyer, Nov. 14, 1832, *CBC*, [1]. Cole, "Seasonal Variation in Sterling Exchange," pp. 209-11. *Price Current*, Nov. 21, 1860, p. 3. Lance Davis and Hughes, "A Dollar-Sterling Exchange," p. 67.
9. H. Lavergne to Gabriel Shaw, Apr. 23, 1841, Letterbook No. 7, DeLavergne Papers. Miller, pp. 72-75, 173-80. Some theorists made the crucial distinction not whether the loan financed some particular "real" transaction but whether it was renewable. Accommodation paper was renewable, but commercial paper was not.
10. Ralph Catterall, p. 32.
11. Cole, "Evolution of the Foreign-Exchange Market," I (1929), 401, 412-13. Roeder, "New Orleans Merchants," pp. 372-74. Ralph Catterall, pp. 32, 158-60. *USC*, [7], p. 658. Baring Brothers to H. Lavergne, Jan. 6, 1840, *CAPC*, folder 35. *CBC*, [3], p. 360. *CBC*, [4], pp. 228-30.
12. Peters, pp. 9, 22. Smith, pp. 43-44, 241-42.
13. Le Long, pp. 18-19.
14. Collector's Office to Levi Woodbury, July 20, 1837, Treasury

Dept., [5]. W. J. Anderson (Columbus, Miss.) to Richard Relf, Apr. 23, 1853, *LSB*, [1], folder 88. Butler, Meeks, & Co. (Natchez) to Louisiana State Bank, Feb. 29, 1856, *ibid.*, folder 95. Thomas Henderson & Co. (Natchez) to Louisiana State Bank, several letters 1859-60, *ibid.*, folders 113, 126.

15. *LS*, [22], pp. 13-14. A full correspondence on the 1836 proposal may be found in *CAPC*, folder 25. This contains both the City Bank resolution (Oct. 22, 1836) and the Citizens Bank reply (Oct. 24, 1836). The Citizens Bank side of the debate is also available in *USC*, [7], pp. 653-58. Commercial Bank, *Annual Report* (1838), pp. 35-37. Peters, pp. 27-28. *LS*, [13], pp. 848-49.

16. Commercial Bank, *Annual Report.* (1838), p. 37. See also Table C.1.

17. *LS*, [2], pp. 52-174. *USC*, [36], No. 471, p. 57. *LS*, [21], 1857, Appendix. Myers, I, 112; she cites the same 1857 Report as her only Louisiana source.

18. See Table 3.1. *Price Current*, June 11, 1853, p. 3. *LS*, [8]. There are several sources in *CBC*: [2], pp. 365, 460; [3], p. 105; [7], pp. 292-97, 325, 395, 412-14; [8], pp. 35, 38, 46, 56. See also *LS*, [22], pp. 13-14.

19. Letters from William G. Hewes to Levi Woodbury (May 17-July 26, 1836) and from the Union Bank to Woodbury (June 14-July 27, 1836); all are in Treasury Dept., [4]. Citizens Bank to Woodbury (Oct. 28-Dec. 3, 1839), Treasury Dept., [5]. *CBC*, [3], pp. 207-8. Lance Davis and Hughes, "A Dollar-Sterling Exchange."

20. For estimates of national capital imports, see Douglass C. North, "The United States Balance of Payments, 1790-1860," in *Trends in the American Economy*, p. 605; see also Jenks, pp. 85, 363. In some years (particularly 1833-34, when the Union Bank had large stock transactions) the Louisiana banks obviously imported more than 12 per cent. Hidy, "The Union Bank of Louisiana Loan."

21. *CBC*: [5], p. 159; [4], p. 34. *LS*, [2], pp. 52-174.

22. *American State Papers*, II, 516-17. Kinley, pp. 23, 35, 52, 60.

23. Kinley, pp. 39, 48. Hammond, *Banks and Politics*, pp. 543-45. Other general studies of the independent treasury system are: Timberlake, "The Independent Treasury"; Taus, *Central Banking Functions*.

24. I am extremely grateful to Frank Gatell for sharing with me his ideas and his research notes on the politics of Louisiana banking in the 1830's. I have attempted to check the original source whenever possible, and otherwise have indicated my reliance on Gatell. Rightor, pp. 583-84. *Ordinance Establishing the Louisiana Bank.* Caldwell, *Banking History*, pp. 26-29. Rowland, pp. 41-42, 160-64. H. B. Trist (customs collector in New Orleans) to Albert Gallatin, June 9, 1804, in Treasury Dept., [9],

No. 245. The Louisiana Bank divided its directorate, and probably its business as well, between the French and American communities. *American State Papers*, II, 218, 516-17.

25. Ralph Catterall, pp. 376, 397. Smith, p. 39.

26. Ralph Catterall, pp. 56, 66, 80. Smith, pp. 126-27. *American State Papers*, IV, 907.

27. Ralph Catterall, pp. 143, 397.

28. Quoted in *USC*, [24], p. 357.

29. On the Western bills, see *USC*, [30], p. 12. Cf. *USC*, [23], pp. 39-41, for a slightly earlier period. Smith, pp. 43-44.

30. *USC*, [24], pp. 316-17, 357. Jaudon to Biddle, Jan. 21, 1833, Biddle Papers.

31. Ralph Catterall, pp. 152-60. *USC*, [25], pp. 148-51. See also Note 29.

32. Ralph Catterall, pp. 5-8, 115, 129. *USC*, [28], p. 3. *USC*, [30], pp. 26-27.

33. Biddle to Charles S. West (cashier of New Orleans branch), Mar. 20, 1823, Apr. 5 and June 29, 1835; all in U.S. Finance Collection. *USC*, [29], No. 98, pp. 40-43. *USC*, [24], pp. 14, 308. Smith, pp. 1, 136.

34. Hidy, "The House of Baring" and "The Union Bank of Louisiana Loan." Smith, pp. 158-59.

35. *USC*, [24], pp. 317-20.

36. Comparisons based on data in Table C.1 and in various *USC* sources: [1], No. 147, pp. 33-34; [2], No. 523, pp. 140-43, 212-15; [5], No. 118, pp. 86-91; [32], No. 8, pp. 27-41; [33], No. 312, pp. 17-20.

37. Ralph Catterall, pp. 83-91. *USC*, [1], Nos. 153, 184. *USC*, [29], No. 108. These memorials were not independently worded, and the third mentions the sending of the other two. They were all solicited, and possibly drafted, by Samuel Jaudon, cashier of the B.U.S. branch (Wilburn, p. 34).

38. Biddle to Charles S. West, Feb. 11, 1823, in U.S. Finance Collection.

39. *USC*, [25], pp. 148-51. Memorials cited in Note 37. Tregle, "Louisiana in the Age of Jackson," pp. 406-8. *Louisiana Courrier*, Nov. 7, 1826.

40. Howard, pp. 33-42. Stephenson, *Alexander Porter*, pp. 80-81. *Biographical Directory of the American Congress*. On Jacksonians in banking, see Tregle, "Louisiana in the Age of Jackson," pp. 407-8. *Price Current*, Dec. 27, 1823, Dec. 2, 1826, and Jan. 9, 1830. Govan, p. 119. Tregle wrongly assumes that Jacksonians on the board of the New Orleans branch were therefore disloyal to the party. Actually, Biddle appointed them at the suggestion of William Lewis, one of Jackson's

"kitchen cabinet," in order to give political balance to the board. See Ralph Catterall, p. 246.

41. Tregle, "Louisiana in the Age of Jackson," pp. 406-11. Norton, pp. 26-27. *USC*, [43], pp. 345-46. *Ibid.*, [21]. Ralph Catterall, pp. 230, 235. *AL*, Mar. 6, 1832, p. 96. *USC*, [21]. Smith, pp. 154-59. Biddle to Jaudon, Apr. 20, 1832, Biddle Papers. Biddle to Jaudon, Jan. 16, 1832, U.S. Finance Collection. Memorials cited in Note 37. John Linton to Josiah S. Johnston, Oct. 5, 1832, Johnston Papers.

42. Ralph Catterall, pp. 314-31. Biddle to W. W. Montgomery, Jan. 24, 1834, Biddle Papers. *Niles' Weekly Register*, XLV, 389 (Feb. 1, 1834), and XLVI, 86 (Apr. 5, 1834). *New Orleans Bee*, Mar. 7, 14, 17, and 22, 1834. Resolution of the Board of the B.U.S., New Orleans Branch, Mar. 14, 1834, Biddle Papers (courtesy of Frank Gatell). Biddle to Joseph Saul, Apr. 5, 1834, U.S. Finance Collection. *USC*, [27], pp. 1011-13.

43. *USC*, [27], pp. 256-58, 1008-9. *Niles' Weekly Register*, XLV, 389 (Feb. 1, 1834). *USC*, [31], No. 187, p. 2.

44. Tregle, "Louisiana in the Age of Jackson," pp. 448-49. Norton, pp. 26-32, 36-37, 85. *New Orleans Bee*, Jan. 29, Feb. 18, 20, and Mar. 18, 1834. *USC*: [2], No. 372; [31], No. 187.

45. Biddle to R. Lenox, Aug. 4, 1835, Biddle Papers. Treasury Dept., [4]: Martin Gordon to President Jackson, Aug. 22, 1835; Union Bank to Levi Woodbury, Aug. 22, 1835; Biddle to Union Bank, Sept. 15, 1835. *USC*: [5], No. 118, p. 61; [36], No. 471, p. 61. Ralph Catterall, pp. 365-69.

46. Biddle Papers: James Erwin to Biddle, June 23, 1836; Biddle to James Erwin, June 25, 1836. *USC*, [13], p. 423.

47. Biddle Papers: Biddle to John Minturn, Jan. 2, 1837; Biddle to W. W. Frazier, May 3, 1837; Biddle to Messrs. Minturn & Yorke, May 4, 1838. *USC*, [36], pp. 56-57.

48. Biddle Papers: Biddle to J. L. Roberts, July 31, 1847; Biddle to Edward C. Biddle, Oct. 1, 1838. Biddle, public letter to John Quincy Adams, Dec. 10, 1838, *Financial Register*, II, 393. *Commercial Bulletin*, Jan. 13, 1838, p. 2. Among the secondary sources that comment on Biddle's cotton transactions are: Matthews, pp. 59-63. Sumner, pp. 298-99. Hidy, *The House of Baring*, pp. 240-42. Bray Hammond, *Banks and Politics*, pp. 468-72, 502-4, 538-39. Smith, pp. 195-202. Temin, *The Jacksonian Economy*, p. 150.

49. Bray Hammond, *Banks and Politics*, p. 471. Smith, pp. 200-201. Sumner, p. 299. Jenks, p. 93.

50. *Financial Register*, II, 29. *USC*, [11], pp. 771, 854, 910, 957, 975-78, 1056-57.

51. Smith, pp. 207-8, 210, 212, 300. Hidy, *House of Baring*, pp. 262, 282-83, 290. Bray Hammond, *Banks and Politics*, pp. 447-78, 538. The quotation comes from Biddle to Samuel J. Peters, Sept. 8, 1838, Woodbury Collection. This letter was published in the New Orleans *Commercial Bulletin*, Oct. 19, 1838, and then copied by another unidentified paper. I located a clipping containing it in the Collections scrapbook "Newspaper Clippings on Banks and Currency."

52. Two previous studies are: Gatell, "Spoils of the Bank War," (especially p. 55); Scheiber, "The Pet Banks." Table 3.5 summarizes all known negotiations for the selection of deposit banks. The four unsuccessful candidates in 1833 are discussed in Treasury Dept., [2]: Martin Gordon to Amos Kendall, Oct. 15, 1833; Samuel Harper to Roger Taney, Oct. 23, 1833; John A. Brown to Reuben Whitney, Oct. 1, 1833 (all courtesy of Gatell). See also J. D. Beers & Co. to Kendall, Sept. 26, 1833, Treasury Dept., [19] (Gatell). On the selection of the Commercial Bank see William G. Hewes to George Poindexter, Mar. 21, 1834, Claiborne Collection. Hewes to Roger Taney, Oct. 7, 1833, USC, [2] (Gatell). Tregle, "The Political Apprenticeship of John Slidell." Slidell to Taney, Oct. 21, 1833, and John Nicholson to Taney, Oct. 29, 1833, Treasury Dept., [19] (Gatell). Although Hewes was a loyal Jacksonian from 1833 on, his background is uncertain; Slidell found it necessary to explain that as a B.U.S. director Hewes had opposed Biddle's policies from within. The leader of the rival Jacksonian faction, Martin Gordon, applied for "pet" status for the Louisiana State Bank, of which he had been a director, and the Mechanics & Traders Bank, which he had founded in April 1833. Furious at his loss in this appeal, he blasted the two banks chosen as enemies of the administration. For evidence of the lack of partisan politics after 1833 see Treasury Dept., [6]: Edmund J. Forstall to Thomas Ewing, Aug. 27 and Sept. 3, 1841; anonymous to Robert Walker, Jan. 6, 1848 [?].

53. See Table 3.5. Bray Hammond, *Banks and Politics*, pp. 420-21. Treasury Dept., [2]: Hewes to Slidell, Oct. 21, 1833; Hewes to Taney, Dec. 30, 1833. *Ibid.*, [3]: Union Bank proposal and resolution, Dec. 13, 1834; Union Bank to Levi Woodbury, Dec. 18, 1834.

54. *U.S. Statutes at Large*, V, 52.

55. Treasury Dept., [4]: Commercial Bank to Levi Woodbury, May 17 and July 26, 1836; Union Bank to Woodbury, July 27, 1836. Scheiber, "The Pet Banks," pp. 206-7. Timberlake, "The Specie Circular."

56. Timberlake, "The Specie Circular." USC, [37], No. 14, pp. 45, 47. Worley, pp. 186-90. Scheiber, "The Pet Banks," pp. 208-9. Scheiber challenges Timberlake but does not clearly distinguish between the bank-to-bank transfers and the bank-to-state payments on the surplus.

Peter Temin (*The Jacksonian Economy*, pp. 133-36) also argues that Treasury transfers did not contribute significantly to the financial difficulties of 1836-37, and that New Orleans in particular felt no pressure. He is quite right for late 1836 (the period to which he specfically refers) but quite wrong for early 1837. I have little doubt that the $2 million of Treasury withdrawals contributed substantially to the pressures that led the New Orleans banks to suspend specie payments in May 1837.

57. Some funds were kept in the banks as "special deposits" during the suspension. Treasury Dept., [13]: Woodbury to Hewes, May 17, July 17, and Aug. 8, 1837; Woodbury to Union and Commercial Banks, May 18 and 30, 1837. *Ibid.*, [5]: Hewes to Woodbury, Oct. 18, 1837; Union Bank to Woodbury, Nov. 6, 1837.

58. *USC*, [35], No. 2, pp. 39-40. Cora Slocomb to Mrs. Harriet Mc-Crindell, July 18, 1837, Johnson Letters.

59. Woodbury to Hewes, Feb. 7, 1839, Woodbury Papers (Gatell). Union Bank to Walter Forward, Dec. 31, 1841, and reply, Jan. 13, 1842, both in Treasury Dept., [6]. Edmund Forstall to T. W. Ward, Aug. 18, 1846, Baring Microfilms, frame 57631.

Chapter Four

1. Trescott, *Financing American Enterprise*, pp. 10-11. In a study of antebellum banking theories, Harry E. Miller (p. 98) finds a similar dualism between the bank's role in providing "media of payment" and its role in "lending purchasing power."

2. For evidence of the pressure for greater guarantees of rural lending, see *LS*, [5]: 10 Leg., 3 sess. (1832), pp. 64, 81-82, 106-8; 11 Leg., 1 sess. (1833), pp. 32, 41; 11 Leg., 2 sess. (1834), pp. 45-46, 76; 12 Leg., 2 sess. (1836), pp. 22-25. 30, 103-5. On stock loans see Redlich, *Molding of American Banking*, I, 12, 48. The property banks used stock loans as their major form of lending, but these were effectively mortgage loans.

3. Bray Hammond, *Banks and Politics*, p. 137.

4. *Ibid.*, pp. 137, 189, 689. Miller, Chapter 11. Redlich, *Molding of American Banking*, II, 7-10. See Appendix A for extended comparisons of antebellum and modern money and banking transactions.

5. Redlich, *Molding of American Banking*, I, 50-55, and II, 4-7. See also: Fenstermaker, pp. 36-39. Redlich and Christman, "Early American Checks"; Baughman, "Early American Checks."

6. *LS*, [6], 11 Leg., 2 sess. (1834), p. 48. As late as the 1850's *DeBow's Review* claimed that the use of deposits was "confined to classes purely commercial." *DeBow's Review*, XII (June 1852), p. 611.

7. *LS*: [5], 12 Leg., 2 sess. (1836), p. 30. *AL*, Mar. 13, 1818, pp. 74-78.

8. *LS*: [5], 6 Leg., 1 sess., p. 21; [3], p. 33.

9. Charters of Bank of Orleans (1823 renewal) and Bank of Louisiana (1824). *LS*, [5]: 6 Leg., 1 sess., pp. 21, 106; 10 Leg., 1 sess., p. 42. A similar argument that expanded banking would eliminate usury was made as early as 1813 (*ibid.*, 1 Leg., 2 sess., p. 67). And the Bank of Louisiana was established partly for such purposes in 1824 (*ibid.*, 7 Leg., 2 sess., p. 124).

10. *LS*: [5], 6 Leg., 2 sess., pp. 11-12; [3], pp. 1-15.

11. James Brown to Josiah Stoddard Johnston, Apr. 11, 1823. Johnston Papers. *LS*: [5], 6 Leg., 1 sess., pp. 69-77, 90-91, 97-100; [3], pp. 17-22.

12. *LS*: [5], 6 Leg., 1 sess., pp. 97, 100; [3], *passim*; [12]; [5], 6 Leg., 2 sess., pp. 11-12.

13. Table 4.1 and sources cited therein. *USBC*, [3], VII, 523, 526. The census data are quite inaccurate for Louisiana.

14. Bank of Louisiana charter. Vincent Nolte to Baring Brothers, Nov. 2, 1824, Baring Microfilms, frame 57131. *Daily Crescent*, Nov. 7, 1856. *LS*, [5]: 6 Leg., 2 sess., pp. 11-12, 29-30; 7 Leg., 1 sess., pp. 4-5. Trotter, pp. 92-93. See Table 4.1 and the property bank charters for basic details. For key amendments see also *AL*: 8 Leg., 2 sess., pp. 30-36; 12 Leg., 2 sess., pp. 16-24. On the Citizens Bank and various other bond negotiations see McGrane, *Foreign Bondholders*, pp. 168-76.

15. For tax exemptions, see the individual bank charters. Stock purchases are also described in the relevant charters, and in: Knox, p. 611; *AL*, 11 Leg., 2 sess., pp. 64-67.

16. On the benefits of incorporation, see Conrad and Meyer, pp. 144-49. On the power of paying interest on deposits see the City Bank charter (1831) and an amendment of Jan. 13, 1832. The quotation is from *LS*, [5], 10 Leg., 1 sess., p. 33.

17. *LS*, [5], 3 Leg., 2 sess., pp. 47-57. Edmund Forstall to Baring Brothers, Oct. 16, 1834, Baring Microfilm, frame 57217.

18. *LS*, [5]: 1 Leg., 2 sess., pp. 67-69; 6 Leg., 2 sess., pp. 11-12. Forstall, p. 7.

19. Forstall, pp. 4-7. *LS*, [5], 1831-39, *passim*. Of the six bank proposals not enacted, three were actually presented during the 1837 session, but before the panic struck.

20. The Gas Light, New Orleans & Carrollton, and Improvement Banks were created by charter amendments to their respective improvement companies. The Atchafalaya Railroad and Banking Company became particularly notorious for failing to construct its railroad. See *LS*, [5]: 14 Leg., 1 sess., p. 59; 15 Leg., 1 sess., pp. 29, 33; 15 Leg., 2 sess., p. 46.

21. See charters of Citizens Bank (and amendment of Jan. 30, 1836), Gas Light Bank (and amendments of Jan. 11 and Mar. 14, 1836), Carrollton Bank, Exchange Bank, and Merchants Bank.

22. Genovese, *The Political Economy of Slavery*, pp. 20-22.

23. For the fullest study of the economic role and power of the merchant groups see Roeder, "New Orleans Merchants." For examples of the controversy between merchants, bankers, and planters, see: *Commercial Bulletin*, Feb. 6, 1838, and Nov. 27, 1855; Forstall, p. 4; and R. M. Davis, *The Southern Planter, the Factor, and the Banker.*

24. Redlich, *Molding of American Banking*, I, 205-8. On the creation of the first property bank, see Neu, "J. B. Moussier and the Property Banks of Louisiana," pp. 550-57.

25. Property bank charters. Edmund Forstall to Baring Brothers, Mar. 1, 1830, Baring Microfilms, frame 57193. *AL*, 12 Leg., 2 sess., pp. 95-96. *LS*, [5], 12 Leg., 1 sess., p. 99.

26. *LS*, [22], p. 10. *LS*, [5], 14 Leg., 1 sess., pp. 98-99.

27. The main fiscal agents of the state were the original Louisiana Bank (1804-19), the Louisiana State Bank (1819-1847 and 1850-?), and the Bank of Louisiana (1847-50, perhaps earlier). See *AL*: 4 Leg., 1 sess., p. 18; 13 Leg., 1 sess., p. 73; 1 Leg., 2 sess. (1847), pp. 16-26; 3 Leg., pp. 75-76. On the profitability of this function see William S. Pike to J. M. Lapeyre, Mar. 7, 1856, *LSB*, [1].

28. The state fought the Bank of Louisiana over the proper division of its profits (arising from its initial bond sales in particular), winning the case in 1834. *LS*, [6], 8 Leg., 2 sess. (1828), pp. 62-65. *LS*, [5]: 11 Leg., 2 sess. (1834), p. 4; 12 Leg., 1 sess. (1835), p. 6 and Appendix after p. 46. Bank of Louisiana, *Resolutions.* In 1850 the state also won a lawsuit by which it finally escaped sharing (as a stockholder) in the losses of the Consolidated Association of Planters. *LS*: [24]; [15], 1850.

29. For authorizations of state borrowing from banks, see *AL*, 1813-14, 1821, 1825-29, 1837, 1839, 1846, 1852, 1859. For the early years of crisis and the borrowing privileges, see *LS*, [5]: 14 Leg., 2 sess., App. following p. 138; 15 Leg., 1 sess., pp. 53-54, App. following p. 106; 15 Leg., 2 sess., App. following p. 54.

30. *Banker's Magazine* (New York, November, 1877), p. 347. Sumner, pp. 388-89. Redlich, *Molding of American Banking*, II, 32. Bray Hammond, *Banks and Politics*, p. 682.

31. *AL*, 15 Leg., 2 sess. (Feb. 5, 1842), pp. 34ff.

32. *Ibid.*

33. On the later dominance of the "commercial loan" theories see Paul Trescott, *Money, Banking, and Economic Welfare* (2d ed.), pp. 311-12, 444-48. On the historical impact of the Act of 1842 see the following: *Banker's Magazine*, Nov. 1877, p. 351; Redlich, *Molding of*

American Banking, II, 8-9, 40, 104; Bray Hammond, "The Louisiana Banking Act," pp. 1-3; Caldwell, "Brief History," p. 32.

34. See the sources cited in Note 33; also Hooper, especially pp. 8-14. The claim of a historical connection between Louisiana's laws and the National Bank Act was made long before 1877. The *New Orleans Times* said as much (Oct. 30, 1863, and Jan. 10, 1866), but only vaguely recognized that reserve requirements were the connection.

35. Hammond, *Banks and Politics,* p. 680.

36. Trescott, *Money, Banking, and Economic Welfare* (1st ed.), p. 311. Phillip Cagan, "The First Fifty Years of the National Banking System—An Historical Appraisal," in Carson, p. 22. Hammond's praise for the commercial loan doctrine is slightly more cautious than Redlich's in that he finds the policy appropriate to the New Orleans commercial "environment," but not necessarily feasible for banks in other circumstances.

37. *Banker's Magazine,* Nov. 1877, p. 352, and Bray Hammond, *Banks and Politics,* p. 680; both briefly cite Forstall as the author. But the most thorough account of his contribution is Redlich, *Molding of American Banking,* II, 32-44. Redlich's account is augmented in Neu, "Louisiana Politics and the Bank Act of 1842" and "Edmond Jean Forstall and Louisiana Banking." I would give somewhat greater emphasis than Redlich and Neu give to the precedent of the Bank of England's "Palmer rule" for a one-third specie reserve, which was widely publicized in 1832. See Fetter, pp. 132-33, 145-46. Forstall's 1837 *Report* specifically refers to the British practice (p. 6).

38. The basic sources for my entire discussion of the Bank Act of 1842 and its background are: *AL,* 1839-42; *LS,* [5], 1837-42, and [6], 1842; *USC,* [9], pp. 486-537, 556-60; *USC,* [11], pp. 645-708. For details on the political background, see my article "The Louisiana Bank Act of 1842."

39. *CBC,* [2], pp. 4-10. *CAPC* (folders 26, 27): J. T. Nisbet to President of Consolidated Association, Apr. 21, 1837; Resolutions of Board of Presidents, May 21, 1837. Redlich, "Bank Money in the United States," p. 215.

40. *LS,* [6], 15 Leg., 2 sess., p. 57.

41. Forstall's subsequent claim that the 1842 rules were "exactly the same" as his 1838 proposals is thus seen to be quite exaggerated. See Forstall to Baring Brothers, Feb. 11, 1847, Baring Microfilm, frame 57661. For criticism of Forstall's rules see *LS,* [17].

42. Robert Palfrey to Enoch Hyde, Feb. 9, 1842, City Bank Collection. Thomas G. Morgan to Walter Forward, Feb. 2, 1842, Treasury Dept., [6].

43. Robert Palfrey to William Palfrey, Mar. 29, 1842, Palfrey Papers.

LS, [17]. *AL*, 15 Leg., 2 sess., Mar. 7, 1842, pp. 214-28. Treasury Dept., [6]: Thomas G. Morgan to Walter Forward, Mar. 3, 8, and 18, 1842; *Morning Advertiser*, Mar. 8, 1842.

44. The outlines of the crisis can be traced most readily in the weekly "money market" reports of *Price Current* throughout 1842.

45. *LS*, [5], 16 Leg., 1 sess., pp. 3-4. *CBC*, [4], pp. 155, 214-19, 234. Smith, Hubbard & Co. to Messrs. Thomas Smith & Co., June 16, 1842, Smith, Hubbard & Co. Correspondence. Thomas Butler to his wife, Feb. 23, 1842, Butler Papers.

46. Norton, p. 197. Robert Palfrey to Enoch Hyde, July 12, 1842, City Bank Collection.

47. Ruffin and McLure, pp. 15, 18-20. Sellers, p. 343. McGrane, *Foreign Bondholders*, p. 183.

48. *AL*, 16 Leg., 1 sess., p. 63. Baring Microfilms: Edmund Forstall to Baring Brothers, Oct. 3, 1843 (frame 57234); Matthias Purton to Baring Brothers, Mar. 1, 1844 (frame 59099). *LS*, [13], pp. 848-49, 856-63. *AL*, 2 Leg., 1 sess. (Mar. 16, 1848), pp. 70-77.

49. Baring Microfilms: Forstall to Baring Brothers, Jan. 23 and July 8, 1844 (frames 57274, 57348); Matthias Purton to Baring Brothers, Feb. 13, 1844 (frame 59059). *AL*, 16 Leg., 1 sess., pp. 56-59.

50. The battles against repudiation are briefly discussed in Hidy, *The House of Barings*, pp. 310, 330-36, and McGrane, *Foreign Bondholders*, pp. 182-92. They can be traced in greater detail in the Baring Microfilms, Letters from New Orleans Agents (reels 52-54), especially the letters from Edmund Forstall to Barings, Feb. 11 and Mar. 18, 1847. Forstall to the stockholders of the Consolidated Association of Planters, Feb. 27, 1847, *CAPC*. *AL*: 16 Leg., 2 sess. (Mar. 25, 1844), pp. 49-54, 81; 17 Leg., 1 sess. (Mar. 10, 1845), pp. 29-30, 33-37; 1 Leg., 2 sess. (Apr. 6, 1847), pp. 76-78. A prohibition of future state debts was inserted into the constitutions of several states that had had fiscal troubles after the panic of 1837.

51. See Table 4.1. *LS*, [15], Jan. 26, 1850. *LS*, [13], pp. 874-80.

52. Greer, pp. 592-96. Robb, No. 1 (Feb. 1, 1856). *DeBow's Review*, X (May 1851), pp. 587-89. Edmund Forstall to Baring Brothers, Nov. 13, 1852, Baring Microfilms, frame 58648. *LS*, [25].

53. *AL*, 4 Leg., Mar. 10, 1852, pp. 109-11. *LS*, [10]. Edmund Forstall to Baring Brothers, Nov. 8, 1851, Baring Microfilms, frame 58534.

54. *LS*, [4], pp. 28, 46-50, 70-80. *DeBow's Review*, XVI (Jan., 1854), pp. 78-80. The constitution also specifically ratified the renewed charter of the Citizens Bank.

55. *LS*, [4].

56. *AL*, 1 Leg., Apr. 30, 1853, pp. 301-11. *LS*, [21], 1857, pp. 10-11.

57. *DeBow's Review*: XII (1852), pp. 610-13; XIII (1852), pp. 127-34; XIV (1853), pp. 28-33, 151-57.

58. Baring Microfilms: Forstall to Baring Brothers, Dec. 11, 1850, and Apr. 30, 1853 (frames 58375, 58680); Forstall to F. S. Wilson, Apr. 11, 1853 (frame 58686).

59. Robb, No. 1 (Feb. 1, 1856). *AL*, 2 Leg., 1 sess. (Mar. 16, 1854), pp. 151-52. *LS*: [11]; [21], 1857, pp. 116-34.

Chapter Five

1. See Chandler, *Economics of Money and Banking*, Chapters 5, 9, and 10.

2. It can be argued that even Biddle was not truly a central banker in the modern sense. See Chapter Three; also Fenstermaker, pp. 69-76.

3. Friedman's monetary theory can be found in his *Studies in the Quantity Theory of Money*. It is applied historically in the monumental study by Friedman and Schwartz, *A Monetary History of the United States, 1867-1960*.

4. Macesich, pp. 428-34. The complete model, with several variations, is presented in Friedman and Schwartz, Appendix B.

5. The first major attempt to apply the model to antebellum history was Macesich, pp. 407-34. The underlying classical framework, by which Macesich primarily explains the quantity of specie, has been criticized by Jeffrey Williamson ("International Trade and United States Economic Development"). Peter Temin has recently used the model in *The Jacksonian Economy*, pp. 71-72 and Appendix.

6. See Minsky: "Longer Waves in Financial Relations," pp. 324-35; "Can 'It' (1929) Happen Again?," in Carson, pp. 101-11. For other examples of cyclical studies in this school, see: Gurley, "Liquidity and Financial Institutions"; Hendershott and Murphy, "The Monetary Cycle and the Business Cycle."

7. On this point see Williamson, "International Trade" and *American Growth and the Balance of Payments*.

8. Minsky, p. 333.

9. See Chapter Three for a detailed discussion of these events.

10. Chandler, *Money and Banking*, pp. 138-43. Trescott, *Money, Banking, and Economic Welfare* (1st ed.), pp.. 400-404. Bray Hammond, *Banks and Politics*, pp. 437-43. For an example of contemporary Louisiana opinion, see *USC*, [11], pp. 684-89.

11. Fenstermaker, pp. 66-75. Table C.1. Temin, *The Jacksonian Economy*, pp. 71-73.

12. Message of Governor Roman to Legislature, *LS*, [6], 11 Leg.,

1 sess., pp. 6-7. Bunner, *History of Louisiana. Niles' Weekly Register*, L (Mar. 5, 1836), p. 2. For statistics, see Table C.1. The capital/notes ratio was more nearly a reserve ratio in Louisiana than in most other states because Louisiana bank shares or bonds were largely sold externally and paid for in specie. But this specie did not remain permanently in the banks, or even in the state.

13. For data on specie flows, see Douglass North, "The United States Balance of Payments," in *Trends in the American Economy*, p. 605. The sources that North cites give further detail, particularly in separating gold and silver flows. See also Temin, *The Jacksonian Economy*, pp. 185-89. For attempts to explain American specie flows, see: McGrane, *The Panic of 1837*, Chapter 1; Macesich, "Sources of Monetary Disturbances"; Williamson, *American Growth*; North, *The Economic Growth of the United States*, pp. 71-73; Temin, "The Causes of Cotton-Price Fluctuations in the 1830's," pp. 463-70. Temin, *The Jacksonian Economy*, pp. 77-112.

14. *Historical Statistics*, p. 245. Temin, *The Jacksonian Economy*, pp. 80-82. *CBC*, [2], p. 365 (also in *USC*, [7], pp. 651-52).

15. *Annual Report of the Comptroller of the Currency*, p. 544. *Price Current*: May 27, July 1, and July 15, 1837; Jan. 13, 1838. On reserve ratios, see Table C.1.

16. Treasury Dept., [4]: Commercial Bank to Levi Woodbury, June 5, 1837; Union Bank to Woodbury, July 27, 1837. *CBC*, [2], p. 365.

17. *Price Current*, Mar. 11, 25, Apr. 8, 22, 1837. Table C.1. *LS*, [21], 1858, p. 10.

18. Edmund J. Forstall to Baring Brothers, Oct. 3, 1843, Apr. 6 and Oct. 30, 1844, Baring Microfilms, frames 57234, 57301, 57341.

19. Tables B.4 and C.1. On state debts see Chapter Four. John L. Lobdell to Lewis Stirling, June 16, 1837, Stirling Papers. Cora Slocomb to Mrs. Harriet McCrindell, Apr. 4, 1837, Johnson Letters.

20. L. Hodge to Josiah S. Johnston, Mar. 8, 1832, Johnston Papers. Bunner, *History of Louisiana*.

21. Lance Davis, "Monopolies, Speculators, Causal Models, Quantitative Evidence, and American Economic Growth." Hughes and Rosenberg, pp. 477-79. Minsky, "Longer Waves in Financial Relations," pp. 331-33.

22. L. Hodge to Josiah S. Johnston, Mar. 8, 1832. Johnston Papers. Thompson, p. 32. John L. Lobdell to Lewis Stirling, June 16, 1837, Stirling Papers. *Price Current*, July 3, 1835. *LS*, [21], 1858, pp. 1-7.

23. For data on growth of the national specie supply, see *Annual Report of the Comptroller of the Currency*, p. 544. Cf. the growth of Louisiana's money income, Table B.4.

24. Message of Governor White, Dec. 11, 1837, *LS*, [5], 13 Leg., 2 sess., p. 2. *LS*, [21], 1858, pp. 1-6. Bunner, *History of Louisiana*. Caldwell, *Banking History*, pp. 56-64. McGrane, *The Panic of 1837*, pp. 93-96, 117-20, 122. Bray Hammond is an exception to the general pattern in his recognition that suspension permitted financial relief to debtors; but he also asserts that it necessarily led to depreciated currency and inflation. Hammond, *Banks and Politics*, p. 478.

25. Waterman and Burgess to C. H. Dabney, Oct. 22, 1842, in "New Orleans Cotton Brokers' Correspondence." Smith, Hubbard & Co. to Messrs. Smith & Co. (Hartford, Conn.), May 20 and 25, 1837, Mar. 6, 1838, and Dec. 24, 1841, in Smith, Hubbard & Co. correspondence. On the cotton exports by the banks, see pp. 95-96.

26. For attempts at legislative control, see Chapter Four. For actions of the Board of Presidents, see below. Most historians have failed to recognize the possibility of regulating money and credit through the voluntary action of the banking community (or a cartel of powerful banks); the Suffolk System of Massachusetts stands almost alone in textbooks as an example of this approach. Fritz Redlich goes to the other extreme, and his extensive and sympathetic treatment of various types of "bank cooperation" perhaps understates the limitations of such voluntary self-control. Redlich, *Molding of American Banking*, II, Chapter 20.

27. *Price Current*, Mar. 11 to May 6, 1837. *CBC*, [2], pp. 460-69 (Apr. 12-15, 1837). Robert J. Palfrey to A. Baudouin, Apr. 1, 1837, in *CAPC*, folder 26. *Louisiana Courier*, May 13, 1837.

28. *CBC*, [3], pp. 31-33. Commercial Bank, *Annual Report*, 1838, pp. 39-42. Hughes Lavergne to Gabriel Shaw, June 16, 1839, DeLavergne Papers.

29. *CBC*, [3], pp. 4-10 (May 14-18, 1837). Resolutions adopted in 1837 by the Board of Presidents (May 21), the Citizens Bank (May 22), and the City Bank (May 24); all in *CAPC*, folder 27. Resolutions of the Board of Presidents, Dec. 9, 1839, *ibid.*, folder 34. *USC*, [36], No. 471, pp. 69-71.

30. Sources listed in previous note. Commercial Bank, *Annual Report*, 1838, pp. 42-46. *Price Current*, Oct. 26, 1839. Circular of Citizens Bank, Dec. 12, 1839, *CAPC*, folder 34. *CBC*, [3], p. 25.

31. Whitney & Burnham to James S. Armory, Dec. 27, 1841, Nashua Papers. *Price Current*: May 14, 21, 25, June 4, 11, 15, July 9, 1842. Smith, Hubbard & Co. to Smith & Co., June 16, 1842, in Smith, Hubbard & Co. Correspondence. New Orleans Collector's office to Walter Forward, May 15, July 5, 1842, in Treasury Dept., [6]. Message of Gov. Roman, *LS*, [5], 16 Leg., 1 sess. (Jan. 3, 1843), p. 4. *LS*, [17], pp. 5-6.

32. *CBC*, [4], p. 22. Thomas Butler to his wife, Feb. 23, 1842, Butler Papers. Message of Governor Roman, Dec. 13, 1841, in *LS*, [5], 15 Leg., 2 sess., pp. 1-5. *LS*, [17], pp. 4-6.

33. Smith, Hubbard & Co. to Messrs. Smith & Co. Mar. 6, 1838, and Mar. 12, 1842, in Smith, Hubbard & Co. Correspondence. *CBC*: [2], pp. 473-74; [4], p. 94. Edward Davis to James Amory, Sept. 21, 1841, and William E. Leverich to James Amory, Dec. 28, 1841; both in Nashua Papers.

34. *CAPC*: Charles Lesseps to President of Consolidated Association, May 17, 1837 (folder 27); Committee of Finance, First Municipality, to President of Consolidated Association, May 14 and 22, 1840, Jan. 7, 1841 (folders 37, 39). *CBC*, [3], p. 319. Rightor, p. 599. *Price Current*, May 21, 1842.

35. Commercial Bank, *Annual Report*, 1838, p. 40. *Commercial Bulletin*, May 15, 1837. Cora Slocomb to Mrs. Harriet McCrindell, May 24 and June 18, 1837, in Johnson Letters.

36. *USC*, [36], No. 508. Commercial Bank, *Annual Report*, 1838, pp. 39-42.

37. *Price Current*, Jan. 15, Feb. 19 and 26, Mar. 12, Dec. 7, 1842. Robert J. Palfrey to Enoch Hyde, Aug. 18 and Dec. 7, 1842, City Bank Collection, folder 64. See also Table C.2.

38. Forstall to Baring Brothers, Jan. 17, 1844; Forstall to T. S. Wilson, Apr. 11, 1853 (copy); both in Baring Microfilms, frames 57245, 58686-90.

39. Robert J. Palfrey to William Palfrey, Oct. 18, 1842, Palfrey Papers. Robert J. Palfrey to Enoch Hyde, June 25, 1842, City Bank Collection, folder 64.

40. *LS*, [17], pp. 2-4. Hughes Lavergne to M. B. Sampson, July 30, 1842, DeLavergne Papers.

41. On the hope for recovery via crop earnings, see Hughes Lavergne to Alexander Gordon, Aug. 3, 1842, DeLavergne Papers.

42. *Price Current*, Sept. 12 to Dec. 30, 1857. *LS*, [21], 1858, pp. 1-7, 138. Martin Gordon, Jr., to Benjamin Tureaud, Oct. 15, 1857, Tureaud Papers. *Daily Crescent*, Oct. 19, 1857. Table 3.1. *DeBow's Review*, XXV (Sept. 1858), p. 561. *USC*, [42], p. 70. Table B.4. Thompson, p. 47.

43. *LS*, [21], 1858, pp. 7-8. *Commercial Bulletin*, Jan. 18, 1855.

44. *AL*: 2 Leg., 2 sess. (Mar. 15, 1855), pp. 214-24; 3 Leg., 2 sess. (Mar. 14, 1857), pp. 104-5. *LS*, [21], 1858, pp. 5, 46, 140-43. "The Banking Systems of Louisiana" (anon.). *Daily Delta*, Feb. 28, 1860. *CBC*, [8], pp. 108-9 (Oct. 29 and Nov. 5, 1857).

Chapter Six

1. Stephen Duncan to William Newton Mercer, Jan. 30 and Aug. 7, 1837, Mercer Papers. John L. Lobdell to Lewis Stirling, June 16, 1837, Stirling Papers. *Hunt's Merchants' Magazine*, XIII (1845), 470-72. Bunner, *History of Louisiana* (see Chapter Five for excerpts). Reed, "Boom or Bust," pp. 36, 41, 49. Rightor, pp. 595-96.

2. McGuire Diary, May 1837. Planters Bank (Natchez) to Levi Woodbury, July 11, 1837, in Treasury Dept., [5]. Winston, pp. 215-16, 221. Babin, p. 259. McGrane, *Foreign Bondholders*, pp. 176-77.

3. Hughes Lavergne to Gabriel Shaw, June 16, 1839, DeLavergne Papers. Reed, "Boom or Bust," p. 53. McGuire Diary, May 1837, Jan., 1842.

4. Hughes and Rosenberg, "The United States Business Cycle Before 1860," pp. 476-82.

5. *Ibid.*, pp. 482-93.

6. For perceptive comments on the application of Friedman's model to economic history, see: Culbertson, "United States Monetary History"; Clower, "Monetary History and Positive Economics."

7. Duesenberry, Chapters 11, 12, and 14, especially pp. 250-53, 269-70, 324-25.

8. See Appendix B.

9. A similar argument is made by Ulrich B. Phillips in "The Economic Cost of Slaveholding in the Cotton Belt," reprinted in Woodman, *Slavery and the Southern Economy*, pp. 43-44.

10. Temin, *The Jacksonian Economy*, pp. 136-47.

11. *Price Current*, 1837-42. See also Table C.2.

12. *Price Current*, Mar. 25, 1837, and Feb. 19, 1842. Ayres P. Merrill to William Newton Mercer, Mar. 29, 1837, Mercer Papers. Merrill was cashier in the Natchez bank of which Mercer was a director.

13. Appendix B. Rightor, pp. 511-17. Smith, Hubbard & Co. to Smith & Co., Feb. 18, 1839, in Smith, Hubbard & Co. Correspondence.

14. USBC, [3], XIX, 267. Foner, pp. 144-47.

15. Russell, pp. 101-4. Foner (p. 147) also mentions lower estimates but seems to accept Hammond's version. For price and output data see Table B.1 and its sources. The counterfactual assumption of stable average prices assumes an increase in British and Northern demand roughly equal to the 5 per cent increase in Southern cotton output.

16. The need to "separate the 'responsibility' of individuals and occupational groups [the planters, the factors, the bankers] from that of a

complex system" is pointed out by William Parker in his review of Woodman's *King Cotton and His Retainers*. Woodman himself made a similar distinction in "The Profitability of Slavery."

17. Genovese, pp. 3-4, 17, 20-26.

18. Conrad and Meyer, pp. 43-92. Genovese (pp. 275-87) seems to doubt that slavery was profitable even for the planters, although he considers the issue of minor importance. Most of the research stimulated by the Conrad and Meyer study seems to confirm their conclusion; see Engerman, "The Effects of Slavery Upon the Southern Economy." The critics of Conrad and Meyer generally admit that slavery was profitable to the slaveholders themselves, but question its benefits for the entire Southern economy and society. See Woodman, "The Profitability of Slavery"; Fischbaum and Rubin, "Slavery and the Economic Development of the American South."

19. Richard Easterlin, "Interregional Differences," in *Trends in the American Economy*, pp. 97-98.

20. Richard Easterlin, "Regional Income Trends, 1840-1950," in Harris, p. 528. Genovese (p. 161) argues quite persuasively that unequal income distribution was an intrinsic and necessary part of the slave society, not only for slaves but among whites as well. This point undermines my convenient distinction between productivity and distribution.

21. See Appendix B. Easterlin's 1860 income estimate extrapolates from 1840 by considering changes in agriculture and manufacturing. It does not measure the growth of commerce; for this, the data in my Table B.3 are helpful. Easterlin, in Harris, pp. 528, 545. *DeBow's Review*, X (May 1851), 589. USBC, [3], XIX, 252, 253, 256. Reed, *New Orleans and the Railroads*, pp. 8, 61, 143. Rightor, pp. 512-16.

22. Allen H. Fenichel, "Growth and Diffusion of Power in Manufacturing, 1838-1919," in *Output, Employment, and Productivity*, pp. 456, 462-64, 470-71. Temin, "Steam and Waterpower," pp. 191-92, 202. Sitterson, *Sugar Country*, pp. 155-56. Rightor, pp. 513, 514.

23. *DeBow's Review*, X (May 1851), 588-89. Clark, "New Orleans and the River." Reed, *New Orleans and the Railroads*, pp. 21-23, 128-30. The lack of any rigorous economic analysis in Reed's study leaves us uncertain about the social value or optimal timing of individual railroad projects. It remains unclear what part of New Orleans' trading hinterland the railroads could economically preserve or extend. See Thomas Brewer's review, pp. 130-31. In 1840 Louisiana actually had in operation about 75 per cent more railroad mileage per capita than the national average. But she did not keep up, and by 1860 she had only half the national average. See Reed, *ibid.*, p. 58; Taylor, *The Transportation Revolution*, p. 79.

24. Engerman, "The Effects of Slavery," pp. 90-91.
25. North, *Economic Growth*, pp. 130-33.

Appendix B

1. Robert E. Gallman: "Commodity Output, 1839-1899," in *Trends in the American Economy*, pp. 13-67; "Gross National Product in the United States, 1834-1909," in *Output, Employment, and Productivity*, pp. 3-76.

2. Richard A. Easterlin, "Interregional Differences," in *Trends in the American Economy*, pp. 73-140; "Regional Income Trends, 1840-1950," in Harris, pp. 525-47.

3. Seaman, pp. 461-62.

4. The government expenditure estimate is from Lance Davis and John Legler, "The Government in the American Economy." Their estimate of $9.40 per capita (for Louisiana and Arkansas) is on p. 548.

5. Most of the cotton data I have used, and many more, are conveniently gathered in Bruchey, *Cotton and the Growth of the American Economy*.

6. The source for this data on value of produce received is Callender, *Selections from the Economic History of the United States*, p. 315. Since Callender headed his table "River Trade of New Orleans, 1813-1860," and gave no details of sources, the meaning of his data is uncertain. But a close comparison with the annual issues of the New Orleans *Price Current* removes this ambiguity. Comparable tables in the source are headed "Value of Produce of the Interior" and include mainly agricultural products, plus such basic commodities as sacking, coal, pig iron, lead, barrel staves, and glass. Louisiana products are included; in fact, cotton and sugar together account for well over half the total value. Ideally, my trade statistics should also include imports from the East Coast and Europe, as well as other types of commodities (especially manufactured goods). But good annual data on these items are not available.

7. See also the brief discussion of the allocation of commercial income between Louisiana and other states in Fishlow, *American Railroads*, pp. 273-75.

8. Paul A. David, "Measuring Real Net Output: A Proposed Index," *Review of Economics and Statistics*, XLVIII (Nov. 1966), 419-25. David does not comment on the usefulness of his approach for the case of the open economy.

Bibliography

Bibliography

SINCE published contemporary works on the economy of antebellum Louisiana are virtually nonexistent, and since the few good modern studies concentrate heavily on such traditional topics as slavery and the plantation economy, most of the evidence for this study has been pieced together from manuscript collections and government documents. The crucial manuscripts, of course, are the surviving records and reports of the banks themselves. These are mostly located at the Tulane University Library and at the Department of Archives and Manuscripts of Louisiana State University (Baton Rouge). The two most valuable collections are Tulane's Canal Bank Collection (which contains the minutebooks of the important Citizens Bank) and the Consolidated Association of the Planters of Louisiana Collection at L.S.U. The same two libraries also have extensive collections of the papers of antebellum planters, merchants, and other businessmen, and many of these contain commentary on banking and finance. Two other large and useful manuscript collections are the Records of the Secretary of the Treasury in the National Archives, especially the Treasury's correspondence with state chartered banks in the 1830's and 1840's, and the papers of Baring Brothers & Company, a London merchant banking firm (microfilm copy in the Library of Congress). I have also made selective use of contemporary newspapers and periodicals; most valuable on economic matters are the New Orleans *Price Current* and *DeBow's Review*.

Louisiana state documents were valuable in studying the legal and political policy aspects of antebellum banking. Bank charters appear in the *Acts of Louisiana*, and the journals and committee reports of the state legislature reveal the politics of banking policy. Federal government publications, particularly the massive Congressional Serial Set (House and Senate reports and documents), provided most of the essential statistics on finance and the economy, for Louisiana and for the rest of the nation. These Congressional records also reproduce various state legislative reports and other documents related to banking, some of which have not survived elsewhere; where other copies do survive, however, there are occasional discrepancies. The published federal census materials were also useful.

The following bibliographical aids proved most useful in locating the primary sources:

Foote, Luci Brown. *Bibliography of the Official Publications of Louisiana, 1803-1934.* Baton Rouge, 1942.

Index to *DeBow's Review.* 2 vols. Typescript, n.p., n.d. (Tulane.)

Jenkins, William Sumner, and Lillian A. Hamrick, eds. *A Guide to the Microfilm Collection of Early State Records.* Washington, D.C., 1950.

Louisiana Historical Record Survey, Works Progress Administration. *Louisiana Newspapers, 1794-1940.* University, La., 1941.

Louisiana Historical Society. *Subject Index to the Publications and Louisiana Historical Quarterly, 1895-1941.* New Orleans, 1941.

McMurtrie, Douglas C. *Early Printing in New Orleans, 1764-1810.* New Orleans, 1929.

Superintendent of Documents. *Tables of and Annotated Index to the Congressional Series of U.S. Public Documents* [1817-1893]. Washington, D.C., 1902.

Thompson, Donald E., ed. *A Bibliography of Louisiana Books and Pamphlets in the T. P. Thompson Collection of the University of Alabama Library.* University, Alabama, 1947.

Even after all possible sources were examined, some large gaps in the evidence remained. I was particularly frustrated by the limited data on chartered banking before 1830 (especially statistics on bank operations), on the operations and impact of private, unchartered banks in Louisiana, on the flow of financial capital between states, and on the political alignments of parties and interest groups in the state legislature.

Acts of Louisiana (AL) 1812-61. The laws passed by the legislature in each session. An indispensable source containing bank charters, insurance company charters, and general laws regulating the banks.

Acts Passed at the 3 Leg., 2 sess., of the Territory of Orleans. Contains charters of the Planters Bank and Bank of Orleans.

Adams, William Harrison, III. "The Louisiana Whig Party." Ph.D. dissertation, Louisiana State University, 1960.

Albion, Robert G. "New York Port and its Disappointed Rivals, 1815-1860." *Journal of Economic and Business History*, III (1930-31), 602-29.

———— *The Rise of New York Port, 1815-1860.* New York, 1939.

American Assembly. *United States Monetary Policy.* New York, 1958.

American State Papers: Finance. Vols. II-V. Washington, D.C., 1832-61.

Andreasson, John C. "Internal Improvements in Louisiana, 1824-1837." M.A. thesis, Louisiana State University, 1935.

Annual Report of the Comptroller of the Currency, 1896, Vol. I. Washington, D.C., 1897.

Atchafalaya Railroad. *Report of the Commissioners of the Atchafalaya Railroad and Banking Company, as made to the Board of Currency on June 22, 1842.* New Orleans, 1842. (Thompson Collection.)

Atherton, Lewis. *The Southern Country Store, 1800-1860.* Baton Rouge, 1949.

Babin, Claude H. "The Economic Expansion of New Orleans before the Civil War." Ph.D. dissertation, Tulane University, 1954.

"The Banking Systems of Louisiana." New Orleans, 1860. (Harvard University). An anonymous pamphlet reprinting excerpts from the *Commercial Bulletin* of New Orleans that compare free banks and chartered banks.

Bank of Louisiana. *Rapport du Comité des Actionnaires de La Banque de la Louisiane.* New Orleans, 1820. (Tulane, Favrot Collection.)

———— *Resolutions Unanimously Adopted by the Board of Directors of the Bank of Louisiana, January 9, 1834.* New Orleans, 1834. (LSU.)

Baring Brothers and Company Manuscripts, 1825-1860. Microfilm Copy, Library of Congress. 78 reels. Reels 51-54 contain reports from Baring agents in New Orleans.

Barker, Jacob. *Incidents in the Life of Jacob Barker, of New Orleans, Louisiana.* Washington, D.C., 1855.

Baughman, James P. "Early American Checks: Forms and Functions." *Business History Review*, XLI (1967), 421-35.

Biddle (Nicholas) Papers, 1823-41. Library of Congress, President's Letterbooks, Vols. CXIV-CXX.

Biographical Directory of the American Congress, 1774-1949. Washington, D.C., 1949.

Blaug, Marc. *Economic Theory in Retrospect.* Homewood, Ill., 1962.

Bodin, Arnold. *Minority Report.* Submitted to the stockholders of the Citizens Bank of Louisiana. New Orleans, 1847. (Thompson Collection.)

Bourne, Edward G. *The History of the Surplus Revenue of 1837.* New York, 1883.

240   BIBLIOGRAPHY

Brewer, Thomas. Review of Merl Reed, *New Orleans and the Railroads.* *Journal of Economic History,* XXVII (1967), 130-31.

Brown, John Crosby. *A Hundred Years of Merchant Banking; A History of Brown Brothers and Company, Brown, Shipley and Company and the Allied Firms.* New York, 1909.

Bruchey, Stuart. *Cotton and the Growth of the American Economy, 1790-1860.* New York, 1967.

Bruton, Henry J. *Principles of Development Economics.* Englewood Cliffs, N.J., 1965.

Buck, Norman S. *The Development of the Organization of Anglo-American Trade, 1800-1850.* New Haven, Conn., 1925.

Bunner, E. *History of Louisiana.* New York, 1861.

Burge, Dennis Fourt. "Louisiana Under Governor André Bienvenu Roman: 1831-1835, 1839-1843." M.A. thesis, Louisiana State University, 1937.

"Business Failures in the Panic of 1857." *Business History Review,* XXXVII (1963), 437-44.

Butler (Thomas and Family) Papers, 1842. (LSU Archives.)

Caldwell, Stephen A. *A Banking History of Louisiana.* Baton Rouge, 1935.

———— "A Brief History of Banking in Louisiana" [1808-1948] *McNeese Review,* II (1949), 31-33.

———— "The Economic Development of the Shreveport Trade Area." *Louisiana Business Bulletin,* V, No. 2 (May 1943). (LSU.)

———— "The New Orleans Trade Area." *University Bulletin,* XXVIII, No. 10 (1936). (LSU.)

Callender, Guy S. "The Early Transportation and Banking Enterprises of the States in Relation to the Growth of the Corporations." *Quarterly Journal of Economics,* XVII (1903), 111-62.

———— *Selections from the Economic History of the United States, 1765-1860.* Boston, 1909.

Cameron, Rondo E. "The Banker as Entrepreneur." *Explorations in Entrepreneurial History,* I (1963), 50-55.

———— "Banking in the Early Stages of Industrialization: A Preliminary Survey." *Scandinavian Economic History Review,* XI (1963), 117-34.

———— *et al. Banking in the Early Stages of Industrialization.* New York, 1967.

Canal Bank Collection (*CBC*), 1830-63. (Tulane.) The largest and most valuable collection of banking materials on antebellum Louisiana. The great bulk of it actually concerns the Citizens Bank of Louisiana. The most useful volumes are listed here.

———— [1] Vol. 103: Canal Bank Letterbook, 1830-32.

———— [2] Vol. 95: Citizens Bank Minutebook 1, 1833-37.

———— [3] Vol. 91: Citizens Bank Minutebook 2, 1837-39. (Citizens Bank Minutebook 3, 1839-41, is missing.)

———— [4] Vol. 99: Citizens Bank Minutebook 4, 1841-42.

———— [5] Vol. 88: Citizens Bank Minutebook 5, 1842-46.

———— [6] Vol. 100: Citizens Bank Minutebook 6, 1846-51.

———— [7] Vol. 101: Citizens Bank Minutebook 7, 1851-56.

———— [8] Vol. 58: Citizens Bank Minutebook 8, 1856-68.

———— [9] Vol. 93: Citizens Bank Stock Book, 1836-78.

———— [10] Vol. 104: Canal Bank, Report of Assets and Liabilities, 1831-33.

———— [11] Vol. 81: Citizens Bank Property Mortgage Book, 1847.

Capers, Gerald M. *Occupied City; New Orleans under the Federals, 1862-1865.* Lexington, Ky., 1965.

Carey, Rita Katherine, "Samuel Jarvis Peters." *Louisiana Historical Quarterly*, XXX (1947), 439-80.

Carson, Deane, ed. *Banking and Monetary Studies.* Homewood, Ill., 1963.

Catterall, Helen Turncliff. *Judicial Cases Concerning American Slavery and the Negro.* Washington, D.C., 1932.

Catterall, Ralph C. H. *The Second Bank of the United States.* Chicago, 1902.

Chandler, Lester V. *Central Banking and Economic Development.* Bombay, 1962.

———— *The Economics of Money and Banking.* 4th ed. New York, 1964.

Citizens Bank of Louisiana (*CBL*). [1] Financial Statements of the Citizens Bank and the Consolidated Association of the Planters of Louisiana, 1849-57. (Tulane.)

———— [2] *Report of the Committee of Investigation (Selected From the Stockholders) Appointed by the Direction of the Citizens Bank of Louisiana, in Conformity with the Resolution of the Board of 18th October, 1838.* New Orleans, 1839. (Tulane.) A critical appraisal of the bank's performance under Edmund Forstall, and particularly of the London agency of F. de Lizardi & Co.

———— [3] *Report of the Committee of Investigation Named by the Stockholders of the Citizens Bank, August 1, 1842.* New Orleans, 1842. (Thompson Collection. French version available at Tulane.) Analyzes reasons for the Bank's decline into forced liquidation between 1839 and 1842.

———— [4] *Report of the President of the Citizens Bank to the Presi-*

dent of the State Senate, February 2, 1844. (Thompson Collection. French version available at Tulane.)

City Bank of New Orleans. *Charter, Rules, &c., of the City Bank of New Orleans.* (Tulane.)

———— City Bank of New Orleans Collection, 1832-1852. (LSU Archives.) Four boxes of correspondence, financial statements, and lists of stockholders. Much of it deals with relations between branches and New Orleans.

Claiborne, John Francis Hamtramck. *Mississippi as a Province, Territory, and State.* Vol. I. Jackson, Miss., 1880.

Claiborne (John F. H.) Collection, 1833-34. (Mississippi State Department of Archives and History). Letters from William G. Hewes to George Poindexter on the selection of the Commercial Bank as a federal deposit bank.

Clark, John G. "The Antebellum Grain Trade of New Orleans: Changing Patterns in the Relation of New Orleans with the Old Northwest." *Agricultural History,* XXXVIII (1964), 131-42.

———— *The Grain Trade in the Old Northwest.* Urbana, Ill., 1966.

———— "New Orleans and the River: A Study in Attitudes and Responses." *Louisiana History,* VIII (1967), 117-35.

Clower, Robert W. "Monetary History and Positive Economics." *Journal of Economic History,* XXIV (1964), 364-80.

Cole, Arthur H. "Evolution of the Foreign-Exchange Market of the United States." *Journal of Economic and Business History,* I (1929), 384-421.

———— "Seasonal Variation in Sterling Exchange." *Journal of Economic and Business History,* II (1929), 203-18.

———— *Wholesale Commodity Prices in the United States, 1700-1861.* Cambridge, Mass., 1938.

Commercial Bank of Natchez Collection, 1836-45. (LSU Archives.) A huge collection of 200 volumes, some 10,000 items. Major use was confined to letterbooks and minutebooks of the Bank's branches.

Commercial Bank of New Orleans. *Annual Report of the President of the Commercial Bank of New Orleans.* New Orleans, 1838. (Thompson Collection.)

———— *Annual Report of the President of the Commercial Bank of New Orleans.* New Orleans, 1848. (Tulane.) Mainly on waterworks operations, little on banking.

———— *Memorial of the Commercial Bank of New Orleans* [to the Louisiana General Assembly]. January 24, 1852. (Tulane.) Requesting legislative relief from municipal taxation.

Commercial Bulletin, 1838, 1855. New Orleans.

Conrad, Alfred H., and John R. Meyer. *The Economics of Slavery and Other Studies in Econometric History.* Chicago, 1964.

Consolidated Association of the Planters of Louisiana. *Charter, Amendments, Rules, and Regulations, Bye-laws of the Consolidated Association of the Planters of Louisiana.* (Tulane.)

———— Consolidated Association of the Planters of Louisiana Collection (*CAPC*), 1827-61. (LSU Archives.) Of the 84 volumes and nearly 10,000 items in the collection, the most useful materials were: 58 folders of miscellaneous unbound papers, 3 volumes of letterbooks, 1829-61; 4 volumes of minutebooks, 1827-59; 1 volume of "Descriptions of Properties Mortgaged, 1847."

Culbertson, John M. "United States Monetary History: Its Implications for Monetary Theory." *National Banking Review*, I (1964), 359-79.

Daily Crescent, 1850-62. New Orleans.

Daily Delta, 1860-62. New Orleans.

Daily True Delta, 1855-62. New Orleans.

Dabney, Thomas Ewing. *One Hundred Years of the Canal Bank and Trust Company.* New Orleans, 1931.

David, Paul A. "Measuring Real Net Output: A Proposed Index." *Review of Economics and Statistics*, XLVIII (1966), 419-25.

———— "The Growth of Real Product in the United States Before 1840: New Evidence, Controlled Conjectures." *Journal of Economic History*, XXVII (1967), 151-97.

Davis, Edwin Adams. *Louisiana: The Pelican State.* Baton Rouge, 1959.

Davis, Lance E. "Capital Immobilities and Finance Capitalism: A Study of Economic Evolution in the United States, 1820-1920." *Explorations in Entrepreneurial History*, I (1963), 88-105.

———— "The Capital Markets and Industrial Concentration: The U.S. and U.K., A Comparative Study." *Economic History Review*, XIX (1966), 255-72.

———— "The Investment Market, 1870-1914: The Evolution of a National Market." *Journal of Economic History*, XXV (1965), 355-99.

———— "Monopolies, Speculators, Causal Models, Quantitative Evidence, and American Economic Growth." Paper read to the Organization of American Historians, Chicago, April 28, 1967.

———— and J. R. T. Hughes. "A Dollar-Sterling Exchange, 1803-1895." *Economic History Review*, XIII (1960), 52-78.

————, J. R. T. Hughes, and Duncan McDougall. *American Economic History.* 3d ed. Homewood, Ill., 1969.

———— and John Legler. "The Government in the American Economy, 1815-1902: A Quantitative Approach." *Journal of Economic History*, XXVI (1966), 514-52.

Davis, Robert M. *Public and Private Credit and Banking and their Abuses.* New Orleans, 1869. (Thompson Collection.)
——— *The Southern Planter, The Factor, and the Banker.* New Orleans, 1871.
DeBow's Review, 1846-66. New Orleans.
DeLaVergne Papers, 1827-42. (Tulane.) Correspondence of banker Hughes LaVergne.
Denison, Edward F. *The Sources of Economic Growth in the United States.* New York, 1962.
Deutsche Zeitung, 1851-67. New Orleans.
Doyle, Elizabeth J. "Greenbacks, Car Tickets, and a Pot of Gold." *Civil War History,* V (1959), 347-62.
Duesenberry, James S. *Business Cycles and Economic Growth.* New York, 1958.
Dufau, Pierre Armand. *Reflexions sur l'influence et le danger des banques de la Louisiane; Sur la nécessité d'une réforme et les moyens de l'operer.* New Orleans, 1823. (Tulane, Favrot Collection.) An English version of this book is available in the Thompson Collection.
Engerman, Stanley L. "The Effects of Slavery upon the Southern Economy: A Review of the Recent Debate." *Explorations in Entrepreneurial History,* IV (1967), 71-97.
Evans, Harry Howard. "James Robb, Banker and Pioneer Railroad Builder of Ante-Bellum Louisiana." *Louisiana Historical Quarterly,* XXIII (1940), 170-258.
Evans (Nathaniel and Family) Papers, 1806-18. (LSU Archives.)
Evening Post, August 3, 1836. New York.
Fenstermaker, Joseph Van. *The Development of American Commercial Banking: 1782-1837.* Kent, Ohio, 1965.
Fetter, Frank Whitson. *Development of British Monetary Orthodoxy, 1797-1875.* Cambridge, Mass., 1965.
Financial Register of the United States, 1837-38. Philadelphia.
Fischbaum, Marvin, and Julius Rubin. "Slavery and the Economic Development of the American South." *Explorations in Entrepreneurial History,* VI (1968), 116-27.
Fishlow, Albert. *American Railroads and the Transformation of the Ante-Bellum Economy.* Cambridge, Mass., 1965.
——— "Antebellum Interregional Trade Reconsidered." *American Economic Review, Proceedings,* LIV (1964), 352-64.
Fogel, Robert William. "The Specification Problem in Economic History." *Journal of Economic History,* XXVII (1967), 283-308.
Folz, William E. "The Financial Crisis of 1819." Ph.D. dissertation, University of Illinois, 1935.

Foner, Philip S. *Business and Slavery; the New York Merchants and the Irrepressible Conflict.* Chapel Hill, N.C., 1941.

Forstall, Edmund J. *Agricultural Productions of Louisiana.* New Orleans, 1845. (LSU.)

Forstall (Eugene) Letterbooks, 1851-64. (Tulane.)

Fortier, Alcée. *History of Louisiana.* Vol. III. New York, 1904.

Foulke, Roy A. *The Sinews of American Commerce.* New York, 1941.

Friedman, Milton. *A Program for Monetary Stability.* New York, 1960.

────── *Studies in the Quantity Theory of Money.* Chicago, 1956.

────── and Anna Jacobson Schwartz. *A Monetary History of the United States, 1867-1960.* Princeton, N.J., 1963.

Gallman, Robert E. "Self-Sufficiency in the Cotton Economy of the Antebellum South." *Agricultural History,* XLIV (1970), 5-23.

Gatell, Frank Otto. "Spoils of the Bank War: Political Bias in the Selection of Pet Banks." *American Historical Review,* LXX (1964), 35-58.

Gayarre, Charles. *History of Louisiana.* Vol. IV. New York, 1866.

General Land Office of the United States. *Annual Reports of the Commissioner of the General Land Office,* 1843-61. Washington, D.C.

Genovese, Eugene D. *The Political Economy of Slavery.* New York, 1965.

Gerstner, Franz Anton Ritter von. *Berichte aus den Vereinigten Staaten von Nord Amerika: Ueber eisenbahnen, dampfschiffahrten, banken und andere offentliche Unternehmungen.* Leipzig, 1837.

Gibson, John. *Gibson's Guide and Directory of the State of Louisiana, and the Cities of New Orleans and Lafayette, Embracing . . . an Historical Notice of the States, Its Boundaries, Products, and Government.* New Orleans, 1838.

Goldsmith, Raymond W. *Financial Structure and Development.* New Haven, Conn., 1969.

Golembe, Carter H. "State Banks and the Economic Development of the West, 1830-1844." Ph.D. dissertation, Columbia University, 1952.

Govan, Thomas Payne. *Nicholas Biddle: Nationalist and Public Banker, 1786-1844.* Chicago, 1959.

Gras, N. S. B., and Henrietta M. Larson. *Casebook in American Business History.* New York, 1939.

Gray, Lewis C. *History of Agriculture in the Southern United States to 1860.* 2 vols. Washington, D.C., 1933.

Green, George D. "The Louisiana Bank Act of 1842." *Explorations in Economic History,* VII (1970), 399-412.

Greer, James Kimmons. "Politics in Louisiana, 1845-1861." *Louisiana Historical Quarterly,* XII (1929), 381-425, 555-610; XIII (1930), 67-116, 257-303, 444-83, 617-54.

Grenier, Emile Phillipe. "The Early Financing of the Consolidated Association of the Planters of Louisiana." M.A. thesis, Louisiana State University, 1938.
────── "Property Banks in Louisiana." Ph.D. dissertation, Louisiana State University, 1942.
Gurley, John G. "Financial Structures in Developing Economies." In David Krivine, ed., *Fiscal and Monetary Problems in Developing States*, pp. 99-120. New York, 1967.
────── "Liquidity and Financial Institutions in the Postwar Economy." 86 Cong., 1 sess., *Study of Employment, Growth and Price Levels*. Joint Economic Committee Study Paper No. 14. 1960.
────── and Edward S. Shaw. "Capital Formation, Decentralization of Decision-Making, and Financial Innovation." Mimeographed.
────── "Financial Aspects of Economic Development." *American Economic Review*, XLV (1955), 515-38.
────── "Financial Intermediaries and the Saving-Investment Process." *Journal of Finance*, XI (1956), 257-76.
────── "Financial Structure and Economic Development." *Economic Development and Cultural Change*, XV (1967), 257-68.
────── "The Growth of Debt and Money in the United States, 1800-1950: A Suggested Interpretation." *Review of Economics and Statistics*, XXXIX (1957), 250-62.
────── *Money in a Theory of Finance*. Washington, D.C., 1960.
Hall, James. *Statistics of the West at the Close of the Year 1836*. Cincinnati, 1836. (Library of Congress.)
Hammond, Bray. *Banks and Politics in America from the Revolution to the Civil War*. Princeton, N.J., 1957.
────── "The Louisiana Banking Act of February 5, 1842." *Federal Reserve Bank of Atlanta Monthly Bulletin*, XXVII (January 1942), 1-3.
Hammond, Matthew Brown. *The Cotton Industry: An Essay in American Economic History*. Part I: *The Cotton Culture and the Cotton Trade*. New York, 1897.
Hansen, Alvin H. *A Guide to Keynes*. New York, 1953.
Harris, Seymour E., ed. *American Economic History*. New York, 1961.
Hawk, Emory Q. *Economic History of the South*. New York, 1934.
Hazard Company Correspondence, 1842-49. (LSU Archives.) New Orleans branch office of Rhode Island textile manufacturer.
Heck, Harold Joseph. "The Development of Banking in Louisiana." M.A. thesis, Louisiana State University, 1931.
────── "A History of Banks and Bank Legislation in Louisiana." Dissertation for Doctorate in Commercial Science, New York University, 1939.
Hendershott, Patric, and James L. Murphy. "The Monetary Cycle and

the Business Cycle: The Flow of Funds Reexamined." *National Banking Review*, I (1964), 531-50.

Hidy, Ralph W. *The House of Baring in American Trade and Finance.* Cambridge, Mass., 1949.

—— "The House of Baring and the Second Bank of the United States, 1826-1836." *Pennsylvania Magazine of History and Biography*, LXVIII (1944), 269-85.

—— "The Union Bank of Louisiana Loan, 1832: A Case Study in Marketing." *Journal of Political Economy*, XLVII (1939), 232-53.

Hooper, Samuel. *An Examination of the Theory and the Effect of Laws Regulating the Amount of Specie in Banks.* Boston, 1860.

Hirschman, Albert O., ed. *Latin American Issues.* New York, 1961.

Howard, Perry H. *Political Tendencies in Louisiana, 1812-1952.* Baton Rouge, 1957.

Hughes, J. R. T., and Nathan Rosenberg. "The United States Business Cycle before 1860: Some Problems of Interpretation." *Economic History Review*, XV (1963), 476-93.

Hunt's Merchants' Magazine, 1839-55. New York.

Jenks, Leland. *The Migration of British Capital to 1875.* New York, 1927.

Johnson (Charles James) Letters and Family Correspondence, 1837. (LSU Archives.)

Johnson, Harry G. "Monetary Theory and Policy." *American Economic Review*, LII (1962), 335-84.

Johnston (Josiah Stoddard) Papers, 1823-32. (Historical Society of Pennsylvania.)

Kent, Frank Richardson. *The Story of Alexander Brown & Sons.* Baltimore, 1925.

Kettell, Thomas P. *Southern Wealth and Northern Profits.* New York, 1860.

Keynes, John Maynard. *The General Theory of Employment, Interest, and Money.* New York, 1936.

Kinley, David. *The History, Organization, and Influence of the Independent Treasury of the United States.* New York, 1893.

Knox, John Jay. *A History of Banking in the United States.* New York, 1900.

Kuznets, Simon. "Notes on the Take-Off." In Walt W. Rostow, ed., *The Economics of Take-Off into Sustained Growth*, pp. 22-43. New York, 1963.

Le Long, Alphonse Annet. *Fifty Years of Banking; Reminiscences Culled from the Annals of the Citizens Bank of Louisiana, the Oldest Financial Institution of the State.* New Orleans, 1911.

Leonard (Jonathan and C. J.) Letter, 1838. (LSU Archives.)

Liddell (Moses, St. John R., and Family) papers, 1842-53. (LSU Archives.)

Lively, Robert A. "The American System: A Review Article." *Business History Review*, XXIX (1955), 81-96.

Longpré, Jean. *An Answer to the Report of the Committee of Stockholders of the Louisiana Bank, Concerning the Deficit and Over-Emission Discovered in that Institution.* New Orleans, 1820. (Thompson Collection.)

Louisiana Advertiser, 1832. New Orleans.

"The Louisiana Bank Act of 1844 [1842]." *Bankers Magazine* (New York), November 1877, pp. 344-53.

Louisiana Bankers' Association. *The Book of the Bankers of Louisiana, Together with a Short History of each Financial Institution in the State, from their Date of Organization down to the year 1902.* New Orleans, 1902.

Louisiana Courier [*Courrier de la Louisiane*], 1829-37. New Orleans.

Louisiana Gazette [*Gazette de la Louisiane*], 1815-24. New Orleans.

Louisiana State Bank (*LSB*). [1] Louisiana State Bank Collection, 1817-60. (LSU Archives.) A large collection (some 187 folders and a few bound volumes) that is most valuable for its general correspondence items and the financial statements of several banks. The letterbook of the St. Martinsville office, 1818-23, is revealing on branch banking policies.

———— [2] Letter of the President of the Louisiana State Bank to the Directors of the Orleans Navigation Company [Samuel J. Peters, October 23, 1849]. New Orleans, 1850. (Tulane.)

———— [3] "Reglemens pour l'administration des affairs de la banque de l'état de la Louisiane." New Orleans, 1818. (Tulane, Favrot Collection.)

Louisiana State Documents (*LS*). [1] *Documents &c., Relative to the Investigation on Banks by the Joint Committee of the Senate and House of Representatives of the State of Louisiana.* 14 Leg., 2 sess., 1840. (Tulane, New Orleans and Carrollton Railroad Company Papers.) This document contains valuable details on the financial condition, the specific debtors and creditors, and the practices of the banks during financial crisis. It is reprinted in *USC* [11].

———— [2] *Documents Relative to the Banks of New Orleans.* By order of the Legislature of Louisiana, 1838. (Tulane.) The first 51 pages of this 174-page document are reprinted in *USC* [9], pp. 609-74. The remainder contain valuable statistical details on most of the banks of New Orleans between 1835 and 1838.

———— [3] *Documents Relative to the Usury Bill.* By order of the Louisiana Senate. New Orleans, 1823. (Tulane.)

——— [4] *Journal of the Convention to Form a New Constitution for the State of Louisiana*. New Orleans, 1852. (New Orleans Public Library.)

——— [5] Louisiana Legislature. *House Journal*, 1812-61. An indispensable source of information on the formulation of state banking policy. The entries contain not only the chronology of debate and voting on legislation, including many roll-call votes, but also some committee reports and other administrative documents.

——— [6] Louisiana Legislature. *Senate Journal*, 1812-61. Same value as *House Journal*. Used selectively.

——— [7] *Louisiana Reports*, IX, May 1836.

——— [8] *Memorial of the General Assembly of the State of Louisiana*, April 18, 1820 [to Congress]. (Tulane.) Opposing continuation of an act regulating circulation of foreign gold coins in the United States.

——— [9] *Minority Report of the Joint Committee on Banks and Banking* [of the Legislature]. 1858. (Tulane.)

——— [10] *Minority Report of the Judiciary Committee on the Citizens Bank Bill*. New Orleans, 1852. (LSU.)

——— [11] *Minority Report of the Senate Committee on the General System of Free Banking in the State of Louisiana*. 1854. (Tulane.)

——— [12] *Observations of Governor Robertson on a Pamphlet published by order of the Senate entitled "Documents Relative to the Usury Bill."* New Orleans, 1823. (Tulane.)

——— [13] *Proceedings and Debates of the Convention of Louisiana Which Assembled at the City of New Orleans, January 14, 1844*. New Orleans, 1845. (LSU.)

——— [14] *Proceedings of the Board of Currency during the Years 1850 and 1851*. New Orleans, 1852. (LSU.)

——— [15] *Report of the Board of Bank Managers on the Affairs of the Citizens Bank of Louisiana and the Consolidated Association*. 1847-50. (Tulane.)

——— [16] *Report of the Board of Bank Managers on the Citizens Bank of Louisiana*. Jan. 15, 1852. (LSU.)

——— [17] *Report of the Committee on Banks* [probably 1843]. (Tulane.)

——— [18] *Report of House Committee on Banks and Banking on House Bill No. 32, An Act to Establish a General System of Free Banking in the State of Louisiana*. 1857. (Tulane.)

——— [19] *Report of the Joint Committee on the Affairs of the Citizens Bank of Louisiana, for the Year 1836*. Submitted to the Legislature in January 1837. New Orleans, 1837. (Thompson Collection.)

——— [20] *Report of the Joint Committee on the Affairs of the Union Bank of Louisiana.* New Orleans, 1833. (LSU.)

——— [21] *Report of the Joint Committee on Banks and Banking.* 1854, 1855, 1857, 1858, 1859, 1860, and 1866. (Tulane.) Each of these annual legislative reports summarizes the financial condition of the banks and investigates the current policy issues—the free banking system, the response of the banks to the financial crisis of 1857, etc. Together, they constitute an indispensable source on banking policy in the 1850's.

——— [22] *Report of the Joint Committee of Finance of the Senate and House of Representatives on the Banking Situation of the Monied Institutions of New Orleans.* New Orleans, 1837. (Tulane.) This report, written by Edmund Forstall, analyzes the background of the crisis of 1837, provides valuable statistics on the banks in 1835 and 1836, and reveals Forstall's theories of "sound banking."

——— [23] *Report of the Louisiana State Bank* (and of its Baton Rouge Branch) to the legislature, 1853. (Tulane.)

——— [24] *Report of the [Senate] Committee of Finance, to Whom Was Referred the Report of the Board of Bank Managers of the Affairs of the Citizens Bank of Louisiana and the Consolidated Association, with Accompanying Documents.* 1848. (Tulane.)

——— [25] *Report of the Standing Committees of the Senate and House of Representatives on Banks and Banking.* 1853. (Tulane.)

——— [26] *Reports of the Citizens Bank and Consolidated Association of the State of Louisiana.* 1853. (Tulane.)

——— [27] *Statement of the Board of Managers of the Citizens Bank, Jan. 25, 1843.* Submitted to the legislature. (LSU.)

Lyon, James. "Enquiry Relative to Banks." New Orleans, 1804. (New York Public Library.) Bound with the *Ordinance Establishing the Louisiana Bank.*

Macesich, George. "Sources of Monetary Disturbances in the United States, 1834-1845." *Journal of Economic History,* XX (1960), 407-34.

Machlup, Fritz. "Plans for Reform of the International Monetary System." Princeton Special Papers in International Economics, No. 3. Princeton, N.J., 1964.

Mandeville (Henry D. and Family) Papers, 1815-38. (LSU Archives.)

Marsten (Henry and Family) Papers, 1839-56. (LSU Archives.) Marsten was cashier of the Union Bank branch at Clinton.

Martin, François Xavier. *The History of Louisiana, from the Earliest Period, to Which Is Appended Annals of Louisiana* [by John F. Condon]. New Orleans, 1882.

Mathews (Charles L. and Family) Papers, 1849-53. (LSU Archives.)

Matthews, Robert Charles Oliver. *A Study in Trade Cycle History; Economic Fluctuations in Great Britain, 1833-1842.* Cambridge, Eng., 1954.

McCormick, Richard Patrick. *The Second American Party System: Party Formation in the Jacksonian Era.* Chapel Hill, N.C., 1966.

McGrane, Reginald C. *The Correspondence of Nicholas Biddle Dealing with National Affairs, 1807-1844.* Boston, 1919.

———— *Foreign Bondholders and American State Debts.* New York, 1935.

———— *The Panic of 1837: Some Financial Problems of the Jacksonian Era.* Chicago, 1924.

McGuire (Dr.) diary, kept at Monroe, Louisiana, 1818-52. (Typescript copy at Tulane.)

Menn, Joseph Karl. *The Large Slaveholders of Louisiana, 1860.* New Orleans, 1964.

Mercer (William Newton) Papers, 1829-54. (Tulane.) Mercer was a wealthy planter who also invested in bank stocks. Letters to Mercer from Stephen Duncan (another planter), Henry W. Huntington (his plantation supervisor), and Ayres P. Merrill (a bank cashier) shed light on banking practices and the panic of 1837.

Merchants Bank Letter File Book, 1857-60. (LSU Archives.) Routine correspondence on collections, remittances, and notifications.

Miller, Harry E. *Banking Theories in the United States before 1860.* Cambridge, Mass., 1927.

Minor (William J. and Family) Papers, 1837-42. (LSU Archives.)

Minsky, Hyman P. "Longer Waves in Financial Relations: Financial Factors in the More Severe Depressions." *American Economic Review, Proceedings,* LIV (1964), 324-35.

Mints, Lloyd W. *A History of Banking Theory in Great Britain and the United States.* Chicago, 1945.

Myers, Margaret Good. *The New York Money Market.* 2 vols. New York, 1921.

Nashua Manufacturing Company Papers, 1841. (LSU Archives.)

Natchez Banking Letters, 1836-39. (Tulane.)

Neu, Irene D. "Edmond Jean Forstall and Louisiana Banking." *Explorations in Economic History,* VII (1970), 383-98.

———— "J. B. Moussier and the Property Banks of Louisiana." *Business History Review,* XXXV (1961), 550-57.

———— "Louisiana Politics and the Bank Act of 1842." Paper read to the American Historical Association, December 28, 1964.

New Orleans Bee, 1834.

New Orleans Canal and Banking Company. *Report of the Committee appointed by the Stockholders of the New Orleans Canal and Banking Company, on the Resolutions Adopted at Their Meetings on the 24th and 31st January, 1835.* New Orleans, 1835. (Tulane, Favrot Collection.)

New Orleans and Carrollton Railroad Company Collection. 1834-60. (Tulane.)

"New Orleans Cotton Brokers Correspondence, 1831-1850." (Tulane.)

New Orleans Savings Bank Book, 1838. (Tulane.)

New Orleans Times, 1863-66.

Niehaus, Earl F. *The Irish in New Orleans, 1800-1860.* Baton Rouge, 1965.

Niles' Weekly Register, 1814-44. Baltimore.

Nolte, Vincent Otto. *Memoirs of Vincent Nolte: Fifty Years in Both Hemispheres.* New York, 1934 (originally published 1854).

North, Douglass C. *The Economic Growth of the United States, 1790-1860.* New York, 1966.

Norton, Leslie Murray. "A History of the Whig Party in Louisiana." Ph.D. dissertation, Louisiana State University, 1940.

Odom, Edwin D. "Louisiana Railroads, 1830-1880: A Study of State and Local Aid." Ph.D. dissertation, Tulane University, 1961.

"One Hundred Years, 1831-1931: The Canal Bank and Trust Company of New Orleans." New Orleans, 1931. (Tulane.)

Ordinance Establishing the Louisiana Bank. New Orleans, 1804. (New York Public Library.)

Output, Employment and Productivity in the United States after 1800. National Bureau of Economic Research, Studies in Income and Wealth, Vol. XXX. New York, 1966.

Palfrey (William T. and Family) Papers, 1812-42. (LSU Archives.)

Parker, William. Review of Harold D. Woodman, *King Cotton and His Retainers. Journal of Economic History,* XXVIII (1968), 752-55.

Patinkin, Don. *Money, Interest, and Prices.* 2d ed. New York, 1965.

Patrick, Hugh T. "Financial Development and Economic Growth in Underdeveloped Countries." *Economic Development and Cultural Change,* XIV (1966), 174-89.

Peters, Samuel Jarvis. *An Address to the Legislature of Louisiana, Showing the Importance of the Credit System on the Prosperity of the United States, and Particularly its Influence on the Agricultural, Commercial, and Manufacturing Interests of Louisiana.* By the New Orleans Chamber of Commerce, December, 1837. New Orleans, 1837. In *LSB* [1].

Peters-LeMonnier-Lastrapes Papers, 1830-80. (Tulane.)

Pontchartrain Railroad Company Minutebook, 1829-37. (Tulane.)

Porter, Alice. "An Economic View of Ante-Bellum New Orleans, 1846-1860." M.A. thesis, Tulane University, 1942.

Poydras Home Collection, Financial Correspondence, 1840-49. (Tulane.)

Price Current, 1823-61. New Orleans.

Puckett, Erastus Paul. "The Attempt of New Orleans to Meet the Crisis in her Trade with the West." *Mississippi Valley Historical Association, Proceedings*, X (1921), 481-95.

Pulwers, Jacob Edward. "Henry Marsten, Ante-Bellum Planter and Businessman of East Feliciana." M.A. thesis, Louisiana State University, 1955.

Ratchford, Benjamin U. *American State Debts.* Durham, N.C., 1941.

Redlich, Fritz. "Bank Money in the United States during the First Half of the Nineteenth Century." *Southern Economic Journal*, X (1944), 212-21.

———— *The Molding of American Banking: Men and Ideas.* 2 vols. New York, 1947.

———— " 'New' and Traditional Approaches to Economic History and Their Interdependence." *Journal of Economic History*, XXV (1965), 480-95.

———— and Webster M. Christman. "Early American Checks and an Example of their Use." *Business History Review*, XLI (1967), 285-302.

Reed, Merl Elwyn. "Boom or Bust: Louisiana's Economy During the 1830's." *Louisiana History*, IV (1963), 35-53.

———— "Louisiana's Transportation Revolution: The Railroads, 1830-1850." Ph.D. dissertation, Louisiana State University, 1957.

———— *New Orleans and the Railroads: The Struggle for Commercial Empire, 1830-1860.* Baton Rouge, 1966.

Reeves, William D. "The Great Port of the South: New Orleans; A Study of Economic Conservatism, 1850-1860." B.A. thesis (Honors in History), Williams College, 1963.

Reinders, Robert Clemens. "A Social History of New Orleans, 1850-1860." Ph.D. dissertation, University of Texas, 1957.

Rightor, Henry, ed. *Standard History of New Orleans.* Chicago, 1900.

Robb, James. *Internal Improvements.* New Orleans, 1856. (Tulane.)

Roeder, Robert E. "Merchants of Ante-Bellum New Orleans." *Explorations in Entrepreneurial History* (old series), X (1958), 113-22.

———— "New Orleans Merchants, 1790-1837." Ph.D. dissertation, Harvard University, 1959.

Rothstein, Morton. "The Antebellum South as a Dual Economy: A Tentative Hypothesis." *Agricultural History*, XLI (1967), 373-82.

———— "Antebellum Wheat and Cotton Exports: A Contrast in Marketing Organization and Economic Development." *Agricultural History*, XL (1966), 91-100.

Rowland, Dunbar, ed. *The Official Letter Books of W. C. C. Claiborne, 1801-1816*. Vol. II. Jackson, Miss., 1917.

Ruffin, Mrs. Minnie Markette, and Miss Lilla McLure. "General Solomon Weathersbee Downs (1801-1854)." *Louisiana Historical Quarterly*, XVII (1934), 5-47.

Russel, Robert Royal. *Economic Aspects of Southern Sectionalism, 1840-1861*. Urbana, Ill., 1924.

St. Georges, A. *Reflexions sur les banques aux Etats Unis envoyees à J.P. Poutz en septembre 1835*. New Orleans, 1843. (Harvard Business School, Baker Library.)

Scheiber, Harry N. *Ohio Canal Era: A Case Study of Government and the Economy, 1820-1861*. Athens, Ohio, 1969.

——— "The Pet Banks in Jacksonian Politics and Finance, 1833-1841." *Journal of Economic History*, XXIII (1963), 196-214 .

Schmidt, Louis B. "Internal Commerce and the Development of National Economy Before 1860." *Journal of Political Economy*, XLVII (1939), 798-822.

Seaman, Ezra Champion. *Essays on the Progress of Nations in Civilization, Productive Industry, Wealth, and Population*. New York, 1852.

"Secrèts Dévoilés De L'Administration Inquisitoriale De La Banque." Written by "A Resident of Attakapas" between 1818 and 1823. Attakapas County Papers (LSU Archives).

Seers, Dudley. "A Theory of Inflation and Growth in Under-Developed Economies, Based on the Experience of Latin America." *Oxford Economic Papers*, XIV (1962), 173-95.

Sellers, Charles G., Jr. "Who Were the Southern Whigs?" *American Historical Review*, LIX (1954), 335-46.

Semi-Weekly Creole, 1854-55. New Orleans.

Sharp, James Roger. *The Jacksonians Versus The Banks; Politics in the States After the Panic of 1837*. New York, 1970.

Shugg, Roger W. *Origins of Class Struggle in Louisiana*. Baton Rouge, 1939.

Sitterson, J. Carlyle. "Financing and Marketing the Sugar Crop of the Old South." *Journal of Southern History*, X (1944), 188-99.

——— "The McCollams: A Planter Family of the Old and New South." *Journal of Southern History*, VI (1940), 347-67.

——— *Sugar Country: The Cane Sugar Industry in the South, 1753-1950*. Lexington, Ky., 1953.

Smith, Hubbard & Company Correspondence, 1834-51. (Tulane.)

Smith (T. and Company) Papers, 1837-39. (LSU Archives.)

Smith, Walter Buckingham. *Economic Aspects of the Second Bank of the United States.* Cambridge, Mass., 1953.

―――― and Arthur H. Cole. *Fluctuations in American Business, 1790-1860.* Cambridge, Mass., 1935.

Solow, Robert M. "Technical Change and the Aggregate Production Function." *Review of Economics and Statistics,* XXXIX (1957), 312-20.

Southern Traveller, 1843. New Orleans.

Stephenson, Wendell H. *Alexander Porter, Whig Planter of Old Louisiana.* Baton Rouge, 1934.

―――― "Ante-Bellum New Orleans as an Agricultural Focus." *Agricultural History,* XV (1941), 161-74.

―――― *Isaac Franklin, Slave Trader and Planter of the Old South.* University, La., 1938.

Stirling (Lewis and Family) Papers, 1837. (LSU Archives.)

Suarez, Raleigh A. "Bargains, Bills, and Bankruptcies: Business Activity in Rural Antebellum Louisiana." *Louisiana History,* V (1966), 189-206.

―――― "Louisiana's Struggling Majority: The Ante-Bellum Farmer." *McNeese Review,* XIV (1963), 14-31.

Sumner, William Graham. *A History of Banking in the United States.* New York, 1896.

Taus, Esther R. *Central Banking Functions of the United States Treasury, 1789-1941.* New York, 1943.

Taylor, George Rogers. "American Urban Growth Preceding the Railway Age." *Journal of Economic History,* XXVII (1967), 309-39.

―――― *The Transportation Revolution, 1815-1860.* New York, 1951.

Temin, Peter. "The Causes of Cotton-Price Fluctuations in the 1830's." *Review of Economics and Statistics,* XLIX (1967), 463-70.

―――― *The Jacksonian Economy.* New York, 1969.

―――― "The Money Supply and Inflation in the 1830's." Paper read at The University of Minnesota, January 25, 1967.

―――― "Steam and Waterpower in the Early Nineteenth Century." *Journal of Economic History,* XXVI (1966), 187-205.

Thompson, T. P. "Early Financing in New Orleans: Being the Story of the Canal Bank, 1831-1915." *Louisiana Historical Society Publications,* VII (1913-14), 11-61.

Thompson (T. P.) Collection, University of Alabama Library.

Timberlake, Richard H., Jr. "The Independent Treasury and Monetary Policy before the Civil War." *Southern Economic Journal,* XXVII (1960), 92-103

———— "The Specie Circular and Distribution of the Surplus." *Journal of Political Economy*, LXVIII (1960), 109-17.

———— "The Specie Standard and Central Banking in the United States before 1860." *Journal of Economic History*, XXI (1961), 318-41.

Treasury Department, Record Group 56, National Archives, Washington, D.C. A vast collection of correspondence to and from government officials. The most valuable part is the correspondence with deposit banks during the 1830's and 1840's. The specific volumes used are:

———— [1] *Letters from Assistant Treasurers*. Philadelphia, Charleston, New Orleans, 1857.

———— *Letters from Banks:*

[2] Apr. 1, 1833, to July 1, 1834.

[3] July 1, 1834, to Dec. 31, 1834.

[4] Ala., Miss., La., Jan. 1835 to July 1837.

[5] Del. . . . , La., Miss., 1837-40.

[6] Va. . . . , La., Miss., Tenn., 1836-48.

———— [7] *Letters from Receivors General and Other Depositories, Under Act of 1840.*

———— [8] *Letters on the State Deposit Act of June, 1836.* 1837-38.

———— [9] *Letters to and from the Collector* [of Customs]. New Orleans, Feb. 27, 1804, to Apr. 29, 1833.

———— *Letters to Banks:*

[10] Nov 17, 1832, to July 20, 1836.

[11] 1834-35.

[12] 1836.

[13] 1837.

[14] 1838.

[15] 1839-40.

[16] July 29, 1839, to Dec. 28, 1843.

[17] Jan. 2, 1844, to Apr. 3, 1849.

———— [18] *Letters to Sub-treasury, Branch Mint, etc.*

———— [19] *Miscellaneous Letters Received, 1837.*

———— [20] *National Banks Correspondence.*

———— [21] *Recommendations of Banks.* Va. . . . , La. . . . , D.C., 1836 to July 1837.

———— Sub-treasury, *Letters from Secretary of the Treasury:*

[22] No. 1: July 6, 1840, to Mar. 8, 1842.

[23] No. 3: Dec. 12, 1853, to Oct. 21, 1857.

[24] No. 4: Oct. 22, 1857, to June 30, 1863.

Tregle, Joseph G., Jr. "Early New Orleans Society: A Reappraisal." *Journal of Southern History*, XVIII (1952), 20-36.

——— "Louisiana in the Age of Jackson: A Study in Ego Politics."
Ph.D. dissertation, University of Pennsylvania, 1954.
——— "The Political Apprenticeship of John Slidell." *Journal of
Southern History*, XXVI (1960), 57-70.
Trends in the American Economy in the Nineteenth Century. National
Bureau of Economic Research, Studies in Income and Wealth, Vol.
XXIV. Princeton, N.J., 1960.
Trescott, Paul B. *Financing American Enterprise.* New York, 1963.
——— *Money, Banking, and Economic Welfare.* 1st ed. New York,
1960. Also 2d ed. New York, 1965.
Triffin, Robert. "The Evolution of the International Monetary System:
Historical Reappraisal and Future Perspectives." *Princeton Studies in
International Finance*, No. 12. Princeton, N.J., 1964.
Trotter, Alexander. *Observations on the Financial Position and Credit
of Such of the States of the North American Union as have Con-
tracted Public Debts.* London, 1839.
Trufant, Samuel A. "Review of Banking in New Orleans, 1830-1840."
Louisiana Historical Society Publications, X (1917), 25-40.
Tureaud (Benjamin F.) Collection, 1849-57. (LSU Archives.)
United States Bureau of the Census (*USBC*). [1] *Compendium of the
Sixth Census of the United States.* Washington, D.C., 1840.
——— [2] *Eighth Census of the United States.* Washington, D.C., 1860.
——— [3] *Tenth Census of the United States.* Washington, D.C., 1880.
——— [4] *Historical Statistics of the United States, 1789-1945.* Washington, D.C., 1945.
——— [5] *Historical Statistics of the United States, Colonial Times to
1957.* Washington, D.C., 1960.
United States Congress (*USC*). [1] *House Documents*, 22 Cong., 1 sess.,
Nos. 147, 153, 184, 218. 1832.
——— [2] *House Documents*, 23 Cong., 1 sess., Nos. 372, 498, 523.
1834.
——— [3] *House Documents*, 23 Cong., 2 sess., No. 38. 1835.
——— [4] *House Documents*, 24 Cong., 1 sess., No. 42. 1836.
——— [5] *House Documents*, 24 Cong., 2 sess., Nos. 65, 77, 118. 1837.
——— [6] *House Documents*, 25 Cong., 1 sess., No. 30. 1838.
——— [7] *House Documents*, 25 Cong., 2 sess., No. 79. 1839. Contains Forstall's *Report on the Banking Situation of the Monied Institutions of New Orleans*, a report on the Citizens Bank for 1836, and
a report on the Commercial Bank, as well as general financial statistics.
——— [8] *House Documents*, 25 Cong., 3 sess., Nos. 72, 201. 1839.
——— [9] *House Documents*, 25 Cong., 3 sess., No. 227. 1839. Con-

tains *Documents Relative to the Banks of New Orleans*, 1838; Forstall letters to the directors of the Citizens Bank; and statistics on the condition of the banks of New Orleans individually and collectively.

——— [10] *House Documents*, 26 Cong., 1 sess., No. 172. 1840.

——— [11] *House Documents*, 26 Cong., 2 sess., No. 111. 1841. Contains *Documents Relative to the Investigation on Banks*, 1840.

——— [12] *House Documents*, 27 Cong., 2 sess., No. 254. 1843.

——— [13] *House Documents*, 29 Cong., 1 sess., No. 226. 1846.

——— [14] *House Documents*, 29 Cong., 2 sess., Nos. 33, 120. 1847.

——— [15] *House Documents*, 30 Cong., 1 sess., No. 77. 1848.

——— [16] *House Documents*, 31 Cong., 1 sess., No. 68. 1850.

——— [17] *House Documents*, 32 Cong., 1 sess., No. 122. 1852.

——— [18] *House Documents*, 35 Cong., 1 sess., No. 107. 1858.

——— [19] *House Documents*, 35 Cong., 2 sess., No. 112. 1859.

——— [20] *House Documents*, 36 Cong., 1 sess., No. 49. 1860.

——— [21] *House Journal*, 22 Cong., 1 sess., pp. 1074-75. 1832.

——— [22] *House Journal*, 23 Cong., 1 sess., pp. 483-89. 1834.

——— [23] *House Reports*, 21 Cong., 1 sess., No. 358. 1830.

——— [24] *House Reports*, 22 Cong., 1 sess., No. 460. 1832.

——— [25] *House Reports*, 22 Cong., 2 sess., No. 121. 1833.

——— [26] *House Reports*, 27 Cong., 2 sess., No. 462. 1843.

——— [27] *Register of Debates in Congress*, 23 Cong., 1 sess., X.

——— [28] *Senate Documents*, 20 Cong., 1 sess., No. 195. 1828.

——— [29] *Senate Documents*, 22 Cong., 1 sess., Nos. 98, 108. 1832.

——— [30] *Senate Documents*, 22 Cong., 2 sess., No. 4. 1833.

——— [31] *Senate Documents*, 23 Cong., 1 sess., Nos. 73, 187, 188. 1834.

——— [32] *Senate Documents*, 23 Cong., 2 sess., Nos. 8, 15. 1835.

——— [33] *Senate Documents*, 24 Cong., 1 sess., Nos. 225, 226, 312. 1836.

——— [34] *Senate Documents*, 24 Cong., 2 sess., No. 29. 1837.

——— [35] *Senate Documents*, 25 Cong., 1 sess., Nos. 2, 7. 1838.

——— [36] *Senate Documents*, 25 Cong., 2 sess., Nos. 420, 457, 471, 508. 1839.

——— [37] *Senate Documents*, 26 Cong., 1 sess., Nos. 14, 72. 1840.

——— [38] *Senate Documents*, 27 Cong., 3 sess., No. 246. 1843.

——— [39] *Senate Documents*, 28 Cong., 2 sess., No. 88. 1845.

——— [40] *Senate Documents*, 33 Cong., 1 sess., No. 42. 1854.

——— [41] *Senate Documents*, 35 Cong., 2 sess., No. 39. 1851.

——— [42] *Senate Documents*, 52 Cong., 2 sess., No. 38. 1893. Banking statistics, 1830-63, for all state-chartered banks; aggregates for each state and for the nation.

——— [43] *Senate Journal*, 22 Cong., 1 sess., pp. 345-46. 1832.

"U.S. Finance" Collection: U.S. Banks, 1774-1856. (Library of Congress.) A collection of papers relating mainly to the Second Bank of the United States.

U.S. Statutes at Large, V, 52. Washington, D.C., 1836. Contains Deposit Act of June 1836.

Watkins, James L. *King Cotton: A Historical and Statistical Review, 1790-1908*. New York, 1908.

Wilburn, Jean Alexander. *Biddle's Bank: The Crucial Years*. New York, 1967.

Williams (Archibald P.) Papers, 1824-69. (Tulane.)

Williamson, Jeffrey G. *American Growth and the Balance of Payments, 1820-1913*. Chapel Hill, N.C., 1963.

——— "International Trade and United States Economic Development: 1827-1843." *Journal of Economic History*, XXI (1961), 372-83.

Winston, James E. "Notes on the Economic History of New Orleans, 1803-1836." *Mississippi Valley Historical Review*, XI (1924), 200-226.

Woodbury (Levi) Collection, 1835-41. (Library of Congress.) Series II, Box 26. Books of newspaper clippings on topics related to banking and finance.

Woodman, Harold D. "Itinerant Cotton Merchants of the Ante-bellum South." *Agricultural History*, XL (1966), 79-90.

——— *King Cotton and His Retainers*. Lexington, Ky., 1968.

——— "The Profitability of Slavery: A Historical Perennial." *Journal of Southern History*, XXIX (1963), 303-25.

——— *Slavery and the Southern Economy*. New York, 1966.

Worley, Ted R. "Arkansas and the Money Crisis of 1836-1837." *Journal of Southern History*, XV (1949), 178-91.

Index

Index

THIS IS THE FIRST BOOK SET

AT STANFORD UNIVERSITY PRESS IN SABON

A TYPE DESIGN BY THE

CONTEMPORARY TYPOGRAPHER JAN TSCHICHOLD

THE BOOK WAS DESIGNED BY

HUMPHREY STONE

Building	60 795 80	117 158
Notes & Bills discounted	2886 284 98	
Credit Loans	1358 897 75	4.272 182
Notes & Bills Protested		✗ 18 034
Suspended Domestic Exchange		✗ 241 198
Domestic Exchange	147 475 16	
Do Do B.	283 58	175 833
Exchange Suspense a/c	£ 9 000	
Thomas Wilson & Co	£ 221 10/	1 073
Fd: Lizardi & Co	£ 166 624 10/4	818 864
Hope & Co	ƒ 165 811	654
	ƒ 440 000	
Office of Deposits		26.0423
Louisiana State Bank	249 245	
City Bank	223 95	
Consolidated Association	323 616	
Canal & Banking Co	538 95	
Commercial Bank	254 334	
Union Bank	36 591	
Gas Light & Bankg Co	95 48	
Improvement Compy	895 06	
Exchange Bank	55.183	10945
Bank of America		1598
Philadelphia Bank		23593
Naumkeag Bank		42
Thibodauaville Branch		267
Poh Gas Light Bk Franklin		465
Special Expenses	114	
Expenses	1958 9 74	19703
Suspense a/c		104
Protest a/c		413
Premium on Checks		1968
Specie from Havana		750
Cash Notes of other Bank	115170	
Specie	3009 3732	416 107